Earth's Structure

interactive SCIENCE

PEARSON

Boston, Massachusetts
Chandler, Arizona
Glenview, Illinois
Upper Saddle River, New Jersey

AUTHORS

You're an author!

As you write in this science book, your answers and personal discoveries will be recorded for you to keep, making this book unique to you. That is why you are one of the primary authors of this book.

✎ **In the space below, print your name, school, town, and state. Then write a short autobiography that includes your interests and accomplishments.**

YOUR NAME

SCHOOL

TOWN, STATE

AUTOBIOGRAPHY

Your Photo

Acknowledgments appear on pages 173–174, which constitute an extension of this copyright page.

ISBN-13: 978-0-13-368484-1
ISBN-10: 0-13-368484-9
11 V011 16 15 14

ON THE COVER
Rock Liner
Do you think all rocks look the same? If you do, look again at the geode on the front cover. The interior of a geode can be lined with perfectly formed crystals of minerals such as amethyst. Amethyst is a type of quartz, which is a common mineral that can be many colors. Scientists believe a geode's crystals slowly take shape after water that contains dissolved minerals seeps into a crack or hollow in a rock.

Program Authors

DON BUCKLEY, M.Sc.
Information and Communications Technology Director,
The School at Columbia University, New York, New York
Mr. Buckley has been at the forefront of K–12 educational technology for nearly two decades. A founder of New York City Independent School Technologists (NYCIST) and long-time chair of New York Association of Independent Schools' annual IT conference, he has taught students on two continents and created multimedia and Internet-based instructional systems for schools worldwide.

ZIPPORAH MILLER, M.A.Ed.
Associate Executive Director for Professional Programs and Conferences, National Science Teachers Association, Arlington, Virginia
Associate executive director for professional programs and conferences at NSTA, Ms. Zipporah Miller is a former K–12 science supervisor and STEM coordinator for the Prince George's County Public School District in Maryland. She is a science education consultant who has overseen curriculum development and staff training for more than 150 district science coordinators.

MICHAEL J. PADILLA, Ph.D.
Associate Dean and Director, Eugene P. Moore School of Education, Clemson University, Clemson, South Carolina
A former middle school teacher and a leader in middle school science education, Dr. Michael Padilla has served as president of the National Science Teachers Association and as a writer of the National Science Education Standards. He is professor of science education at Clemson University. As lead author of the *Science Explorer* series, Dr. Padilla has inspired the team in developing a program that promotes student inquiry and meets the needs of today's students.

KATHRYN THORNTON, Ph.D.
Professor and Associate Dean, School of Engineering and Applied Science, University of Virginia, Charlottesville, Virginia
Selected by NASA in May 1984, Dr. Kathryn Thornton is a veteran of four space flights. She has logged over 975 hours in space, including more than 21 hours of extravehicular activity. As an author on the *Scott Foresman Science* series, Dr. Thornton's enthusiasm for science has inspired teachers around the globe.

MICHAEL E. WYSESSION, Ph.D.
Associate Professor of Earth and Planetary Science, Washington University, St. Louis, Missouri
An author on more than 50 scientific publications, Dr. Wysession was awarded the prestigious Packard Foundation Fellowship and Presidential Faculty Fellowship for his research in geophysics. Dr. Wysession is an expert on Earth's inner structure and has mapped various regions of Earth using seismic tomography. He is known internationally for his work in geoscience education and outreach.

Instructional Design Author

GRANT WIGGINS, Ed.D.
President, Authentic Education, Hopewell, New Jersey
Dr. Wiggins is a co-author with Jay McTighe of *Understanding by Design, 2nd Edition* (ASCD 2005). His approach to instructional design provides teachers with a disciplined way of thinking about curriculum design, assessment, and instruction that moves teaching from covering content to ensuring understanding.
UNDERSTANDING BY DESIGN® and UbD™ are trademarks of ASCD, and are used under license.

Planet Diary Author

JACK HANKIN
Science/Mathematics Teacher, The Hilldale School, Daly City, California Founder, Planet Diary Web site
Mr. Hankin is the creator and writer of Planet Diary, a science current events Web site. He is passionate about bringing science news and environmental awareness into classrooms and offers numerous Planet Diary workshops at NSTA and other events to train middle and high school teachers.

ELL Consultant

JIM CUMMINS, Ph.D.
Professor and Canada Research Chair, Curriculum, Teaching and Learning department at the University of Toronto
Dr. Cummins focuses on literacy development in multilingual schools and the role of technology in promoting student learning across the curriculum. *Interactive Science* incorporates essential research-based principles for integrating language with the teaching of academic content based on his instructional framework.

Reading Consultant

HARVEY DANIELS, Ph.D.
Professor of Secondary Education, University of New Mexico, Albuquerque, New Mexico
Dr. Daniels is an international consultant to schools, districts, and educational agencies. He has authored or coauthored 13 books on language, literacy, and education. His most recent works are *Comprehension and Collaboration: Inquiry Circles in Action* and *Subjects Matter: Every Teacher's Guide to Content-Area Reading*.

REVIEWERS

Contributing Writers

Edward Aguado, Ph.D.
Professor, Department of Geography
San Diego State University
San Diego, California

Elizabeth Coolidge-Stolz, M.D.
Medical Writer
North Reading, Massachusetts

Donald L. Cronkite, Ph.D.
Professor of Biology
Hope College
Holland, Michigan

Jan Jenner, Ph.D.
Science Writer
Talladega, Alabama

Linda Cronin Jones, Ph.D.
Associate Professor of Science and Environmental Education
University of Florida
Gainesville, Florida

T. Griffith Jones, Ph.D.
Clinical Associate Professor of Science Education
College of Education
University of Florida
Gainesville, Florida

Andrew C. Kemp, Ph.D.
Teacher
Jefferson County Public Schools
Louisville, Kentucky

Matthew Stoneking, Ph.D.
Associate Professor of Physics
Lawrence University
Appleton, Wisconsin

R. Bruce Ward, Ed.D.
Senior Research Associate
Science Education Department
Harvard-Smithsonian Center for Astrophysics
Cambridge, Massachusetts

Content Reviewers

Paul D. Beale, Ph.D.
Department of Physics
University of Colorado at Boulder
Boulder, Colorado

Jeff R. Bodart, Ph.D.
Professor of Physical Sciences
Chipola College
Marianna, Florida

Joy Branlund, Ph.D.
Department of Earth Science
Southwestern Illinois College
Granite City, Illinois

Marguerite Brickman, Ph.D.
Division of Biological Sciences
University of Georgia
Athens, Georgia

Bonnie J. Brunkhorst, Ph.D.
Science Education and Geological Sciences
California State University
San Bernardino, California

Michael Castellani, Ph.D.
Department of Chemistry
Marshall University
Huntington, West Virginia

Charles C. Curtis, Ph.D.
Research Associate Professor of Physics
University of Arizona
Tucson, Arizona

Diane I. Doser, Ph.D.
Department of Geological Sciences
University of Texas
El Paso, Texas

Rick Duhrkopf, Ph.D.
Department of Biology
Baylor University
Waco, Texas

Alice K. Hankla, Ph.D.
The Galloway School
Atlanta, Georgia

Mark Henriksen, Ph.D.
Physics Department
University of Maryland
Baltimore, Maryland

Chad Hershock, Ph.D.
Center for Research on Learning and Teaching
University of Michigan
Ann Arbor, Michigan

Jeremiah N. Jarrett, Ph.D.
Department of Biology
Central Connecticut State University
New Britain, Connecticut

Scott L. Kight, Ph.D.
Department of Biology
Montclair State University
Montclair, New Jersey

Jennifer O. Liang, Ph.D.
Department of Biology
University of Minnesota–Duluth
Duluth, Minnesota

Candace Lutzow-Felling, Ph.D.
Director of Education
The State Arboretum of Virginia
University of Virginia
Boyce, Virginia

Cortney V. Martin, Ph.D.
Virginia Polytechnic Institute
Blacksburg, Virginia

Joseph F. McCullough, Ph.D.
Physics Program Chair
Cabrillo College
Aptos, California

Heather Mernitz, Ph.D.
Department of Physical Science
Alverno College
Milwaukee, Wisconsin

Sadredin C. Moosavi, Ph.D.
Department of Earth and Environmental Sciences
Tulane University
New Orleans, Louisiana

David L. Reid, Ph.D.
Department of Biology
Blackburn College
Carlinville, Illinois

Scott M. Rochette, Ph.D.
Department of the Earth Sciences
SUNY College at Brockport
Brockport, New York

Karyn L. Rogers, Ph.D.
Department of Geological Sciences
University of Missouri
Columbia, Missouri

Laurence Rosenhein, Ph.D.
Department of Chemistry
Indiana State University
Terre Haute, Indiana

Sara Seager, Ph.D.
Department of Planetary Sciences and Physics
Massachusetts Institute of Technology
Cambridge, Massachusetts

Tom Shoberg, Ph.D.
Missouri University of Science and Technology
Rolla, Missouri

Patricia Simmons, Ph.D.
North Carolina State University
Raleigh, North Carolina

William H. Steinecker, Ph.D.
Research Scholar
Miami University
Oxford, Ohio

Paul R. Stoddard, Ph.D.
Department of Geology and Environmental Geosciences
Northern Illinois University
DeKalb, Illinois

John R. Villarreal, Ph.D.
Department of Chemistry
The University of Texas–Pan American
Edinburg, Texas

John R. Wagner, Ph.D.
Department of Geology
Clemson University
Clemson, South Carolina

Jerry Waldvogel, Ph.D.
Department of Biological Sciences
Clemson University
Clemson, South Carolina

Donna L. Witter, Ph.D.
Department of Geology
Kent State University
Kent, Ohio

Edward J. Zalisko, Ph.D.
Department of Biology
Blackburn College
Carlinville, Illinois

Museum of Science.

Special thanks to the Museum of Science, Boston, Massachusetts, and Ioannis Miaoulis, the Museum's president and director, for serving as content advisors for the technology and design strand in this program.

CONTENTS

Lab zone® Enter the Lab zone
for hands-on inquiry.

Chapter Lab Investigation:
• Directed Inquiry: Modeling Mantle
Convection Currents
• Open Inquiry: Modeling Mantle Convection
Currents

Inquiry Warm-Ups: • What Is a System?
• Earth's Interior • Tracing Heat Flow

Quick Labs: • Parts of Earth's System • What
Forces Shape Earth? • How Do Scientists Find
Out What's Inside Earth? • Build a Model
of Earth • How Can Heat Cause Motion in a
Liquid?

Go to MyScienceOnline.com to
interact with this chapter's content.
Keyword: Introducing Earth

> UNTAMED SCIENCE
• Beyond the Dirt

> PLANET DIARY
• Introducing Earth

> INTERACTIVE ART
• Earth's System • Heat Transfer

> ART IN MOTION
• Convection in Earth's Mantle

> REAL-WORLD INQUIRY
• Exploring Earth's Layers

CHAPTER 2

Minerals and Rocks

Lab zone® Enter the Lab zone for hands-on inquiry.

Chapter Lab Investigation:
• Directed Inquiry: Testing Rock Flooring
• Open Inquiry: Testing Rock Flooring

Inquiry Warm-Ups: • How Does the Rate of Cooling Affect Crystals? • How Do Rocks Compare? • Liquid to Solid • Earth's Coral Reefs • A Sequined Rock • Recycling Rocks

Quick Labs: • Classifying Objects as Minerals • What Is the True Color of a Mineral? • Classify These Rocks • How Do Igneous Rocks Form? • The Rocks Around Us • How Does Pressure Affect Particles of Rock? • What Causes Layers? • How Do Grain Patterns Compare? • Which Rock Came First?

my science online.com

Go to MyScienceOnline.com to interact with this chapter's content.
Keyword: Minerals and Rocks

> **UNTAMED SCIENCE**
• Climbing Through the Rock Cycle

> **PLANET DIARY**
• Minerals and Rocks

> **INTERACTIVE ART**
• Crystal Systems • Rock Cycle

> **ART IN MOTION**
• Formation of Igneous Rock

> **REAL-WORLD INQUIRY**
• What Would You Build With?

CONTENTS

Lab zone® **Enter the Lab zone for hands-on inquiry.**

Chapter Lab Investigation:
• Directed Inquiry: Modeling Sea-Floor Spreading
• Open Inquiry: Modeling Sea-Floor Spreading

Inquiry Warm-Ups: • How Are Earth's Continents Linked Together? • What Is the Effect of a Change in Density? • Plate Interactions

Quick Labs: • Moving the Continents • Mid-Ocean Ridges • Reversing Poles • Mantle Convection Currents

my science online .com

Go to MyScienceOnline.com to interact with this chapter's content. Keyword: Plate Tectonics

> **UNTAMED SCIENCE**
• Diving Toward Divergence

> **PLANET DIARY**
• Plate Tectonics

> **INTERACTIVE ART**
• Continental Drift • Sea-Floor Spreading

> **ART IN MOTION**
• Changing Earth's Crust

> **REAL-WORLD INQUIRY**
• Predicting Plate Motion

Lab® zone Enter the Lab zone for hands-on inquiry.

Chapter Lab Investigation:
• Directed Inquiry: Finding the Epicenter
• Open Inquiry: Finding the Epicenter

Inquiry Warm-Ups: • How Does Stress Affect Earth's Crust? • How Do Seismic Waves Travel Through Earth? • How Can Seismic Waves Be Detected?

Quick Labs: • Effects of Stress • Modeling Faults • Modeling Stress • Properties of Seismic Waves • Measuring Earthquakes • Design a Seismograph • Earthquake Patterns

my science ONLINE .com

Go to MyScienceOnline.com to interact with this chapter's content.
Keyword: Earthquakes

> **UNTAMED SCIENCE**
• Why Quakes Shake

> **PLANET DIARY**
• Earthquakes

> **INTERACTIVE ART**
• Seismic Waves • Earthquake Engineering

> **ART IN MOTION**
• Stresses and Faults

> **REAL-WORLD INQUIRY**
• Placing a Bay Area Stadium

CONTENTS

CHAPTER 5

Volcanoes

Lab zone® Enter the Lab zone for hands-on inquiry.

Chapter Lab Investigation:
• Directed Inquiry: Gelatin Volcanoes
• Open Inquiry: Gelatin Volcanoes

Inquiry Warm-Ups: • Moving Volcanoes
• How Fast Do Liquids Flow? • How Do
Volcanoes Change Land?

Quick Labs: • Where Are Volcanoes
Found on Earth's Surface? • Volcanic Stages
• Identifying Volcanic Landforms • How Can
Volcanic Activity Change Earth's Surface?

my science online.com

**Go to MyScienceOnline.com to
interact with this chapter's content.
Keyword: Volcanoes**

> **UNTAMED SCIENCE**
• Why Some Volcanoes Explode

> **PLANET DIARY**
• Volcanoes

> **INTERACTIVE ART**
• Composite Volcano • Volcanoes and
Volcanic Landforms

> **ART IN MOTION**
• Volcanic Boundaries and Hot Spots

> **REAL-WORLD INQUIRY**
• Monitoring a Volcano

Video Series: Chapter Adventures

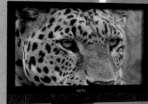

Untamed Science created this captivating video series for interactive SCIENCE featuring a unique segment for every chapter of the program.

Featuring videos such as

Beyond the Dirt
Chapter 1 Rock. Water. Air. Life. Join the Untamed Science crew as they reveal how Earth's cliffs, lakes, skies, and wildlife are all connected to one another.

Climbing Through the Rock Cycle
Chapter 2 Join the Untamed Science crew as they dig into the world of rocks and minerals.

Diving Toward Divergence
Chapter 3 Earth is cracking up—literally! Join one of our ecogeeks for a dive into the icy waters of Iceland, where a huge underwater crack is forming as two pieces of Earth's crust pull slowly away from each other.

Why Quakes Shake
Chapter 4 Follow Danni as she travels to the historic town of New Madrid, Missouri, in a quest to unlock the mysteries of earthquakes.

Why Some Volcanoes Explode
Chapter 5 Why did Mount St. Helens in Washington State erupt so explosively in 1980? Join the Untamed Science crew as they re-enact the eruption and try to discover the answer!

interactive SCIENCE

This is your book.
You can write in it!

THE BIG
?Q

Get Engaged!

At the start of each chapter, you will see two questions: an Engaging Question and the Big Question. Each chapter's Big Question will help you start thinking about the Big Ideas of Science. Look for the Big Q symbol throughout the chapter!

HOW CAN WIND KEEP YOUR LIGHTS ON?

THE BIG ? What are some of Earth's energy sources?

This man is repairing a wind turbine at a wind farm in Texas. Most wind turbines are at least 30 meters off the ground where the winds are fast. Wind speed and blade length help determine the best way to capture the wind and turn it into power. **Develop Hypotheses** Why do you think people are working to increase the amount of power we get from wind?

Wind energy collected by the turbine does not cause air pollution.

▶ **UNTAMED SCIENCE** Watch the Untamed Science video to learn more about energy resources.

174 Energy Resources

Untamed Science™

Follow the Untamed Science video crew as they travel the globe exploring the Big Ideas of Science.

Interact with your textbook.   **Interact with inquiry.**   **Interact online.**

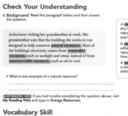

Build Reading, Inquiry, and Vocabulary Skills

In every lesson you will learn new ⟲ Reading and ▲ Inquiry skills. These skills will help you read and think like a scientist. Vocabulary skills will help you communicate effectively and uncover the meaning of words.

my SCIENCE online.com

Go Online!

Look for the MyScienceOnline.com technology options. At MyScienceOnline.com you can immerse yourself in amazing virtual environments, get extra practice, and even blog about current events in science.

Explore the Key Concepts.

Each lesson begins with a series of Key Concept questions. The interactivities in each lesson will help you understand these concepts and Unlock the Big Question.

MY PLANET DIARY

At the start of each lesson, My Planet Diary will introduce you to amazing events, significant people, and important discoveries in science or help you to overcome common misconceptions about science concepts.

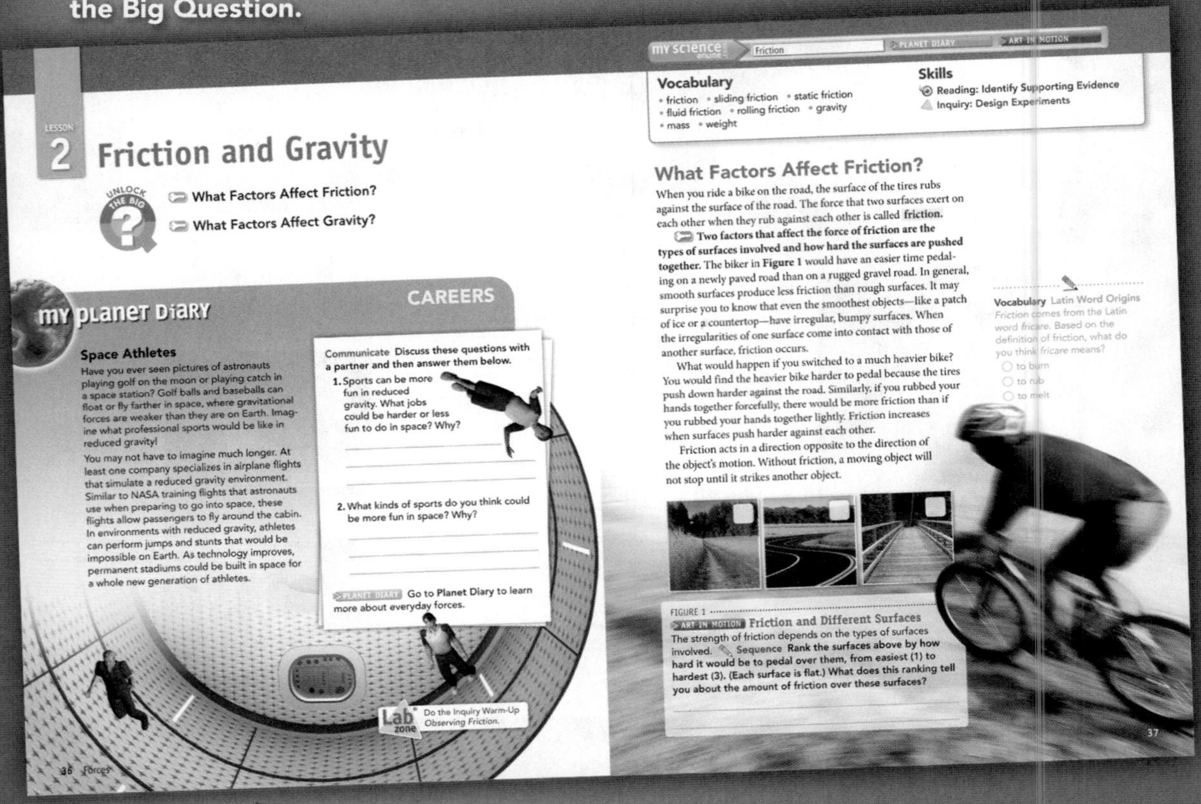

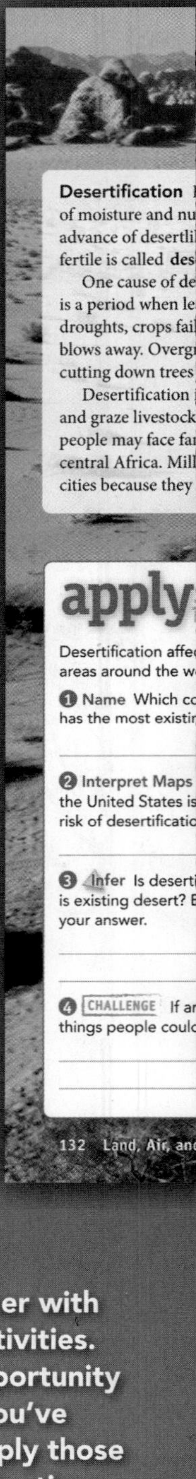

Desertification of moisture and nu advance of desertli fertile is called **des**

One cause of de is a period when le droughts, crops fail blows away. Overgr cutting down trees

Desertification and graze livestock people may face fa central Africa. Mill cities because they

---

LESSON
2 Friction and Gravity

☐ What Factors Affect Friction?
☐ What Factors Affect Gravity?

MY PLANET DIARY   CAREERS

Space Athletes

Have you ever seen pictures of astronauts playing golf on the moon or playing catch in a space station? Golf balls and baseballs can float or fly farther in space, where gravitational forces are weaker than they are on Earth. Imagine what professional sports would be like in reduced gravity!

You may not have to imagine much longer. At least one company specializes in airplane flights that simulate a reduced gravity environment. Similar to NASA training flights that astronauts use when preparing to go into space, these flights allow passengers to fly around the cabin. In environments with reduced gravity, athletes can perform jumps and stunts that would be impossible on Earth. As technology improves, permanent stadiums could be built in space for a whole new generation of athletes.

Communicate Discuss these questions with a partner and then answer them below.

1. Sports can be more fun in reduced gravity. What jobs could be harder or less fun to do in space? Why?

2. What kinds of sports do you think could be more fun in space? Why?

▷ PLANET DIARY Go to Planet Diary to learn more about everyday forces.

Lab zone Do the Inquiry Warm-Up Observing Friction.

MY SCIENCE ▷ Friction   ▷ PLANET DIARY   ▷ ART IN MOTION

Vocabulary
• friction • sliding friction • static friction
• fluid friction • rolling friction • gravity
• mass • weight

Skills
▷ Reading: Identify Supporting Evidence
▷ Inquiry: Design Experiments

What Factors Affect Friction?

When you ride a bike on the road, the surface of the tires rubs against the surface of the road. The force that two surfaces exert on each other when they rub against each other is called **friction**. **Two factors that affect the force of friction are the types of surfaces involved and how hard the surfaces are pushed together.** The biker in **Figure 1** would have an easier time pedaling on a newly paved road than on a rugged gravel road. In general, smooth surfaces produce less friction than rough surfaces. It may surprise you to know that even the smoothest objects—like a patch of ice or a countertop—have irregular, bumpy surfaces. When the irregularities of one surface come into contact with those of another surface, friction occurs.

What would happen if you switched to a much heavier bike? You would find the heavier bike harder to pedal because the tires push down harder against the road. Similarly, if you rubbed your hands together forcefully, there would be more friction than if you rubbed your hands together lightly. Friction increases when surfaces push harder against each other.

Friction acts in a direction opposite to the direction of the object's motion. Without friction, a moving object will not stop until it strikes another object.

Vocabulary Latin Word Origins Friction comes from the Latin word *fricare*. Based on the definition of friction, what do you think *fricare* means?
○ to burn
○ to rub
○ to melt

FIGURE 1
▷ ART IN MOTION **Friction and Different Surfaces**
The strength of friction depends on the types of surfaces involved. ✎ Sequence Rank the surfaces above by how hard it would be to pedal over them, from easiest (1) to hardest (3). (Each surface is flat.) What does this ranking tell you about the amount of friction over these surfaces?

36 Forces   37

---

apply

Desertification affe areas around the w

❶ **Name** Which co has the most existin

❷ **Interpret Maps** the United States is risk of desertificatio

❸ **Infer** Is deserti is existing desert? E your answer.

❹ **CHALLENGE** If ar things people coul

132 Land, Air, an

Explain what you know.

Look for the pencil. When you see it, it's time to interact with your book and demonstrate what you have learned.

Elaborate further with the Apply It activities. This is your opportunity to take what you've learned and apply those skills to new situations.

Lab Zone

Look for the Lab zone triangle. This means it's time to do a hands-on inquiry lab. In every lesson, you'll have the opportunity to do a hands-on inquiry activity that will help reinforce your understanding of the lesson topic.

Land Reclamation Fortunately, it is possible to replace land damaged by erosion or mining. The process of restoring an area of land to a more productive state is called **land reclamation.** In addition to restoring land for agriculture, land reclamation can restore habitats for wildlife. Many different types of land reclamation projects are currently underway all over the world. But it is generally more difficult and expensive to restore damaged land and soil than it is to protect those resources in the first place. In some cases, the land may not return to its original state.

FIGURE 4 ·······························

Land Reclamation
These pictures show land before and after it was mined.

✎ **Communicate** Below the pictures, write a story about what happened to the land.

Assess Your Understanding

1a. Review Subsoil has (less/more) plant and animal matter than topsoil.

b. Explain What can happen to soil if plants are removed?

c. Apply Concepts ...
that could prev...
land reclama...

got it?

○ I get it! Now I know that soil management is important becau...

○ I need extra help with _____
Go to MY SCIENCE 🔍 COACH online for help with this subject.

Do the Quick Lab
Modeling Soi...

---

depleted
rt. The
usly were
un).
e, a **drought**
During
soil easily
heep and
ion, too.
grow crops
d. As a result,
n is severe in
ng to the
on the land.

Europe Asia
Atlantic
Ocean
Africa Indian
Ocean
Australia

Key
- Existing desert
- High-risk area
- Moderate-risk area

e there
o support

t are some

---

got it?

Evaluate Your Progress.

After answering the Got It question, think about how you're doing. Did you get it or do you need a little help? Remember, MY SCIENCE 🔍 COACH is there for you if you need extra help.

Explore the Big Question.

At one point in the chapter, you'll have the opportunity to take all that you've learned to further explore the Big Question.

Pollution and Solutions

EXPLORE THE BIG ?

What can people do to use resources wisely?

FIGURE 4 ....

▶ **REAL-WORLD INQUIRY** All living things depend on land, air, and water. Conserving these resources for the future is important. Part of resource conservation is identifying and limiting sources of pollution.

✎ **Interpret Photos** On the photograph, write the letter from the key into the circle that best identifies the source of pollution.

Land
Describe at least one thing your community could do to reduce pollution on land.
_____
_____
_____
_____
_____

Pollution Sources

A. Sediments

B. Municipal solid waste

C. Runoff from development

C.

Air
Describe at least one thing your community could do to reduce air pollution.
_____
_____
_____
_____
_____

Water
Describe at least one thing your community could do to reduce water pollution.
_____
_____
_____
_____
_____

Assess

1a. Define What

b. Explain How
spill in the oc

c. **ANSWER** What
reso

d. **CHALLENGE**
to recycle t
would redu
_____
_____

got it?

○ I get it! N
can be rec

○ I need ex

Go to **my s**
with this su

ANSWER THE BIG ?

Answer the Big Question.

Now it's time to show what you know and answer the Big Question.

Review What You've Learned.

Use the Chapter Study Guide to review the Big Question and prepare for the test.

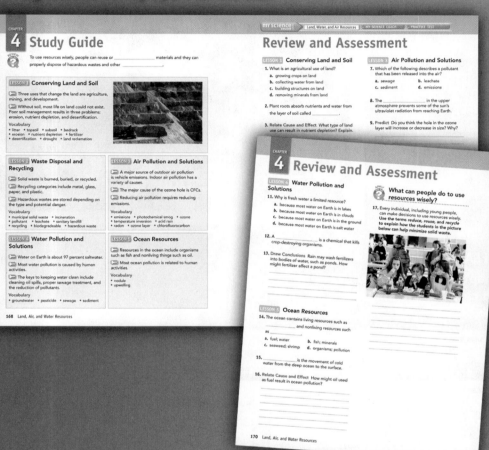

Practice Taking Tests.

Apply the Big Question and take a practice test in standardized test format.

INTERACT... WITH YOUR TEXTBOOK...

Go to **MyScienceOnline.com** and immerse yourself in amazing virtual environments.

> THE BIG QUESTION

Each online chapter starts with a Big Question. Your mission is to unlock the meaning of this Big Question as each science lesson unfolds.

Unit 4 > Chapter 1 > Lesson 1

<< The Big Question | Unlock the Big Question | Explore the Big Question | >>

The Big Question | Check Your Understanding | Vocabulary Skill

Populations and Communities

The Big Question

Unit 2 > Chapter 4 > Less

Engage & Explore

Planet Diary

my planet di

> VOCAB FLASH CARDS

Practice chapter vocabulary with interactive flash cards. Each card has an image, definitions in English and Spanish, and space for your own notes.

Unit 4 > Chapter 1 > Lesson 1

<< The Big Question | Unlock the Big Question | Explore the Big Question | >>

The Big Question | Untamed Science | Check Your Understanding | Vocabulary Skill | Vocabulary Flashcards

Vocabulary Flashcards

Tools

Card List | Create-a-Card | 10 Cards Left | Test Me

Lesson Cards | My Cards

Birth Rate
Carrying Capacity
Commensalism
Community
Competition
Death Rate
Ecology
Ecosystem
Emigration
Habitat
Host
Immigration
Limiting Factor

Science Vocabulary

Term: **Community**

Definition: **All the different populations that live together in a particular area.**

View Spanish

Add Notes

Card 5 of

Unit 6 > Chapte

Engage & E

Apply It | Direc

Color in Lig

Exit

Reset Lab

Unit 6 > Chapter 1 > Lesson 1

Engage & Explore | Explain | Elaborate | Evaluate

Apply It | Do the Math | Art in Motion | Interactive Art | Real World Inquiry

The Nebraska Plains

▶ Bald Eagle

Information | Media

Haliaeetus leucocephalus
Bald Eagles are 80-95 cm tall with a wingspan of 180-230 cm. These birds are born with all brown feathers but grow white feathers on their head, neck, and tail.

Layers List | ▲ Show

> INTERACTIVE ART

At MyScienceOnline.com, many of the beautiful visuals in your book become interactive so you can extend your learning.

▶ Next

22 of 22

Back

GO ONLINE

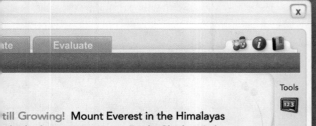

↻   +   🌐 http://www.myscienceonline.com/

> PLANET DIARY

My Planet Diary online is the place to find more information and activities related to the topic in the lesson.

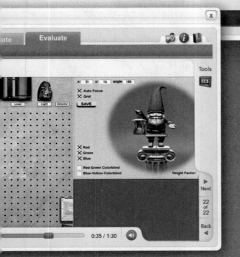

...till Growing! Mount Everest in the Himalayas is the highest mountain on Earth. Climbers who reach the peak stand 8,850 meters above sea level. You might think that mountains never change. But forces inside Earth push Mount Everest at least several millimeters higher each year. Over time, Earth's forces slowly but constantly lift, stretch, bend, and break Earth's crust in dramatic ways!

Planet Diary   Go to Planet Diary to learn more about forces in the Earth's crust.

> VIRTUAL LAB

Get more practice with realistic virtual labs. Manipulate the variables on-screen and test your hypothesis.

Find Your Chapter

1 Go to www.myscienceonline.com.

2 Log in with username and password.

3 Click on your program and select your chapter.

Keyword Search

1 Go to www.myscienceonline.com.

2 Log in with username and password.

3 Click on your program and select Search.

4 Enter the keyword (from your book) in the search box.

Other Content Available Online

> **UNTAMED SCIENCE** Follow these young scientists through their amazing online video blogs as they travel the globe in search of answers to the Big Questions of Science.

> **MY SCIENCE COACH** Need extra help? My Science Coach is your personal online study partner. My Science Coach is a chance for you to get more practice on key science concepts. There you can choose from a variety of tools that will help guide you through each science lesson.

> **MY READING WEB** Need extra reading help on a particular science topic? At My Reading Web you will find a choice of reading selections targeted to your specific reading level.

? BIG IDEAS OF SCIENCE

Have you ever worked on a jigsaw puzzle? Usually a puzzle has a theme that leads you to group the pieces by what they have in common. But until you put all the pieces together you can't solve the puzzle. Studying science is similar to solving a puzzle. The big ideas of science are like puzzle themes. To understand big ideas, scientists ask questions. The answers to those questions are like pieces of a puzzle. Each chapter in this book asks a big question to help you think about a big idea of science. By answering the big questions, you will get closer to understanding the big idea.

✎ **Before you read each chapter, write about what you know and what more you'd like to know.**

BIGIDEA

Earth's land, water, air, and life form a system.

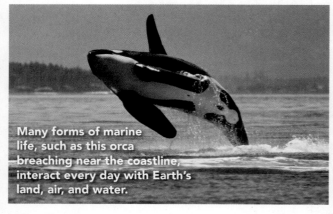

Many forms of marine life, such as this orca breaching near the coastline, interact every day with Earth's land, air, and water.

What do you already know about how land, water, air, and life interact on Earth?

✎ **What would you like to know?**

_____

_____

_____

Big Question

❷ What is the structure of Earth? Chapter 1

✎ **After reading the chapter, write what you have learned about the Big Idea.**

_____

_____

_____

_____

Over millions of years, forces inside Earth can slowly change a flat plain into hills made of folded rock, such as the rock shown here in Greece.

Earth is a continually changing planet.

In 2009, this eruption of an underwater volcano off the coast of Tonga formed a small new island in the Pacific Ocean.

What do you already know about how Earth changes every day?

✏ **What would you like to know?**

_____

_____

_____

_____

Big Questions

❓ How do rocks form? Chapter 2

❓ How do moving plates change Earth's crust? Chapter 3

❓ Why do earthquakes occur more often in some places than in others? Chapter 4

❓ How does a volcano erupt? Chapter 5

✏ **After reading the chapters, write what you have learned about the Big Idea.**

_____

_____

_____

_____

_____

_____

HOW DEEP INTO EARTH CAN THIS CLIMBER GO?

THE BIG ? What is the structure of Earth?

Descending into a canyon, this climber will get nearer to the center of Earth. But how close will he get? As climbers move down through narrow, dark passages of rock and dirt, they sometimes have to dig their way through. Some spelunkers, or cave explorers, have even descended into caves over 2,000 meters deep—the length of nearly 22 football fields!

Predict If this climber could go all the way down to Earth's center, what materials other than dirt and solid rock might he find along the way? Explain your answer.

_____

_____

_____

_____

> **UNTAMED SCIENCE** Watch the **Untamed Science** video to learn more about Earth's structure.

Introducing Earth

 1 Getting Started

Check Your Understanding

1. **Background** Read the paragraph below and then answer the question.

On a field trip, Paula sees that beach cliffs near the sea have worn away. "Where do the cliffs go?" she asks. Her teacher says, "The cliffs are exposed to natural **forces** all year. The harsh weather breaks the cliffs into pieces. **Gravity** causes the pieces to fall to the sea. Waves then shape the pieces into small **particles,** which wash away."

> A **force** is a natural power that acts on an object.
>
> **Gravity** is the force that makes objects fall toward Earth's center.
>
> A **particle** is a very small fragment of a much larger object.

• What forces change the beach cliffs each year?

_____

_____

> **MY READING WEB** If you had trouble answering the question above, visit **My Reading Web** and type in *Introducing Earth*.

Vocabulary Skill

Identify Related Word Forms You can increase your vocabulary by learning related word forms. If you know that the noun *energy* means "the ability to do work," you can figure out the meaning of the adjective *energetic*.

Verb	Noun	Adjective
destroy to reduce to pieces	destruction the process of reducing to pieces	destructive tending to cause damage or to reduce to pieces
radiate to release energy	radiation energy released in the form of rays or waves	radiant released as waves or rays

2. **Quick Check** Review the words related to *destroy*. Then circle the correct form of the word *destroy* in the following sentence.

• The (destruction/destructive) winds of a hurricane can be very dangerous.

system

hydrosphere

basalt

convection current

Chapter Preview

LESSON 1
- system
- energy
- atmosphere
- geosphere
- hydrosphere
- biosphere
- constructive force
- destructive force

↻ **Ask Questions**
△ **Draw Conclusions**

LESSON 2
- seismic wave
- pressure
- crust
- basalt
- granite
- mantle
- lithosphere
- asthenosphere
- outer core
- inner core

↻ **Identify Supporting Evidence**
△ **Interpret Data**

LESSON 3
- radiation
- convection
- conduction
- density
- convection current

↻ **Relate Cause and Effect**
△ **Communicate**

➤ **VOCAB FLASH CARDS** For extra help with vocabulary, visit **Vocab Flash Cards** and type in *Introducing Earth.*

The Earth System

UNLOCK
THE BIG
?

🔑 **What Are the Main Parts of the Earth System?**

🔑 **How Do Constructive and Destructive Forces Change Earth?**

my PLANeT DiaRY

Posted by: Nicole

Location: Medfield, Massachusetts

This past summer my family and I went to the Grand Canyon. The Grand Canyon was carved by the Colorado River. It was so cool, looking down from the edge and seeing a small line that is the river and the rock layers in all different colors. I was amazed that mules could carry you down into the canyon.

Lab zone® Do the Inquiry Warm-Up *What Is a System?*

BLOG

Read the text and answer the questions.

1. How did the Colorado River change the landscape that existed before the Grand Canyon formed?

_____

_____

2. What else would you like to learn about the Colorado River?

_____

_____

_____

_____

> **PLANET DIARY** Go to **Planet Diary** to learn more about how natural forces change Earth's features.

What Are the Main Parts of the Earth System?

The Grand Canyon is made up of different parts. Rock forms the canyon walls. Water flows through the canyon in the form of a river, which carves away the rock. Animals such as deer drink the river's water. And air fills the canyon, allowing the animals to breath. All these parts work together. So the environment of the Grand Canyon can be thought of as a system. A **system** is a group of parts that work together as a whole. **Figure 1** shows how air, water, rock, and life work together in another part of Earth.

Vocabulary

- system • energy • atmosphere • geosphere
- hydrosphere • biosphere • constructive force
- destructive force

Skills

Reading: Ask Questions

Inquiry: Draw Conclusions

Earth as a System The Earth system involves a constant flow of matter through different parts. For example, you may know that in the *water cycle,* water evaporates from the ocean, rises into the atmosphere, and then falls from the sky as rain. The rainwater then flows into and over Earth, and then back into the ocean.

You might be surprised to learn that rock, too, cycles through the Earth system. For example, new rock can form from molten material inside Earth called *magma.* This material can rise to the surface and harden on land to form new rock. The new rock can then erode into small pieces. The pieces can be washed into the ocean, where they may sink to the bottom as small particles, or *sediment.* If enough of the small particles collect, the weight of the sediment can crush all the particles together. The particles can then be cemented together to form new rock. The flow of rock through the Earth system is called the *rock cycle.*

The constant flow, or cycling, of matter through the Earth system is driven by energy. **Energy** is the ability to do work. The energy that drives the Earth system has two main sources: heat from the sun and heat flowing out of Earth as it cools.

FIGURE 1 ·······························

All Systems Go!

The many parts of the Earth system all work together.

✎ **Develop Hypotheses** Look at the photograph. Choose one part of the Earth system—rock, water, air, or life—and describe how the other parts might be affected if the first part were removed.

_____
_____
_____
_____
_____
_____
_____
_____
_____
_____
_____
_____
_____

5

FIGURE 2 ·······················

▶ INTERACTIVE ART **The Earth System**

Earth's four spheres can affect one another.

✎ **Interpret Photos** Read the descriptions of Earth's four spheres. On the lines in each box, write the spheres that are interacting with each other in the small photograph next to the box.

Parts of the Earth System Earth contains air, water, land, and life. Each of these parts forms its own part, or "sphere." 🔑 **The Earth system has four main spheres: the atmosphere, the hydrosphere, the geosphere, and the biosphere. As a major source of energy for Earth processes, the sun can be considered part of the Earth system as well.** Each part of the Earth system can be studied separately. But the four parts are interconnected, as shown in **Figure 2**.

One of the most important parts of the Earth system is—you! Humans greatly affect the air, water, land, and life of Earth. For instance, the amount of paved land, including roads and parking lots, in the United States is now larger than the state of Georgia.

Atmosphere

Earth's outermost layer is a mixture of gases—mostly nitrogen and oxygen. It also contains dust particles, cloud droplets, and the rain and snow that form from water vapor. It contains Earth's weather, and is the foundation for the different climates around the world. Earth's **atmosphere** (AT muh sfeer) is the relatively thin envelope of gases that forms Earth's outermost layer.

_____

_____

Geosphere

Nearly all of Earth's mass is found in Earth's solid rocks and metals, in addition to other materials. Earth's **geosphere** (GEE uh sfeer) has three main parts: a metal core, a solid middle layer, and a rocky outer layer.

_____

_____

Hydrosphere

About three quarters of Earth is covered by a relatively thin layer of water. Earth's water can take the form of oceans, glaciers, rivers, lakes, groundwater, and water vapor. Of the surface water, most is the salt water of the ocean. Only a tiny part of the hydrosphere is fresh water that is drinkable by humans. The **hydrosphere** (HY druh sfeer) contains all of Earth's water.

_____

_____

Feedback Within a System For years, the ice in glaciers at Glacier National Park in Montana has been melting. The melting is caused by rising temperatures. As the volume of ice in the glaciers has decreased, the land around the glaciers has become warmer. The warmer land melts the glaciers even faster.

Melting of the glaciers in Glacier National Park is an example of a process called *feedback*. When feedback occurs, a system returns—or feeds back—to itself data about a change in the system. In Glacier National Park, the ground around the melting glaciers feeds back warmer temperatures to the glaciers. Feedback can increase the effects of a change, as in the case of warming glaciers, or slow the effects down. Feedback demonstrates how changes in one part of the Earth system might affect the other parts. For example, the feedback of melting glaciers affects the geosphere (the ground), hydrosphere (glaciers), and atmosphere (climate).

Ask Questions Write a question about feedback. Then read the text and answer your question.

_____

_____

_____

_____

_____

_____

_____

Do the Quick Lab
Parts of Earth's System.

Assess Your Understanding

1a. Review The Earth system consists of the sun and four main _____

b. Classify The sphere that contains humans is the _____

c. Evaluate the Impact on Society Give one example of how humans affect the hydrosphere. Then explain how this change impacts society.

_____

_____

_____

got it?

O **I get it!** Now I know that the main parts of the Earth system are _____

_____

_____

O **I need extra help with** _____

Go to **MY SCIENCE COACH** online for help with this subject.

Biosphere
Life exists at the tops of mountains, deep underground, at the bottom of the ocean, and high up in the atmosphere. In fact, life exists in all kinds of conditions. But life as we know it cannot exist without water. The parts of Earth that contain living organisms make up the **biosphere** (BI uh sfeer).

_____

_____

_____

How Do Constructive and Destructive Forces Change Earth?

Suppose you left a movie camera running in one spot for the next 100 million years and then you watched the movie in fast motion. You would see lands forming and mountains rising up—but you would also see them eroding back down again. 🔑 **Lands are constantly being created and destroyed by competing forces.**

Constructive Forces The Himalayas are Earth's highest mountains. But rock in the Himalayas contains *fossils,* or remains, of ocean animals such as ammonites. How could creatures that once lived at the bottom of the sea be found at the top of the world?

The Himalayas are the result of the collision of two sections of Earth's *lithosphere,* or Earth's top layer of stiff, solid rock. This layer is broken into huge pieces, or *plates,* that move slowly over Earth. The slow movement of Earth's plates is called *plate tectonics.*

The Himalayas are the result of the collision of the plate that carries India with the plate that carries China. Over millions of years, as these plates collided, their edges were squeezed slowly upward. This process lifted up the ocean floor and formed the Himalayas, shown in **Figure 3.**

Forces that construct, or build up, mountains are called **constructive forces.** 🔑 **Constructive forces shape the land's surface by building up mountains and other landmasses.** Volcanoes build up Earth's surface by spewing lava that hardens into rock. Earthquakes build landmasses by lifting up mountains and rock.

Ammonite

FIGURE 3 ·····························

From Sea to Mountain

Constructive forces raised the Himalaya Mountains.

✎ **Answer the questions.**

1. **Explain** Why are ammonite fossils found in the Himalayas?

   _____

   _____

   _____

   _____

   _____

   _____

   _____

   _____

2. **Calculate** Many peaks in the Himalayas are 7,300 meters or more above sea level. About how high above India's capital, New Delhi, are these peaks?

   _____

Key
— Plate boundary
Elevation
Meters
4,500
3,000
1,800
900
300
150
0

Destructive Forces While the Himalayas are being built up, they are also being torn down. Ice, rain, wind, and changing temperatures tear the rock apart. This process is called *weathering*. After the rock is torn apart, gravity pulls it downward. Eventually, rivers and streams carry away most of the eroded material.

Because forces such as ice, rain, wind, and changing temperatures wear down, or destroy, landmasses, they are called **destructive forces.** **Destructive forces destroy and wear away landmasses through processes like erosion and weathering.** *Erosion* is the wearing down and carrying away of land by natural forces such as water, ice, or wind.

Vocabulary Identify Related Word Forms Use the text and your knowledge of the word *weather* to write a definition of *weathering.*

_____

_____

_____

_____

_____

apply it!

Since 1983, lava from Kilauea has covered more than 100 square kilometers of land in Hawaii. Here, lava flows into the Pacific Ocean. When it reaches the water, it cools quickly. The cooled lava hardens to form new rock.

❶ **Draw Conclusions** The forces that cause lava to erupt are (constructive/destructive) forces.

❷ **CHALLENGE** Other than the weather, what force wears down the new rock formed by the magma from Kilauea?

_____

_____

Lab zone Do the Quick Lab *What Forces Shape Earth?*

Assess Your Understanding

2a. Review Forces that erode mountains are called (constructive/destructive) forces.

b. List List the destructive forces that act on mountains to erode them.

_____

_____

c. Relate Cause and Effect How do destructive forces change Earth?

_____

_____

_____

_____

_____

got it?

○ **I get it!** Now I know that constructive and destructive forces change Earth by _____

_____

○ **I need extra help with** _____

Go to **my science COACH** online for help with this subject.

Earth's Interior

UNLOCK THE BIG ?

🔑 **How Do Geologists Learn About Earth's Interior?**

🔑 **What Are the Features of Earth's Crust, Mantle, and Core?**

my pLaNeT DiaRY

Inside Earth

Deep inside Earth, our planet is constantly changing. Dr. Samuel B. Mukasa, a geochemist at the University of Michigan, studies some of these changes. He examines rocks in Antarctica that have been brought up to Earth's surface by magma. When he examines these rocks, he looks for elements that occur only in very small amounts. These elements can offer telltale signs of processes occurring near the boundary between Earth's crust and its mantle—or even at deeper levels. By studying rocks at Earth's surface, Dr. Mukasa is helping us understand Earth's interior.

CAREERS

Read the text and then answer the question.

How is Dr. Mukasa able to study Earth's interior without actually seeing it?

_____

_____

_____

_____

_____

> PLANET DIARY Go to **Planet Diary** to learn more about Earth's interior.

Lab zone® Do the Inquiry Warm-Up *Earth's Interior.*

How Do Geologists Learn About Earth's Interior?

Processes that affect Earth's surface are often a result of what's going on inside Earth. But what's inside Earth? This question is very difficult to answer, because geologists are unable to see deep inside Earth. But geologists have found other methods to study the interior of Earth. 🔑 **Geologists have used two main types of evidence to learn about Earth's interior: direct evidence from rock samples and indirect evidence from seismic waves.**

Vocabulary

- seismic wave • pressure • crust • basalt
- granite • mantle • lithosphere • asthenosphere
- outer core • inner core

Skills

- Reading: Identify Supporting Evidence
- Inquiry: Interpret Data

Evidence From Rock Samples Geologists have drilled holes as deep as 12.3 kilometers into Earth. The drills bring up samples of rock. These rocks give geologists clues about Earth's structure and conditions deep inside Earth, where the rocks formed. In addition, volcanoes sometimes blast rock to the surface from depths of more than 100 kilometers. These rocks provide more information about Earth's interior. Also, in laboratories, geologists have re-created conditions inside Earth to see how rock behaves. For instance, they focus laser beams on pieces of rock while squeezing the rock with great force.

Evidence From Seismic Waves To study Earth's interior, geologists use an indirect method. When earthquakes occur, they produce **seismic waves** (syz mik). Geologists record the seismic waves and study how they travel through Earth. The speed of seismic waves and the paths they take give geologists clues about the structure of the planet. That is, the paths of seismic waves reveal areas inside Earth where the makeup or form of material changes. To better understand how seismic waves can reveal Earth's interior, look at how the paths of ocean waves "reveal" the island shown in **Figure 1**.

Direction of ocean waves

FIGURE 1 ·······································

Waves
Paths of ocean waves change when the waves reach an island.

✎ **Infer** Geologists have found that the paths of seismic waves change when the waves reach specific depths inside Earth. What can you infer about Earth's structure from this observation?

 Lab zone Do the Quick Lab *How Do Scientists Find Out What's Inside Earth?*

🗝 Assess Your Understanding

got it? ···

○ **I get it!** Now I know that to learn about Earth's interior, geologists use two main types of evidence:

_____

○ **I need extra help with** _____

Go to **my science COACH** *online for help with this subject.*

What Are the Features of Earth's Crust, Mantle, and Core?

Today, scientists know that Earth's interior is made up of three main layers. Each of Earth's layers covers the layers beneath it, much like the layers of an onion. 🔑 **The three main layers of Earth are the crust, the mantle, and the core. These layers vary greatly in size, composition, temperature, and pressure.**

Although each layer of Earth has its own characteristics, some properties apply throughout all of Earth. For example, the deeper inside Earth, the greater the mass of the rock that is pressing down from above. **Pressure** results from a force pressing on an area. Because of the weight of the rock above, pressure inside Earth increases with depth. 🔑 **The deeper down inside Earth, the greater the pressure.** Look at **Figure 2**. Pressure inside Earth increases much like pressure in the swimming pool increases.

The mass of rock that presses down from above affects the temperature inside Earth. 🔑 **The temperature inside Earth increases as depth increases.** Just beneath Earth's surface, the surrounding rock is cool. But at about 20 meters down, the rock starts to get warmer. For every 40 meters of depth from that point, the temperature typically rises 1 Celsius degree. The rapid rise in temperature continues for several tens of kilometers. Eventually, the temperature increases more slowly, but steadily. The high temperatures inside Earth are the result of the great pressures squeezing rock and the release of energy from radioactive substances. Some heat is also left over from the formation of Earth 4.6 billion years ago.

FIGURE 2 ·······························

Pressure and Depth

The deeper that this swimmer goes, the greater the pressure from the surrounding water.

✎ **Compare and Contrast**
How is the water in the swimming pool similar to Earth's interior? How is it different? (*Hint:* Consider both temperature and pressure in your answer.)

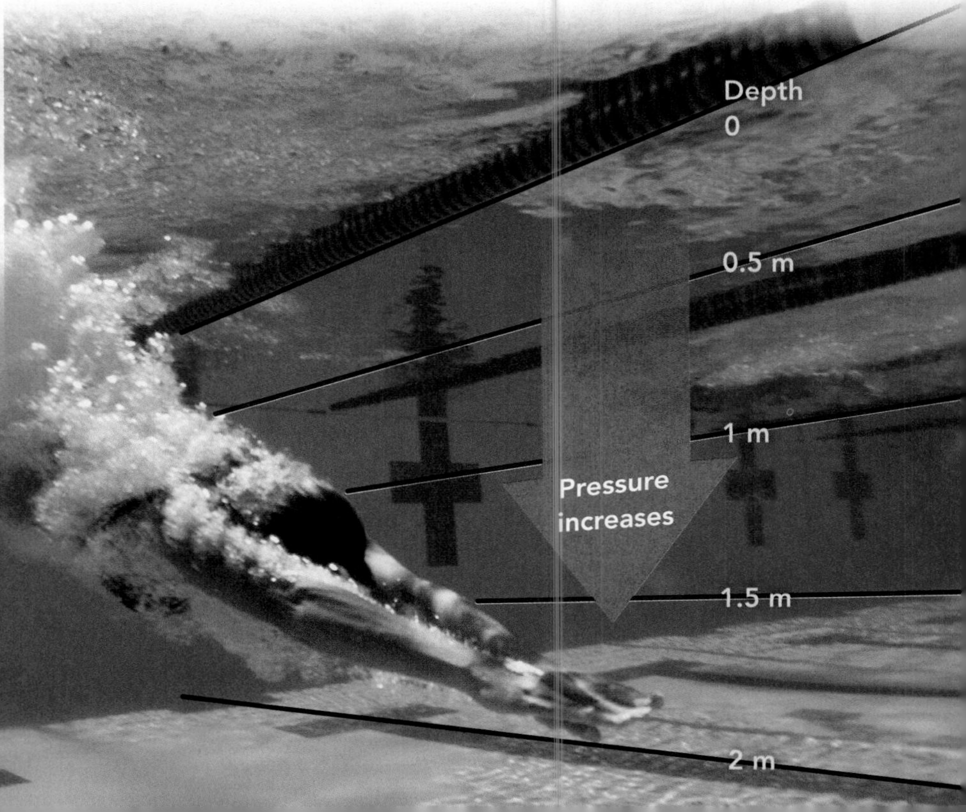

_____

_____

_____

_____

_____

_____

_____

_____

Depth
0

0.5 m

1 m

Pressure increases

1.5 m

2 m

The Crust

In the summer, you might climb a mountain or hike down into a shaded valley. During each of these activities, you are interacting with Earth's **crust**, the layer of rock that forms Earth's outer skin. ⊶ **The crust is a layer of solid rock that includes both dry land and the ocean floor.** The main elements in the crust are oxygen and silicon, as shown in **Figure 3.**

The crust is much thinner than the layer that lies beneath it. In most places, the crust is between 5 and 40 kilometers thick. It is thickest under high mountains—where it can be as thick as 80 kilometers—and thinnest beneath the ocean.

The crust that lies beneath the ocean is called oceanic crust. The composition of oceanic crust is nearly constant. Its overall composition is much like basalt, with small amounts of ocean sediment on top. **Basalt** (buh SAWLT) is a dark, fine-grained rock.

Continental crust, the crust that forms the continents, contains many types of rocks. So, unlike oceanic crust, its composition varies greatly. But overall the composition of continental crust is much like granite. **Granite** is a rock that usually is a light color and has coarse grains. Both granite and basalt have more oxygen and silicon than they have any other element.

Read the text on this page and then fill in the missing information below.

Layer: _____

Thickness: _____

FIGURE 3 ·······································
Earth's Crust
The crust is Earth's outer layer of solid rock.

The Earth's Crust

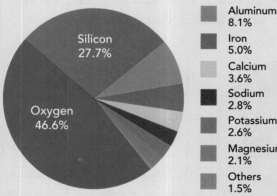

- Aluminum 8.1%
- Iron 5.0%
- Calcium 3.6%
- Sodium 2.8%
- Potassium 2.6%
- Magnesium 2.1%
- Others 1.5%

Silicon 27.7%

Oxygen 46.6%

Note: Percentages given are by weight.

The circle graph above shows the composition of Earth's crust.

✎ **Use the graph and the text on this page to complete the activities below.**

1. **Read Graphs** In total, how much of Earth's crust is made up of oxygen and silicon?

   _____

2. **Summarize** Fill in the missing information in the two charts at the right.

Oceanic crust

Oceanic crust

Typical rock: _____

Relative grain size: _____

Color: _____

Continental crust

Typical rock: _____

Relative grain size: _____

Color: _____

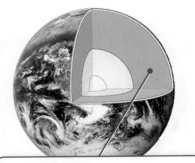

Read the text on this page and then fill in the missing information below.

Layer: _____

Thickness: _____

_____

The Mantle

About 40 kilometers beneath dry land, the rock in Earth's interior changes. Rock here contains more magnesium and iron than rock above it. The rock below the boundary is the solid material of the **mantle**, a layer of hot rock. 🔑 **The mantle is made of rock that is very hot, but solid. Scientists divide the mantle into layers based on the physical characteristics of those layers. Overall, the mantle is nearly 3,000 kilometers thick.**

The Lithosphere The uppermost part of the mantle is brittle rock, like the rock of the crust. Both the crust and the uppermost part of the mantle are strong, hard, and rigid. So geologists often group the crust and uppermost mantle into a single layer called the **lithosphere** (LITH uh sfeer). As shown in **Figure 4,** Earth's lithosphere averages about 100 kilometers thick.

The Asthenosphere Below the lithosphere, the material is hotter and under increasing pressure. As a result, the part of the mantle just beneath the lithosphere is less rigid than the rock above. Over thousands of years this part of the mantle can bend like a metal spoon. But it's still solid. If you kicked it, you would stub your toe. This soft layer is called the **asthenosphere** (as THEN uh sfeer).

The Mesosphere Beneath the asthenosphere, the mantle is hot but more rigid. The stiffness of the *mesosphere* is the result of increasingly high pressure. This layer includes a region called the transition zone, which lies just beneath the asthenosphere. It also includes the lower mantle, which extends down to Earth's core.

FIGURE 4 ·······························

Mantle Piece
Earth's mantle is nearly 3,000 kilometers thick. The rigid lithosphere rests on the softer material of the asthenosphere.

✏️ **Describe** Fill in the information in the boxes next to the diagram of the upper mantle.

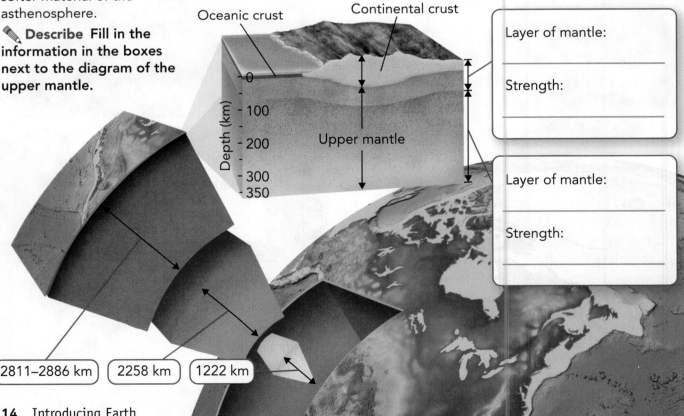

Oceanic crust

Continental crust

Depth (km)
- 0
- 100
- 200
- 300
- 350

Upper mantle

Layer of mantle:
_____
Strength:
_____

Layer of mantle:
_____
Strength:
_____

2811–2886 km   2258 km   1222 km

The Core Below the mantle lies Earth's core. 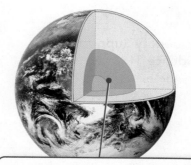 **The core is made mostly of the metals iron and nickel. It consists of two parts—a liquid outer core and a solid inner core.** The outer core is 2,258 kilometers thick. The inner core is a solid ball. Its radius is 1,222 kilometers. The total radius of the core is 3,480 kilometers. Earth's core occupies the center of the planet.

Outer Core and Inner Core The outer core is a layer of molten metal surrounding the inner core. Despite enormous pressure, the outer core is liquid. The inner core is a dense ball of solid metal. In the inner core, extreme pressure squeezes the atoms of iron and nickel so much that they cannot spread out to become liquid.

Currently, most evidence suggests that both parts of the core are made of iron and nickel. But scientists have found data suggesting that the core also contains oxygen, sulfur, and silicon.

> **Read the text on this page and then fill in the missing information below.**
>
> Layer: _____
>
> Radius: _____

FIGURE 5

The Core of It
Earth's core consists of two separate layers.

✎ **Review** Put each term below in its proper place in the Venn diagram.

solid metal	molten metal
iron	nickel
dense ball	liquid layer

Outer Core   Both   Inner Core

do the
math! Analyzing Data

Temperature Inside Earth

The graph shows how temperatures change between Earth's surface and the core.

❶ Read Graphs Between what depths does Earth's temperature increase the slowest?

_____

❷ CHALLENGE Why does the graph show a temperature of 16°C at 0 meters of depth?

_____

_____

❸ Interpret Data How does temperature change with depth in Earth's interior?

_____

_____

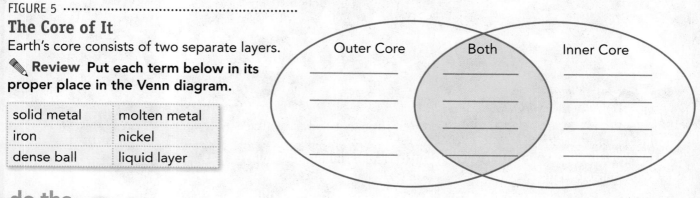

Temperature and Depth

Boundary between lithosphere and asthenosphere

Boundary between lower mantle and core

Temperature (°C)

Depth (km)

15

🖙 Identify Supporting Evidence How can iron filings provide evidence that a bar magnet has a magnetic field?

_____

_____

_____

_____

_____

The Core and Earth's Magnetic Field Scientists think that movements in the liquid outer core create Earth's magnetic field. Because Earth has a magnetic field, the planet acts like a giant bar magnet. Earth's magnetic field affects the whole planet.

To understand how a magnetic field affects an object, look at the bar magnet shown in **Figure 6.** If you place the magnet on a piece of paper and sprinkle iron filings on the paper, the iron filings line up with the bar's magnetic field. If you could surround Earth with iron filings, they would form a similar pattern.

When you use a compass, the compass needle aligns with the lines of force in Earth's magnetic field. These lines meet at Earth's magnetic poles. So the needle points to Earth's _magnetic_ north pole, which is not the same location as Earth's _geographic_ North Pole.

EXPLORE THE BIG ❓ _Earth's Interior_

What is the structure of Earth?

FIGURE 7 ··

▶ **REAL-WORLD INQUIRY** Earth is divided into distinct layers. Each layer has its own characteristics.

1. **Summarize** Draw each of Earth's layers. Include both the outer core and the inner core. Label each layer. Then, complete the chart below.

	Thickness/Radius	Composition	Solid/Liquid
Crust:			
Mantle:			
Outer core:			
Inner core:			
TOTAL:	6,371 km		

2. **Compare and Contrast** Pick any two points inside Earth and label them A and B. Compare and contrast Earth at those two points.

My Point A is in the _____

My Point B is in the _____

_____

_____

_____

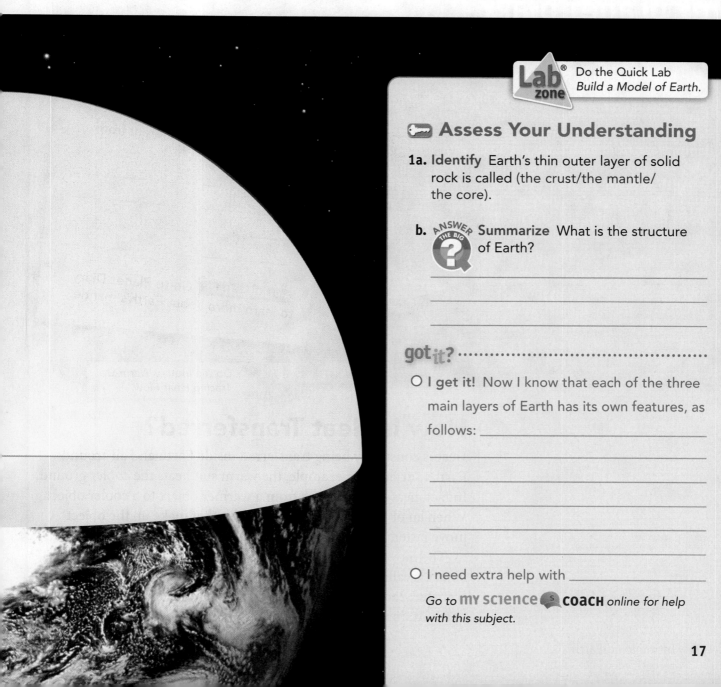

FIGURE 6 ··············

Earth's Magnetic Field

Earth's magnetic field has a north and south pole, like the magnetic field at each end of a magnet.

✎ **Name** Which pole will a compass needle in North America point to? (Underline the correct label for the pole on the globe.)

Magnetic pole   Geographic North Pole

Geographic South Pole   Magnetic pole

Lab® zone Do the Quick Lab *Build a Model of Earth.*

🔑 Assess Your Understanding

1a. Identify Earth's thin outer layer of solid rock is called (the crust/the mantle/ the core).

b. ANSWER THE BIG ? **Summarize** What is the structure of Earth?

_____

_____

_____

got it? ···

○ **I get it!** Now I know that each of the three main layers of Earth has its own features, as follows: _____

_____

_____

_____

_____

_____

○ **I need extra help with** _____

Go to MY SCIENCE ⬤ COACH *online for help with this subject.*

17

Convection and the Mantle

UNLOCK THE BIG Q?

🔑 **How Is Heat Transferred?**

🔑 **How Does Convection Occur in Earth's Mantle?**

MY PLANET DiARY

Lighting Up the Subject

Misconception: Rock cannot flow.

Did you know that the solid rock in Earth's mantle can flow like a fluid? To learn how, look at this image of a lava lamp. Heat from a bulb causes solid globs of wax at the bottom of the lamp to expand. As they expand, the globs become less dense. The globs then rise through the more dense fluid that surrounds them.

In Earth's mantle, great heat and pressure create regions of rock that are less dense than the rock around them. Over millions of years, the less dense rock slowly rises—like the solid globs in the lava lamp!

MISCONCEPTION

✏️ **Compare and Contrast** Think about your own observations of liquids that flow. Then answer the question below.

How is flowing rock different from flowing water?

_____

_____

_____

_____

▶ PLANET DIARY Go to **Planet Diary** to learn more about Earth's mantle.

Lab zone® Do the Inquiry Warm-Up *Tracing Heat Flow.*

How Is Heat Transferred?

Heat is constantly being transferred inside Earth and all around Earth's surface. For example, the warm sun heats the cooler ground. In fact, heat always moves from a warmer object to a cooler object. When an object is heated, the particles that make up the object move faster. The faster-moving particles have more energy.

The movement of energy from a warmer object to a cooler object is called heat transfer. 🔑 **There are three types of heat transfer: radiation, convection, and conduction.** Look at **Figure 1** to see examples of heat transfer.

Vocabulary
- radiation • convection
- conduction • density
- convection current

Skills
⤸ Reading: Relate Cause and Effect

△ Inquiry: Communicate

Radiation
The sun constantly transfers light and heat through the air, warming your skin. The transfer of energy that is carried in rays like light is called **radiation**.

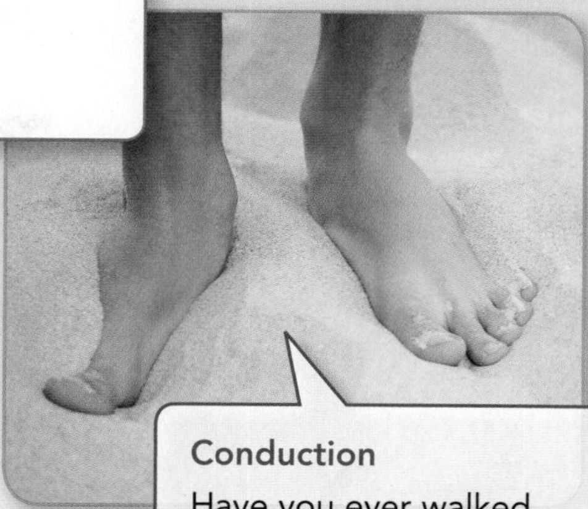

Conduction
Have you ever walked barefoot over hot sand? Your feet can feel as if they are burning! That is because the sand transfers its heat to your skin. Heat transfer between materials that are touching is called **conduction**.

Convection
Seagulls often soar on warm air currents. The currents are created as warm air rises from the ground. The warm air heats cooler air above it. Heat transfer by the movement of a fluid is called **convection**.

FIGURE 1 ·······················
⟩ INTERACTIVE ART **Heat Transfer**
In each type of heat transfer, heat moves from a warmer object to a colder object.

△Communicate Work with a classmate to think of other examples of conduction, convection, and radiation. (*Hint*: Think of different ways to cook food.) Write your answers in the spaces provided.

Radiation
_____
_____

Conduction
_____
_____

Convection
_____
_____

 Do the Quick Lab *How Can Heat Cause Motion in a Liquid?*

🔑 Assess Your Understanding

got it? ··

○ **I get it!** Now I know that the three types of heat transfer are _____
_____

○ **I need extra help with** _____
Go to **my science ⟨s⟩ coach** *online for help with this subject.*

How Does Convection Occur in Earth's Mantle?

Recall that Earth's mantle and core are extremely hot. How is heat transferred within Earth?

Convection Currents When you heat soup on a stove, convection occurs in the soup. That is, the soup at the bottom of the pot gets hot and expands. As the soup expands, its density decreases. **Density** is a measure of how much mass there is in a given volume of a substance. For example, most rock is more dense than water because a given volume of rock has more mass than the same volume of water.

The warm, less dense soup above the heat source moves upward and floats over the cooler, denser soup, as shown in **Figure 2.** Near the surface, the warm soup cools, becoming denser. Gravity then pulls the colder soup back down to the bottom of the pot. Here, it is reheated and rises again.

A constant flow begins. Cooler, denser soup sinks to the bottom of the pot. At the same time, warmer, less dense soup rises. The flow that transfers heat within a fluid is called a **convection current.** **Heating and cooling of a fluid, changes in the fluid's density, and the force of gravity combine to set convection currents in motion.** Without heat, convection currents eventually stop.

Relate Cause and Effect
What three processes or forces combine to set convection currents in motion?

_____

_____

_____

_____

_____

FIGURE 2 ·······················
Convection Currents
In a pot of soup, convection currents flow as the hotter, less dense soup rises and the cooler, more dense soup sinks.

apply it!

Hot springs are common in Yellowstone National Park. Here, melted snow and rainwater seep to a depth of 3,000 meters, where a shallow magma chamber heats the rock of Earth's crust. The rock heats the water to over 200°C and keeps it under very high pressure.

① **Compare and Contrast** The heated water is (more/less) dense than the melted snow and rainwater.

② [CHALLENGE] What might cause convection currents in a hot spring?

_____

_____

Convection Currents in Earth

Inside Earth, heat from the core and the mantle act like the stove that heats the pot of soup. That is, large amounts of heat are transferred by convection currents within the core and mantle. 🔑 **Heat from the core and the mantle itself causes convection currents in the mantle.** To see how these currents work in the core and mantle, look at **Figure 3.**

How is it possible for mantle rock to flow? Over millions of years, the great heat and pressure in the mantle have caused solid mantle rock to warm and flow very slowly. Many geologists think plumes of mantle rock rise slowly from the bottom of the mantle toward the top. The hot rock eventually cools and sinks back through the mantle. Over and over, the cycle of rising and sinking takes place. Convection currents like these have been moving inside Earth for more than four billion years!

There are also convection currents in the outer core. These convection currents cause Earth's magnetic field.

FIGURE 3 ⋯⋯⋯⋯⋯⋯⋯⋯⋯⋯⋯⋯⋯⋯⋯⋯⋯⋯⋯
ART IN MOTION **Mantle Convection**
✏️ **Interpret Diagrams** Place the following labels in the boxes for Points A and B:

hotter	less dense	sinks
colder	more dense	rises

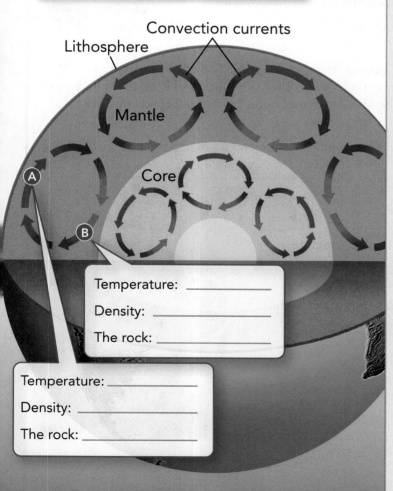

Convection currents

Lithosphere

Mantle

Core

A

B

Temperature: _____
Density: _____
The rock: _____

Temperature: _____
Density: _____
The rock: _____

Lab zone ® Do the Lab Investigation *Modeling Mantle Convection Currents.*

🔑 **Assess Your Understanding**

1a. Explain A convection current transfers (heat /air) within a fluid.

b. Infer In which part of Earth's core do convection currents occur? _____

c. Predict What would happen to the convection currents in the mantle if Earth's interior eventually cooled down? Why?

_____
_____
_____
_____
_____

got it? ⋯⋯⋯⋯⋯⋯⋯⋯⋯⋯⋯⋯⋯⋯⋯⋯

○ **I get it!** Now I know that convection currents in the mantle are caused by_____
_____
_____

○ **I need extra help with** _____

Go to **my science** ˢ **coach** *online for help with this subject.*

1 Study Guide

Earth consists of three main layers. The _____ is the outermost layer. The _____ is made up of rock that is hot but solid. The _____ occupies Earth's center.

LESSON 1 The Earth System

🔑 The Earth system has four main spheres: the atmosphere, the hydrosphere, the geosphere, and the biosphere. As a major source of energy for Earth processes, the sun can be considered part of the Earth system as well.

🔑 Lands are constantly being created and destroyed by competing forces. Constructive forces shape the land's surface by building up mountains and other landmasses. Destructive forces destroy and wear away landmasses through processes like erosion and weathering.

Vocabulary
• system • energy • atmosphere • geosphere • hydrosphere
• biosphere • constructive force • destructive force

LESSON 2 Earth's Interior

🔑 Geologists have used two main types of evidence to learn about Earth's interior: direct evidence from rock samples and indirect evidence from seismic waves.

🔑 The deeper down inside Earth, the greater the pressure. The temperature inside Earth increases as depth increases.

🔑 The three main layers of Earth are the crust, the mantle, and the core. The crust is a layer of solid rock that includes dry land and ocean floor. The mantle is about 3,000 km thick and is made of very hot, solid rock. The core is mostly iron and nickel. It consists of a liquid outer core and a solid inner core.

Vocabulary
• seismic wave • pressure • crust • basalt • granite • mantle
• lithosphere • asthenosphere • outer core • inner core

LESSON 3 Convection and the Mantle

🔑 There are three types of heat transfer: radiation, convection, and conduction.

🔑 Heating and cooling of a fluid, changes in the fluid's density, and the force of gravity combine to set convection currents in motion.

🔑 Heat from the core and the mantle itself causes convection currents in the mantle.

Vocabulary
• radiation • convection • conduction • density • convection current

Review and Assessment

LESSON 1 **The Earth System**

1. Which is part of Earth's hydrosphere?

   a. liquid outer core   **b.** solid inner core

   c. granite   **d.** ocean water

2. Earth's system has two sources of energy, which are _____

   _____

   _____

3. **Infer** Explain how the hydrosphere and biosphere interact in this swamp.

   _____

   _____

   _____

4. **Classify** Are the forces that cause lava to erupt from a volcano and flow over Earth's surface constructive or destructive forces? Explain.

   _____

   _____

   _____

   _____

5. **Write About It** If the amount of paved land in the United States continues to increase, how might the biosphere be affected?

LESSON 2 **Earth's Interior**

6. What is the relatively soft layer of the upper mantle called?

   a. continental crust   **b.** lithosphere

   c. asthenosphere   **d.** inner core

7. To learn about Earth's structure, geologists use seismic waves, which are _____

   _____

   _____

8. **Relate Cause and Effect** What do scientists think produces Earth's magnetic field?

   _____

   _____

   _____

   _____

9. **Sequence** Name each layer of Earth, starting from Earth's center. Include both layers of the core and all layers of the mantle.

   _____

   _____

   _____

   _____

10. **Summarize** What is the relationship between temperature and depth inside Earth? Is this relationship the same for pressure?

    _____

    _____

    _____

    _____

11. **Write About It** Compare and contrast oceanic crust with continental crust. In your answer, be sure to consider the composition and thickness of both types of crust.

1 Review and Assessment

Convection and the Mantle

12. What is the transfer of heat by direct contact of particles of matter called?

   a. conduction   **b.** radiation

   c. convection   **d.** pressure

13. Compared to air and water, most rock has a

high density, which means it has _____

_____

_____

14. Identify Name the two layers below Earth's surface in which convection takes place.

_____

15. Explain What conditions allow rock in the mantle to flow?

_____

_____

_____

16. Develop Hypotheses Suppose a certain part of the mantle is cooler than the parts surrounding it. What might happen to the cooler rock? In your answer, discuss the role of gravity.

_____

_____

_____

_____

 What is the structure of Earth?

17. Suppose you could travel to the center of Earth. You must design a special vehicle for your journey. What equipment should your vehicle include so that it could travel through each layer of Earth shown below? Also, what conditions should your vehicle be able to withstand? Consider temperature, pressure, and the hardness of each layer of Earth.

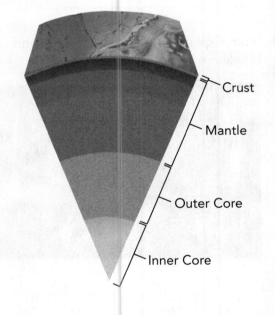

Crust

Mantle

Outer Core

Inner Core

_____

_____

_____

_____

_____

_____

_____

_____

_____

_____

_____

_____

_____

Standardized Test Prep

Multiple Choice

Circle the letter of the best answer.

1. The illustration below shows a pot of boiling water.

   What process is heating the water?

   A radiation
   B conduction
   C convection
   D destruction

2. Which part of Earth's system is made up of plants and animals?

   A biosphere
   B hydrosphere
   C atmosphere
   D geosphere

3. Which part of Earth's interior is made mostly of nickel and iron and has liquid and solid parts?

   A lithosphere
   B crust
   C asthenosphere
   D core

4. What is one result of convection currents in Earth's outer core?

   A erosion
   B Earth's magnetic field
   C melted glaciers
   D Earth's force of gravity

5. How do pressure and temperature change inside Earth as depth increases?

   A pressure and temperature decrease
   B pressure increases; temperature decreases
   C pressure decreases; temperature increases
   D pressure and temperature increase

Constructed Response

Use the illustration below and your knowledge of science to help you answer Question 6. Write your answer on a separate piece of paper.

6. Describe how Earth's spheres are interacting in the scene pictured below. Also describe any notable constructive and destructive forces.

A Slice of Earth

If you could dig a hole that went straight through to the other side of the world, on your way down you'd see all of the layers underneath Earth's surface.

Of course, digging that kind of hole would be impossible. But if we want to see a slice of Earth, and all its layers, we have another tool. Seismic tomography lets us see Earth's layers as 3-D images. A computer uses data on the size and speed of seismic waves to make these images.

The sudden release of stored energy under Earth's crust sends seismic waves in all directions and causes an earthquake. The waves travel out from the center of the earthquake. Density, pressure, and temperature affect how quickly these seismic waves move through the layers of rock underground. Waves can also bend or bounce back where they meet a boundary between layers.

Scientists are able to record the speed and size of the seismic waves from thousands of earthquakes. Combining data recorded at different places allows scientists to use computers to create models of Earth's interior.

Knowing exactly what is lying beneath our feet is helping scientists learn more about tectonic processes, such as mountain building, as well as helping us find important mineral resources.

Research It Seismic tomography has been compared to CAT (computerized axial tomography) scans. How are they similar? How are they different? Research them both and create a graphic organizer outlining the similarities and differences.

This seismic tomography image shows a cross-section of Earth's crust and mantle. The colors show materials of different densities that are rising or sinking as part of convection currents in the mantle. The blue line on the map shows that this "slice" of Earth extends from the Pacific Ocean eastward to western Africa. ▶

Save the Seeds, Save the World

Bananas may be in trouble. So may some species of wheat. In fact a number of species of plants face threats to their survival. Scientists think that Earth's climate is changing. And as it changes, so does the biosphere. Some plants are becoming more vulnerable to disease or to insect pests. Human development also threatens some plants' habitats. With all these changes to the biosphere, plant species are becoming extinct at an increasing rate.

The Svalbard Global Seed Vault may be helping to preserve samples of important resources. Tucked into the permafrost in Svalbard—an island north of Norway that is farther north than almost any other landmass on Earth—the Seed Vault protects seeds that come from almost every important food crop in the world. The seeds of bananas, strawberries, rice, and beans are all preserved (along with many other species) in case they go extinct. Many seeds come from developing countries, which have a lot of biodiversity. Because the Seed Vault is in the cryosphere—the frozen portion of the hydrosphere—scientists think that Svalbard will remain frozen even if climate change continues to cause the glaciers farther south to melt.

The Seed Vault can store up to 4.5 million seeds at –18°C. Even if the power goes out, the seeds will stay frozen because the permafrost will keep the temperature of the vaults below –3.5°C.

Inside the Svalbard Global Seed Vault ▲

Write About It Scientists have observed signs of global climate change. Changes to Earth's climate are affecting many other Earth systems. For example, sea levels are rising, and sea ice is melting. Write an essay explaining how these changes might lead to the extinction of a specific plant species.

HOW DID THIS ROCK GET HERE?

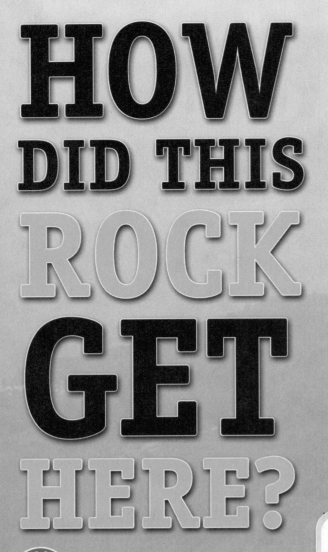

How do rocks form?

The famous naturalist John Muir first climbed to the summit of Cathedral Peak in 1869. Located in the Sierra Nevada Range in California, it is 3,308 meters in elevation. Cathedral Peak is mostly composed of granite, a mixture of quartz, feldspar, and other minerals such as hornblende and mica. Looking down from this tall, narrow peak, you would probably feel like you were on top of the world!

△ **Develop Hypotheses** How might this towering piece of rock have gotten here?

_____

_____

_____

_____

_____

▷ UNTAMED SCIENCE   Watch the **Untamed Science** video to learn more about minerals and rocks.

Minerals and Rocks

Getting Started

Check Your Understanding

1. **Background** Read the paragraph below and then answer the question.

Judy filled a glass jar with water. She put a lid on the jar and put the jar in the freezer. Overnight, the water, which was a **liquid,** froze into ice, which is a **solid.** But Judy had forgotten that ice occupies a larger **volume** than the same mass of water. So when the water froze, it expanded and cracked the jar.

A **liquid** is a substance that flows and whose shape, but not volume, can be changed.

A **solid** is a substance that resists changing shape.

Volume is the amount of space that matter occupies.

• What variable changed to turn the liquid water into solid ice?

_____

_____

> **MY READING WEB** If you had trouble completing the question above, visit **My Reading Web** and type in *Minerals and Rocks.*

Vocabulary Skill

Latin Word Origins Many science words in English come from Latin. For example, *granite* comes from the Latin *granum,* meaning "grain." Granite is a rock that has large, visible grains.

Latin Word	Meaning of Latin Word	Example
erosus	eaten away	erosion, *n.* a process by which a mountain is broken into pieces
folium	leaf	foliated, *adj.* with thin, flat layers
caementum	stones and chips from a quarry	cementation, *n.* process in which bits of rock are glued together

2. **Quick Check** Choose the word from the table that best completes the sentence.

• Rocks that have their grains arranged in flat layers are said to be

_____

crystal

texture

clastic rock

rock cycle

Chapter Preview

LESSON 1
- mineral • inorganic • crystal
- streak • luster
- Mohs hardness scale • cleavage
- fracture • geode • crystallization
- solution • vein

↻ **Relate Text and Visuals**
△ **Form Operational Definitions**

LESSON 2
- rock-forming mineral • granite
- basalt • grain • texture
- igneous rock • sedimentary rock
- metamorphic rock

↻ **Identify the Main Idea**
△ **Observe**

LESSON 3
- extrusive rock
- intrusive rock

↻ **Relate Cause and Effect**
△ **Interpret Data**

LESSON 4
- sediment • weathering • erosion
- deposition • compaction
- cementation • clastic rock
- organic rock • chemical rock

↻ **Identify the Main Idea**
△ **Infer**

LESSON 5
- foliated

↻ **Relate Cause and Effect**
△ **Observe**

LESSON 6
- rock cycle

↻ **Sequence**
△ **Classify**

▷ **VOCAB FLASH CARDS** For extra help with vocabulary, visit **Vocab Flash Cards** and type in *Minerals and Rocks.*

UNLOCK THE BIG ?

🔑 **What Is a Mineral?**

🔑 **How Are Minerals Identified?**

🔑 **How Do Minerals Form?**

MY PLANET DIARY

Posted by: MacKenzie

Location: Brewerton, New York

I used to go to summer camp. We went on a good field trip to an underground cavern. When we got inside, I thought I was in a dragon's mouth. Later, I found out that those teeth were stalactites and stalagmites. Stalactites hang from the ceiling and stalagmites grow from the ground.

BLOG

Communicate Discuss the question with a partner. Write your answer below.

Stalactites and stalagmites are usually made up of the mineral calcite. This mineral dissolves easily in acidic water. How do you think calcite hardened to form the features in the cave?

_____

_____

_____

_____

_____

▸ PLANET DIARY Go to **Planet Diary** to learn more about minerals.

Lab zone® Do the Inquiry Warm-Up *How Does the Rate of Cooling Affect Crystals?*

What Is a Mineral?

Look at the two substances in **Figure 1.** On the left is a hard chunk of coal. On the right are beautiful quartz crystals. Both are solid materials that form beneath Earth's surface. But which is a mineral?

Defining Minerals How are minerals defined? 🔑 **A mineral is a naturally occurring solid that can form by inorganic processes and that has a crystal structure and a definite chemical composition.** For a substance to be a **mineral,** it must have all five of these characteristics. So, is either quartz or coal a mineral?

Vocabulary

- mineral • inorganic • crystal • streak • luster
- Mohs hardness scale • cleavage • fracture
- geode • crystallization • solution • vein

Skills

↻ Reading: Relate Text and Visuals

△ Inquiry: Form Operational Definitions

Naturally Occurring

All minerals are substances that are formed by natural processes. Quartz forms naturally as molten material called magma cools and hardens beneath Earth's surface. Coal forms naturally from the remains of plants that are squeezed tightly together.

Forms by Inorganic Processes

All minerals must be able to form by **inorganic** processes. That is, every mineral must be able to form from materials that were not a part of living things. Quartz can form naturally as magma cools. Coal comes only from living things—the remains of plants that lived millions of years ago. But some minerals that can form from inorganic processes may also be produced by living things.

Solid

A mineral is always a solid, with a definite volume and shape. The particles that make up a solid are packed together very tightly, so they cannot move like the particles that make up a liquid. Coal and quartz are solids.

Definite Chemical Composition

A mineral has a definite chemical composition. This means that a mineral always contains certain elements in definite proportions. An element is a substance composed of a single kind of atom.

Quartz always contains one atom of silicon for every two atoms of oxygen. The elements in coal can vary over a wide range.

Crystal Structure

The particles of a mineral line up in a pattern that repeats over and over again. The repeating pattern of a mineral's particles forms a solid called a **crystal.** A crystal has flat sides, called faces, that meet at sharp edges and corners. The quartz in **Figure 1** has a crystal structure. In contrast, most coal lacks a crystal structure.

Quartz

Coal

FIGURE 1 ·······························

Are They or Aren't They?

To be classified as a mineral, a substance must satisfy five requirements.

✎ **Classify Complete the checklist. Are quartz and coal minerals or only naturally occurring substances?**

_____

_____

Mineral Characteristics	Quartz	Coal
Naturally occurring	✔	✔
Can form by inorganic processes		
Solid		
Crystal structure		
Definite chemical composition		

Minerals, Compounds, and Elements

Almost all minerals are compounds. In a compound, two or more elements are combined so that the elements no longer have distinct properties. For example, the mineral cinnabar is composed of the elements sulfur and mercury. Sulfur is bright yellow. Mercury is a silvery liquid at room temperature. But cinnabar has solid, shiny, red crystals.

Different minerals have a different combination of elements. For example, a crystal of quartz has one atom of silicon for every two atoms of oxygen. This ratio is constant for all varieties of quartz. Each mineral in the garnet group of minerals has three atoms of silicon for every twelve atoms of oxygen. But garnets also contain other elements, in set ratios. **Figure 2** shows one variety of garnet.

Some elements occur in nature in a pure form, and not as part of a compound. Elements such as copper, silver, and gold are also minerals. Almost all pure, solid elements are metals.

FIGURE 2 ····························

Elements and Compounds in Minerals

Quartz and the garnet minerals contain the elements silicon and oxygen. At room temperature, pure silicon is a hard, dark gray solid. Oxygen is a colorless gas.

✎ **Describe** Choose either quartz or garnet. Then, choose silicon or oxygen. When your element is part of a mineral, how is it different from its pure form?

_____

_____

_____

_____

_____

_____

_____

Rose quartz   **Almandine garnet**

Lab zone® Do the Quick Lab *Classifying Objects as Minerals.*

🔑 Assess Your Understanding

1a. Summarize All minerals must be able to form from (organic/inorganic) processes.

b. Explain What, specifically, makes a process inorganic?

_____

_____

c. Classify Amber is a material used in jewelry. It forms only by the process of pine tree resin hardening into stone. Is amber a mineral? Explain.

_____

_____

_____

---

got it? ·······················

○ **I get it!** Now I know that to be classified as a mineral, a substance must be _____

_____

_____

○ **I need extra help with** _____

Go to **MY SCIENCE** ⓢ **COACH** online for help with this subject.

How Are Minerals Identified?

Geologists have identified more than 4,000 minerals. But telling these minerals apart can often be a challenge. 🔑 **Each mineral has characteristic properties that can be used to identify it.**

Color

Both minerals shown here are the color gold. But only one is the mineral gold. In fact, only a few minerals have their own characteristic color.

B

A

FIGURE 3 ···
Is All That Glitters Really Gold?
Both minerals shown here are gold in color.

✏️ **Identify** Circle the mineral that you think is gold. (Answer at bottom of page.)

Streak

The **streak** of a mineral is the color of its powder. Although the color of a mineral can vary, its streak does not. However, the streak color and the mineral color are often different. For example, pyrite has a gold color but its streak is greenish black.

FIGURE 4 ···
Scratching the Surface
The color of any particular mineral's streak does not vary.

✏️ **Infer** Which is more useful when identifying a mineral: the mineral's color or the mineral's streak?

_____

Malachite

Galena   Hematite

Luster

Luster is the term used to describe how light is reflected from a mineral's surface. For example, minerals such as galena that contain metals often have a metallic luster. Quartz has a glassy luster. Other terms used to describe luster include earthy, silky, waxy, and pearly.

Metallic	Silky	Waxy, greasy, or pearly

Galena   Malachite   Talc

FIGURE 5 ···
Upon Reflection
Geologists use many terms to describe the luster of minerals.

✏️ **Describe** Choose any item in your classroom that reflects light. In one word, describe its luster.

Item: _____

Luster: _____

A. Gold B. Pyrite

know?

Apatite is a mineral included in the Mohs hardness scale. Enamel on mature teeth consists mainly of apatite crystals.

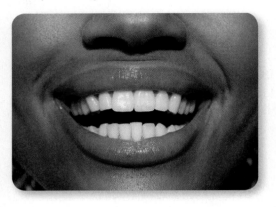

Hardness When you want to identify a mineral, one of the most useful clues to use is the mineral's hardness. In 1812, Austrian Friedrich Mohs, a mineral expert, invented a scale to help identify minerals by how hard they are. The **Mohs hardness scale** is used to rank the hardness of minerals. The scale assigns a mineral's hardness a ranking from 1 to 10, as shown in **Figure 6.**

Hardness can be determined by a scratch test. A mineral can scratch any mineral softer than itself, but can be scratched by any mineral that is harder. For example, suppose you found a deposit of azurite. Azurite is not on the Mohs scale, but you would like to determine its hardness. So you take a small sample and try to scratch it with talc, gypsum, and calcite. But none of these minerals scratch your sample. Apatite, rated 5 on the scale, does scratch it. Therefore, the hardness of azurite is probably about 4.

FIGURE 6
Mohs Hardness Scale

Geologists determine a mineral's hardness by comparing it to the hardness of the minerals on the Mohs scale.

✏️ **Explain Read the description of each mineral at the right. Place each mineral's name in its proper location in the scale.**

Topaz It can scratch quartz but not corundum.

Gypsum A fingernail can easily scratch it.

Apatite A steel knife can scratch it.

Diamond Extremely hard, it can scratch all known common minerals.

Quartz It can scratch feldspar but not topaz.

1 Talc The softest mineral, talc flakes when scratched by a fingernail.

2 _____

3 Calcite A fingernail cannot scratch it, but a copper penny can.

4 Fluorite A steel knife can easily scratch it.

5 _____

Increasing hardness

do the math!

Calculating Density

For many minerals, different samples of a mineral all have the same density. So geologists can use density to help identify mineral samples. To do so, they use the following formula.

$$\text{Density} = \frac{\text{Mass}}{\text{Volume}}$$

You find a sample of the mineral magnetite. The sample has a mass of 151.0 g and a volume of 29.0 cm³. What is the density of magnetite?

_____

_____

_____

Density   Each mineral has a characteristic density. Recall that density is the mass in a given space, or mass per unit volume. No matter how large or small the mineral sample is, the density of that mineral always remains the same. For example, the density of quartz is 2.6 g/cm³. The density of diamond is 3.5 g/cm³.

To measure density, geologists use a balance to first determine the precise mass of a mineral sample. Then they place the mineral in water to determine how much water the sample displaces. The volume of the displaced water equals the volume of the sample. The mineral's density can then be calculated using the formula below.

$$\text{Density} = \frac{\text{Mass}}{\text{Volume}}$$

You can compare the density of two mineral samples of about the same size. Just pick them up and heft them, or feel their weight, in your hands. The sample that feels heavier is probably also denser.

6 Feldspar
It can't be scratched by a steel knife but can scratch window glass.

7 _____

8 _____

9 Corundum
It can scratch topaz.

10 _____

Halite

Quartz

Crystal Structure

The atoms that make up a mineral line up in a regular pattern. This pattern repeats over and over. The repeating pattern of a mineral's atoms forms a mineral's crystal structure. All the crystals of a mineral have the same crystal structure. Scientists can use crystal structure to identify very small mineral samples. For example, scientists can bounce a powerful beam of particles off very small crystals. Because the atoms that make up minerals line up in regular patterns, these beams produce distinct patterns of light.

As shown in **Figure 7,** different minerals have crystals that are shaped differently. Halite crystals are cubic. That is, they are shaped like a cube. You can break a large piece of halite into smaller pieces. But the smaller pieces still contain crystals that are perfect cubes.

Geologists classify crystals by the number of faces, or sides, on the crystal. They also measure the angles at which the faces meet.

What Do You Know?

✎ **Interpret Photographs** The photograph shows crystals of the mineral stibnite. Read the text about how minerals are identified. Then identify which of stibnite's characteristic properties you can infer from the photograph. Which properties would you need to test before being able to identify the mineral?

_____

_____

_____

_____

_____

_____

_____

_____

Cleavage and Fracture

You may be familiar with how the mineral mica can split apart to form flat sheets. A mineral that splits easily along flat surfaces has the property called **cleavage.**

Whether a mineral has cleavage depends on how the atoms in its crystals are arranged. The way atoms are arranged in mica allows it to split easily in one direction. **Figure 8** shows cleavage in mica.

Most minerals do not split apart evenly. Instead, they have a characteristic type of fracture. **Fracture** describes how a mineral looks when it breaks apart in an irregular way. For example, when quartz breaks, it produces curved, shell-like surfaces.

Special Properties

Some minerals can be identified by special physical properties. Calcite bends light to produce double images, as shown in **Figure 9.** Other minerals conduct electricity, glow when placed under ultraviolet light, or are magnetic.

Mica

Quartz

FIGURE 8 ....
Fracture and Cleavage

How a mineral breaks apart can help to identify it.

⚐ **Form Operational Definitions** Observe the examples of cleavage and fracture above. Based on your observations, write a definition of cleavage in your own words.

_____

_____

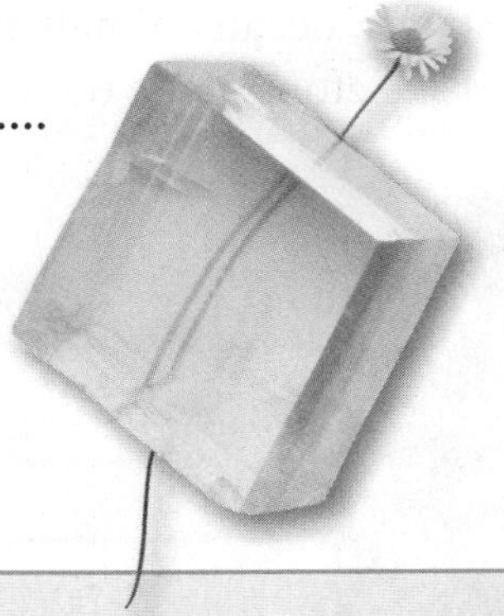

FIGURE 9 ....
Special Properties

Calcite bends light to produce a double image.

 Lab zone® Do the Quick Lab *Identifying Minerals.*

🔑 Assess Your Understanding

2a. Summarize Geologists identify minerals by examining their _____

_____

_____

_____

b. Design Experiments Lodestone is magnetic. How might you identify whether a mineral sample might be lodestone?

_____

_____

_____

got it? ....

O **I get it!** Now I know that the characteristic properties used to identify minerals are _____

_____

O **I need extra help with** _____

Go to MY SCIENCE Ⓢ COACH online for help with this subject.

How Do Minerals Form?

On a rock-collecting field trip, you find an egg-shaped rock about the size of a football. Later, at a geologic laboratory, you split the rock open. The rock is hollow! Its inside surface sparkles with large amethyst crystals. Amethyst is a type of quartz.

You have found a geode, as shown in **Figure 10**. A **geode** (JEE ohd) is a rounded, hollow rock that is often lined with mineral crystals. Geologists believe that crystals probably form inside a geode when water containing dissolved minerals seeps into a crack or hollow in a rock. Slowly, crystallization occurs, lining the inside with large crystals that are often perfectly formed. **Crystallization** is the process by which atoms are arranged to form a material that has a crystal structure. 🔑 **In general, minerals can form in three ways. Some minerals form from organic processes. Other minerals can crystallize from materials dissolved in solutions. Finally, many minerals crystallize as magma and lava cool.**

Organic Minerals All minerals can form by inorganic processes. 🔑 **However, some minerals can also form by organic processes.** For instance, ocean animals such as clams and corals produce shells and skeletons made out of the mineral calcite.

FIGURE 10 ·······························

Geodes

Water seeping into a crack in a rock can result in the formation of a geode.

✏ **Sequence Complete the graphic organizer to show how a geode forms in four steps.**

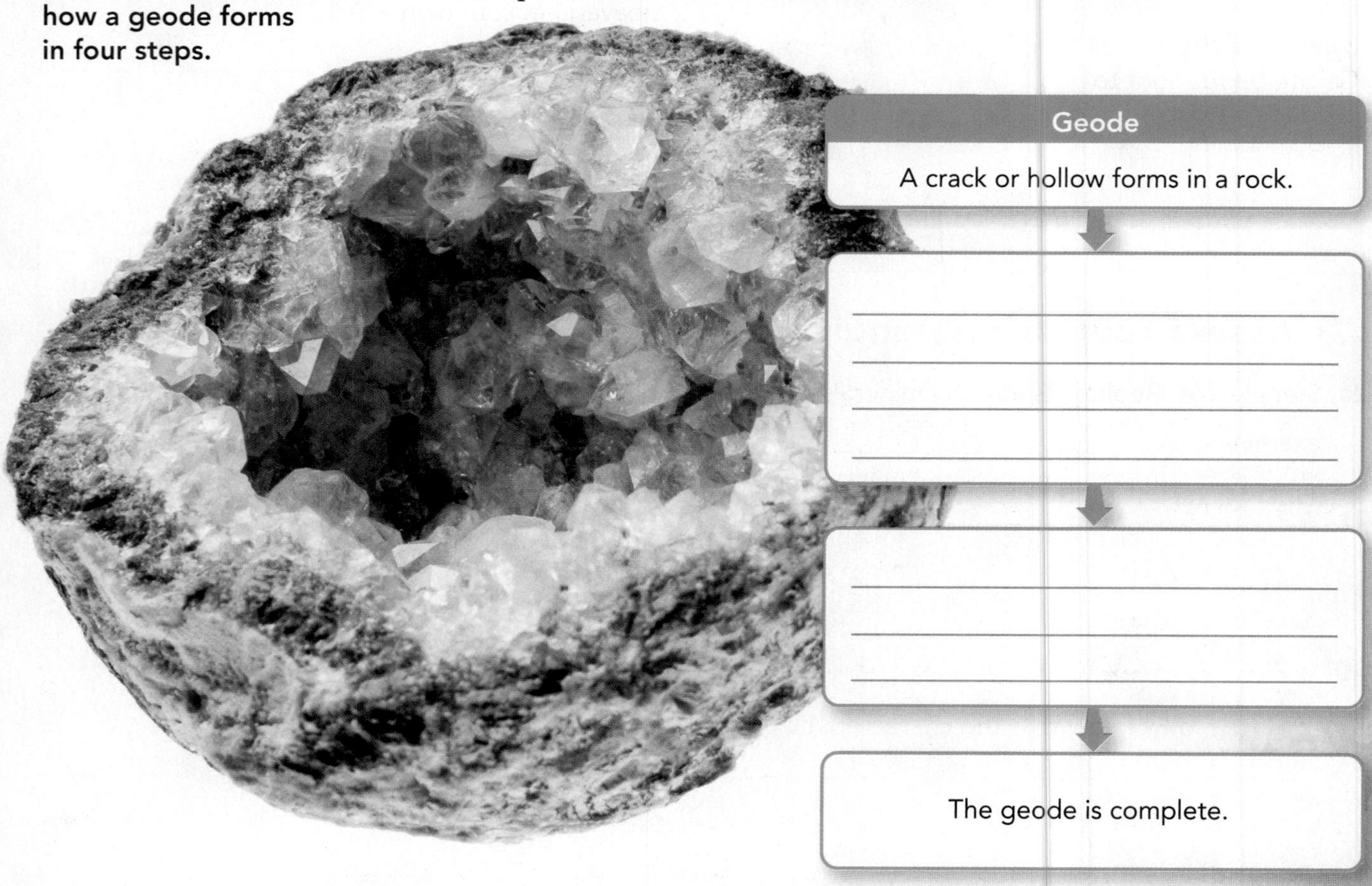

Geode
A crack or hollow forms in a rock.

↓

↓

↓

The geode is complete.

Minerals From Solutions

Sometimes the elements and compounds that form minerals can be dissolved in water to form solutions. A **solution** is a mixture in which one substance is dissolved in another. 🔑 **When elements and compounds that are dissolved in water leave a solution, crystallization occurs.** Minerals can form in this way in bodies of water on Earth's surface. But the huge selenite crystals shown in **Figure 11** formed from a solution of hot water that cooled underground.

Minerals Formed by Evaporation

Some minerals form when solutions evaporate. For example, when the water in salt water evaporates, it leaves behind salt crystals.

In a similar way, deposits of the mineral halite formed over millions of years when ancient seas slowly evaporated. Such halite deposits are found in the American Southwest and along the Gulf Coast. Gypsum and calcite can also form by evaporation. Sometimes, gypsum forms in the shape of a rose.

A gypsum "rose"

Minerals From Hot Water Solutions

Deep underground, magma can heat water to a high temperature. The hot water can dissolve the elements and compounds that form minerals. When the hot water solution begins to cool, the elements and compounds leave the solution and crystallize as minerals. For example, quartz can crystallize from out of a hot water solution. Pure silver is also often deposited from a hot water solution. Gold, too, can be deposited in this way.

Pure metals that crystallize from hot water solutions underground often form veins. A **vein** is a narrow channel or slab of a mineral that is different from the surrounding rock.

Silver

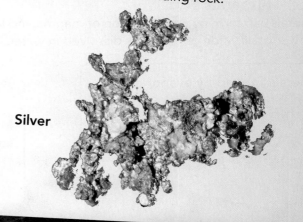

FIGURE 11 ·················
Selenite
These huge selenite crystals in a cave in Mexico formed from the crystallization of minerals in a solution.

41

✏️ ....

🔁 **Relate Text and Visuals**
Review the text on this page and on the previous page. Underline the name of each mineral the first time it is mentioned. Then place each mineral in its correct place in **Figure 12.**

Minerals From Magma and Lava Many minerals form from magma and lava. 💬 **Minerals form as hot magma cools inside the crust, or as lava hardens on the surface. When these liquids cool to a solid state, they form crystals.** The size of the crystals depends on several factors. The rate at which the magma cools, the amount of gas the magma contains, and the chemical composition of the magma all affect crystal size.

Magma and lava are often rich in oxygen and silicon. Minerals that contain these elements are called *silicates*. Together, silicates make up a majority of Earth's crust.

Minerals From Magma
Magma that remains deep below the surface cools slowly over thousands of years. Slow cooling leads to the formation of large crystals. Quartz, feldspar, tourmaline, and mica are common silicate minerals that form from magma.

Tourmaline

Minerals From Lava
If magma erupts to the surface and becomes lava, the lava will cool quickly. There will be no time for large crystals to form. Instead, small crystals form. Leucite and olivine are silicate minerals that can form in lava.

Olivine

FIGURE 12 ·······································
Where Minerals Form
Minerals can form by crystallization of magma and lava or by crystallization of materials dissolved in water.

Minerals formed as lava cools
_____

Minerals formed by evaporation
_____
_____

Minerals formed in hot water solutions
_____
_____

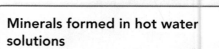

Veins

Minerals formed as magma cools
_____
_____

Water containing dissolved minerals

Cooling magma

Where Mineral Resources Are Found

Earth's crust is made up mostly of the common rock-forming minerals combined in various types of rock. Less common minerals are not found evenly throughout the crust. Instead, several processes can concentrate these minerals, or bring them together, in deposits. An *ore* is a deposit of valuable minerals contained in rocks. Iron ores may contain the iron-bearing minerals pyrite, magnetite, and hematite. Lead ores may contain galena. These ores are mined and the iron or lead is separated from the rock. Graphite and sulfur are sometimes also mined. **Figure 13** shows some major mining areas.

FIGURE 13 ·············

Ores

Interpret Maps Copper, aluminum, zinc, iron, and nickel can be used in making refrigerators. Which of these metals might the United States need to import for its refrigerators?

_____

_____

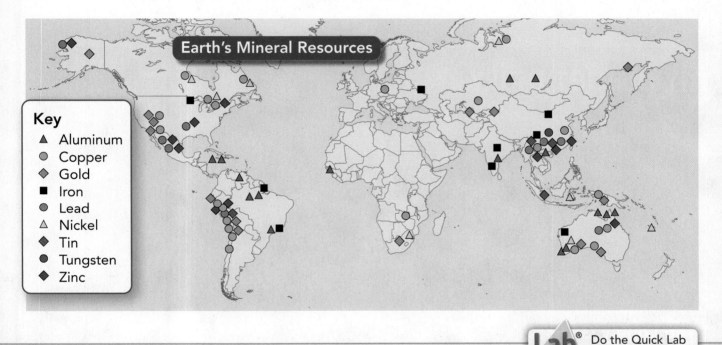

Earth's Mineral Resources

Key
- ▲ Aluminum
- ● Copper
- ◆ Gold
- ■ Iron
- ● Lead
- △ Nickel
- ◆ Tin
- ● Tungsten
- ◆ Zinc

Lab zone® Do the Quick Lab *Crystal Hands.*

Assess Your Understanding

3a. Review Magma below Earth's surface cools (slowly/quickly).

b. Predict Slow cooling of magma leads to what size mineral crystals?

_____

_____

c. Develop Hypotheses A certain rock has large crystals of feldspar, mica, and quartz. Explain how and where the rock might have formed.

_____

_____

_____

got it? ·············

○ **I get it!** Now I know that the three general ways minerals form are when _____

_____

_____

○ **I need extra help with** _____

Go to **MY SCIENCE** ⬤ **COACH** online for help with this subject.

Classifying Rocks

🔑 **How Do Geologists Classify Rocks?**

my planeT DiaRY

FIELD TRIP

The Lonely Giant

In the midst of Wyoming stands a lonely giant: Mount Moran. Its peak stands more than 3,800 meters above sea level. If you climb Mount Moran, you'll crawl across slabs of rock. These slabs formed deep beneath Earth's surface. Here, great temperatures and pressures changed one type of rock into the rock of the slabs. As you continue to climb, a thick, vertical strip of darker stone suddenly appears. This rock is volcanic rock. Finally, when you reach the top, you find a 15-meter cap of sandstone. This rock formed when many tiny particles were squeezed tightly together over millions of years. So Mount Moran contains rocks that formed in three different ways.

Read the text and then answer the questions.

1. In your own words, describe one way in which rocks formed on Mount Moran.

_____

_____

2. If you were climbing Mount Moran, how might you be able to tell one rock from another?

_____

_____

Lab zone Do the Inquiry Warm-Up *How Do Rocks Compare?*

▷ **PLANET DIARY** Go to **Planet Diary** to learn more about the three main groups of rocks.

Vocabulary
- rock-forming mineral • granite • basalt • grain
- texture • igneous rock • sedimentary rock
- metamorphic rock

Skills
- Reading: Identify the Main Idea
- Inquiry: Observe

How Do Geologists Classify Rocks?

If you were a geologist, how would you examine a rock for the first time? You might look at the outside surfaces. But you would also probably use a hammer to break open a small sample of the rock and look at the inside. **To study a rock sample, geologists observe the rock's mineral composition, color, and texture.**

Mineral Composition and Color Rocks are made of mixtures of minerals and other materials. Some rocks contain only a single mineral. Other rocks contain several minerals. The granite in **Figure 1,** for example, is made up of quartz, feldspar, mica, and hornblende. About 20 minerals make up most of the rocks of Earth's crust. These minerals are known as **rock-forming minerals.** The minerals that make up granite are rock-forming minerals.

A rock's color provides clues to the rock's mineral composition. For example, **granite** is generally a light-colored rock that has high silica content. That is, it is rich in the elements silicon and oxygen. **Basalt** is a dark-colored rock that has a lower silica content than granite has. But unlike granite, basalt has mineral crystals that are too small to be seen with the naked eye. As with minerals, color alone does not provide enough information to identify a rock.

FIGURE 1 ⋯⋯⋯⋯⋯⋯⋯⋯
Granite
Granite is generally made up of only a few common minerals.

△ **Observe** How would you describe the overall color of this rock? What minerals cause the color (or colors) you chose?

_____
_____
_____
_____

_____
_____

Feldspar

Hornblende

Quartz

Mica

Granite

45

Texture Most rocks are made up of particles of minerals or other rocks, which geologists call **grains.** Grains give the rock its texture. **Texture** is the look and feel of a rock's surface. To describe the texture of a rock, geologists use terms that are based on the size, shape, and pattern of the grains.

Grain Size

Rocks with grains that are large and easy to see are said to be coarse grained. Fine-grained rocks have grains that are so small they can be seen only with a microscope.

Fine grain	Coarse grain	No visible grain
Slate	Diorite	Flint

Grain Shape

In some rocks, grain shape results from the shape of the mineral crystals that form the rock. Other rocks have a grain shape that results from rounded or jagged bits of several rocks.

Rounded grain	Jagged grain
Conglomerate	Breccia

Grain Pattern

In banded rocks, grains can lie in a pattern of flat layers or can form swirls or colored bands. Nonbanded rocks have grains that do not lie in any visible pattern.

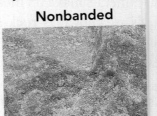

Nonbanded	Banded
Quartzite	Gneiss

apply it!

This photograph shows part of a coarse-grained rock. Read the text on this page and then answer the questions.

1 Observe Is this rock banded or nonbanded? _____

2 Infer Based on this rock's appearance, what type of rock might it be? _____

3 CHALLENGE Gneiss forms when very high pressure and temperature are applied to existing rock. How might these conditions explain the wavy pattern in this rock?

_____

_____

_____

_____

Origin Using the characteristics of color, texture, and mineral composition, geologists can classify a rock according to its origin. A rock's origin is the way that the rock formed. 🔑 **Geologists have classified rocks into three major groups: igneous rock, sedimentary rock, and metamorphic rock.**

Each of these groups of rocks forms in a different way, as shown in **Figure 2.** **Igneous rock** (IG nee us) forms from the cooling of magma or lava. The magma hardens underground to form rock. The lava erupts, cools, and hardens to form rock on Earth's surface.

Most **sedimentary rock** (sed uh MEN tur ee) forms when small particles of rocks or the remains of plants and animals are pressed and cemented together. Sedimentary rock forms in layers that are buried below the surface. **Metamorphic rock** (met uh MAWR fik) forms when a rock is changed by heat or pressure, or by chemical reactions. Most metamorphic rock forms deep underground.

✎ **Identify the Main Idea**
Read the text on this page. Underline how each of the three major groups of rocks forms.

FIGURE 2 ·····················
Rock Origins
Rocks are classified by the way they formed.

✎ **Interpret Diagrams** Using the sentences you underlined, label each diagram with the rock origin it represents.

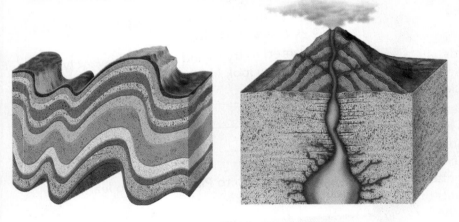
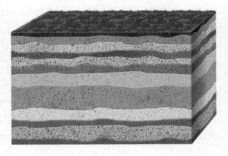

_____   _____   _____

 Do the Quick Lab *Classify These Rocks.*

🔑 Assess Your Understanding

1a. Review Geologists classify rocks according to their _____

b. Explain How do igneous rocks form?

_____

_____

c. Classify Pumice is a type of rock that forms from molten material that erupts violently from a volcano. To what group of rock does pumice belong?

_____

_____

got it? ···

○ **I get it!** Now I know that geologists classify rocks into three major groups called _____

_____

○ **I need extra help with** _____

Go to **MY SCIENCE** ⓢ **COACH** online for help with this subject.

🔑 **How Do Geologists Classify Igneous Rocks?**

🔑 **How Are Igneous Rocks Used?**

UNLOCK THE BIG **?**

my planet diary

Arctic Diamonds

If you were looking for diamonds, where would you start? Maybe in a helicopter flying over the Arctic Circle?

In the 1980s, a pair of geologists used a helicopter to search for diamonds in Canada. The pair knew that diamonds form more than 100 kilometers under Earth's surface. They also knew that after diamonds form, powerful eruptions of magma can thrust the diamonds to the surface through volcanic pipes. As the magma cools and hardens, the diamonds are trapped inside volcanic rock.

The geologists found a source for diamonds after searching for several years. Now, diamond mines in Canada produce one of the world's most valuable crops of diamonds!

DISCOVERY

Discuss this question with a group of classmates. Write your answer below.

If you wanted to try to find diamonds, what type of rock might you look for? Why?

_____

_____

_____

▷ PLANET DIARY Go to **Planet Diary** to learn more about volcanic rocks.

 Do the Inquiry Warm-Up *Liquid to Solid.*

How Do Geologists Classify Igneous Rocks?

Look at **Figure 1.** All the rocks shown in the figure are igneous rocks. But do all these rocks look the same? No, because even though all igneous rocks form from magma or lava, igneous rocks can look vastly different from each other. 🔑 **Igneous rocks are classified by their origin, texture, and mineral composition.**

Vocabulary
- extrusive rock
- intrusive rock

Skills
↻ Reading: Relate Cause and Effect
△ Inquiry: Interpret Data

Origin Igneous rock may form on or beneath Earth's surface. **Extrusive rock** is igneous rock formed from lava that erupted onto Earth's surface. Basalt is the most common extrusive rock.

Igneous rock that formed when magma hardened beneath the surface of Earth is called **intrusive rock.** The most abundant type of intrusive rock in continental crust is granite. Granite forms tens of kilometers below Earth's surface and over hundreds of thousands of years or longer.

Texture Different igneous rocks may have similar mineral compositions and yet have very different textures. The texture of an igneous rock depends on the size and shape of its mineral crystals. The only exceptions to this rule are the different types of volcanic glass—igneous rock that lacks a crystal structure.

Rapidly cooling lava forms fine-grained igneous rocks with small crystals or no crystals at all. Slowly cooling magma forms coarse-grained rocks, such as granite, with large crystals. So, intrusive and extrusive rocks usually have different textures. For example, intrusive rocks have larger grains than extrusive rocks. Extrusive rocks have a fine-grained or glassy texture. **Figure 1** shows the textures of different igneous rocks.

Vocabulary Latin Word Origins *Ignis* means "fire" in Latin. What is "fiery" about igneous rocks?

_____

_____

_____

_____

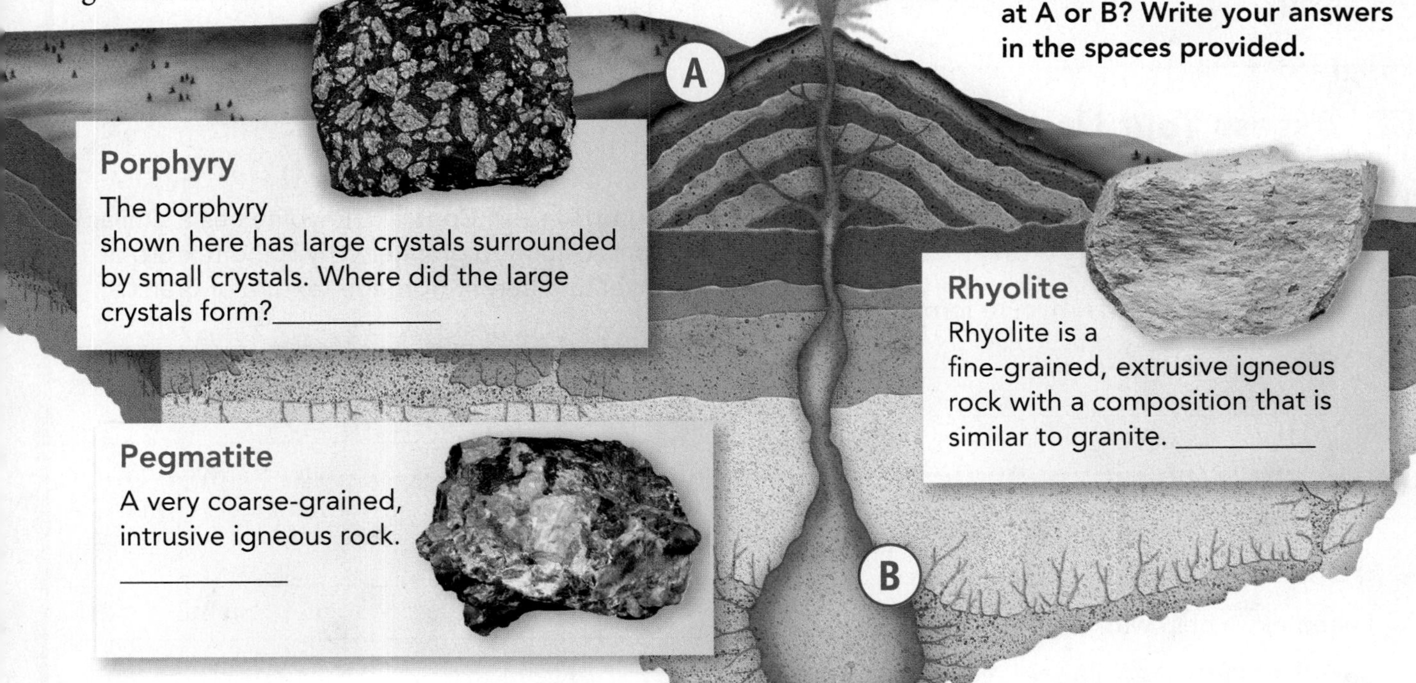

FIGURE 1 ·····························

> ART IN MOTION **Igneous Rock Origins and Textures** The texture of igneous rock varies according to its origin.

✏ **Interpret Diagrams** Did the rocks in the photographs form at A or B? Write your answers in the spaces provided.

Porphyry
The porphyry shown here has large crystals surrounded by small crystals. Where did the large crystals form?_____

Pegmatite
A very coarse-grained, intrusive igneous rock.
_____

Rhyolite
Rhyolite is a fine-grained, extrusive igneous rock with a composition that is similar to granite. _____

A

B

apply it!

Diorite is a coarse-grained intrusive igneous rock. It is a mixture of feldspar and dark-colored minerals such as hornblende and mica. The proportion of feldspar and dark minerals in diorite can vary.

1 ⚠ **Interpret Data** What mineral is most abundant in the sample of diorite illustrated by the graph?

_____

2 [CHALLENGE] How would the color of the diorite change if it contained less hornblende and more feldspar? Explain.

_____

_____

_____

_____

Mineral Composition of Diorite

Feldspar 67%

33%

Dark minerals (mica, hornblende)

Mineral Composition

Recall that the silica content of magma and lava can vary. Lava that is low in silica usually forms dark-colored rocks such as basalt. Basalt contains feldspar as well as certain dark-colored minerals, but does not contain quartz.

Magma that is high in silica usually forms light-colored rocks, such as granite. Granite's mineral composition determines its color, which can be light gray, red, or pink. Granite that is rich in reddish feldspar is a speckled pink. But granite rich in hornblende and dark mica is light gray with dark specks. Quartz crystals in granite add light gray or smoky specks.

✏️

↩ Relate Cause and Effect
What determines the color of granite?

○ Its mineral composition

○ Its density

Lab zone Do the Quick Lab *How Do Igneous Rocks Form?*

🔑 Assess Your Understanding

1a. Identify Rhyolite is an (intrusive/extrusive) igneous rock.

b. Summarize How does rhyolite form?

_____

_____

c. Compare and Contrast Rhyolite has a similar composition to granite. Why is the texture of rhyolite different from the texture of granite?

_____

_____

_____

got it?

○ **I get it!** Now I know that igneous rocks are classified according to their _____

_____

○ **I need extra help with** _____

Go to **my science** Ⓢ **COACH** *online for help with this subject.*

How Are Igneous Rocks Used?

Many igneous rocks are hard, dense, and durable. **People throughout history have used igneous rock for tools and building materials.**

Granite has a long history of use as a building material. More than 3,500 years ago, the ancient Egyptians used granite to build statues. About 600 years ago, the Incas of Peru built fortresses out of great blocks of granite and other igneous rock. You can see part of one of their fortresses in **Figure 2.** In the United States during the 1800s and early 1900s, granite was widely used to build bridges and public buildings. Today, thin, polished sheets of granite are used in curbstones and floors. Another igneous rock, basalt, can be used for cobblestones. It can also be crushed and used as a material in landscaping and in roads.

Igneous rocks such as pumice and obsidian also have important uses. The rough surface of pumice forms when gas bubbles are trapped in fast-cooling lava, leaving spaces in the rock. The rough surface makes pumice a good abrasive for cleaning and polishing. Ancient Native Americans used obsidian to make sharp tools for cutting and scraping. Obsidian cools very quickly, without forming crystals. So it has a smooth, shiny texture like glass. Perlite, formed by the rapid cooling of magma or lava, is often mixed with soil and used for starting vegetable seeds.

FIGURE 2 ·····················
Building Blocks

Igneous rock has long been used as a building material, such as for this Incan fortress in Peru.

✎ **Work With Design Constraints** A fortress must be strong enough to withstand violent attacks. Why might the Incas have chosen igneous rock to build their fortress near Ollantaytambo in Peru?

_____

_____

_____

_____

▲ Ollantaytambo

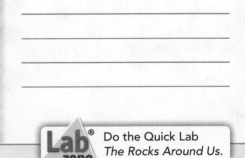

Lab zone ® Do the Quick Lab
The Rocks Around Us.

☞ Assess Your Understanding

got it? ·····················

○ **I get it!** Now I know that throughout history, people have used igneous rocks for ____

_____

○ I need extra help with _____

Go to my science ⓢ coach *online for help with this subject.*

51

Sedimentary Rocks

UNLOCK THE BIG **?**

🔑 **How Do Sedimentary Rocks Form?**

🔑 **What Are the Three Major Types of Sedimentary Rocks?**

🔑 **How Are Sedimentary Rocks Used?**

MY PLANET DIARY

The Cutting Edge

If you had to carve tools out of stone, would you know which rocks to use? Dr. Beverly Chiarulli, an archaeologist at Indiana University of Pennsylvania, studies stone tools that were used by people in Pennsylvania 10,000 years ago. Dr. Chiarulli has found that these people crafted spearheads out of the sedimentary rocks called chert and jasper. Chert is hard and has a very fine texture. It is brittle, but does not fracture along thin, even planes. So, chert can be shaped somewhat easily by flaking off chips, producing the sharp edges needed for spearheads.

CAREERS

Read the text and then answer the question.

What properties of chert allow it to be carved into sharp spearheads?

_____

_____

_____

_____

▷ **PLANET DIARY** Go to **Planet Diary** to learn more about sedimentary rocks.

Lab zone® Do the Inquiry Warm-Up *Acid Test for Rocks.*

How Do Sedimentary Rocks Form?

The banks of a cool stream may be made up of tiny sand grains, mud, and pebbles. Shells, leaves, and even bones may also be mixed in. All of these particles are examples of sediment. **Sediment** is small, solid pieces of material that come from rocks or living things.

Sedimentary rocks form when sediment is deposited by water and wind, as shown in **Figure 1.** 🔑 **Most sedimentary rocks are formed through a sequence of processes: weathering, erosion, deposition, compaction, and cementation.**

Vocabulary

- sediment • weathering • erosion • deposition
- compaction • cementation • clastic rock
- organic rock • chemical rock

Skills

- Reading: Identify the Main Idea
- Inquiry: Infer

Deposition

Water can carry sediment to a lake or ocean. Here, the material is deposited in layers as it sinks to the bottom. **Deposition** is the process by which sediment settles out of the water or wind carrying it.

Weathering and Erosion

Rock on Earth's surface is constantly broken up by **weathering**—the effects of freezing and thawing, plant roots, acid, and other forces on rock. After the rock is broken up, the fragments are carried away as a result of **erosion**—the process by which running water, wind, or ice carry away bits of broken-up rock.

Compaction

Thick layers of sediment build up gradually over millions of years. The weight of new layers can squeeze older sediments tightly together. The process that presses sediments together is **compaction.**

Cementation

While compaction is taking place, some minerals in the rock slowly dissolve in the water. **Cementation** is the process in which dissolved minerals crystallize and glue particles of sediment together.

FIGURE 1 ·······························

How Sedimentary Rock Forms

Sedimentary rocks form through a series of processes over millions of years.

✎ **Sequence** Put the terms listed in the word bank in the proper sequence to show how mountains can change into sedimentary rock.

| Compaction |
| Cementation |
| Weathering and erosion |
| Deposition |

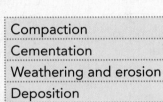

Lab zone ® Do the Quick Lab *How Does Pressure Affect Particles of Rock?*

🔑 Assess Your Understanding

got it? ···

○ **I get it!** Now I know that most sedimentary rocks are formed through the processes of _____

_____

○ **I need extra help with** _____

Go to my science ⑤ COACH *online for help with this subject.*

What Are the Three Major Types of Sedimentary Rocks?

Geologists classify sedimentary rocks according to the type of sediments that make up the rock. 🔑 **The three major groups of sedimentary rocks are clastic rocks, organic rocks, and chemical rocks.** Different processes form each of these types of rocks.

Clastic Rocks   Most sedimentary rocks are made up of broken pieces of other rocks. A **clastic rock** is a sedimentary rock formed when rock fragments are squeezed together. The fragments can range in size from clay particles that are too small to be seen without a microscope to large, heavy boulders. Clastic rocks are grouped by the size of the rock fragments, or particles, of which they are made. Some common clastic rocks, shown in **Figure 2,** are shale, sandstone, conglomerate, and breccia (BRECH ee uh).

Shale forms from tiny particles of clay. Water deposits the clay particles in thin, flat layers. Sandstone forms from the sand on beaches, the ocean floor, riverbeds, and sand dunes. Most sand particles consist of quartz.

Some clastic sedimentary rocks contain rock fragments that are of different sizes. If the fragments have rounded edges, they form conglomerate. Fragments with sharp edges form breccia.

✏️ **Identify the Main Idea**

Clastic rocks are grouped by the size of the _____ _____ they contain.

FIGURE 2

Clastic Rocks

Clastic rocks are sedimentary rocks that form from particles of other rocks.

✏️ **Identify** Match the clastic rocks to the four photographs below them. Write your answer in the spaces provided.

Shale
Fossils are often found in shale, which tends to split into flat pieces.
_____

Sandstone
Many small holes between sand grains allow sandstone to absorb water.
_____

Conglomerate
Rock fragments with rounded edges make up conglomerate.
_____

Breccia
Rock fragments with sharp edges form breccia.
_____

1

2

3

4

Organic Rocks You may be familiar with the rocks called coal and limestone, shown in **Figure 3.** Both are sedimentary rocks. But instead of forming from particles of other rocks, they form from the remains of material that was once living. **Organic rock** forms where the remains of plants and animals are deposited in layers. The term "organic" refers to substances that once were part of living things or were made by living things.

Coal forms from the remains of swamp plants buried in water. As layer upon layer of plant remains build up, the weight of the layers squeezes the decaying plants together. Over millions of years, they slowly change into coal.

Limestone forms in the ocean, where many living things, such as coral, clams, and oysters, have hard shells or skeletons made of calcite. When these ocean animals die, their shells pile up on the ocean floor. Over millions of years, compaction and cementation can change the thick sediment into limestone.

FIGURE 3 ·······························

Organic Rocks
Organic rocks such as limestone and coal are sedimentary rocks that form from the remains of living things.

✎ **Sequence Complete the graphic organizers to show how coal and limestone form.**

Coal

Remains of swamp plants are buried in water.

⬇

⬇

Over millions of years, coal forms.

Limestone

Ocean animals with hard shells or skeletons die.

⬇

⬇

Sediment is slowly changed to limestone.

These rock "towers" in Mono Lake, California, are made of tufa, a form of limestone. Tufa forms from water solutions that contain dissolved materials. The towers formed under water. They became exposed when the water level in the lake dropped as a result of water needs for the city of Los Angeles. Read the text about the major types of sedimentary rocks. Then answer the questions.

1 **Classify** Tufa is a (clastic/organic/chemical) sedimentary rock.

2 **Infer** What mineral was dissolved in the waters of Mono Lake and later crystallized to form the rock towers?

_____

3 **CHALLENGE** When acid comes into contact with calcite, the acid bubbles. How can geologists use acid to confirm that the rock towers are made of limestone?

_____

_____

_____

_____

Chemical Rocks Limestone can also form when calcite that is dissolved in lakes, seas, or underground water comes out of a solution and forms crystals. This kind of limestone is considered a chemical rock. **Chemical rock** forms when minerals dissolved in a water solution crystallize. Chemical rocks can also form from mineral deposits that are left when seas or lakes evaporate. For example, rock salt is made of the mineral halite, which forms by evaporation.

Do the Quick Lab
What Causes Layers?

🔑 Assess Your Understanding

1a. Review Shale forms from tiny particles of (clay/sand/mica).

b. Describe How is clay deposited to form shale?

_____

_____

_____

c. Infer You come across a thick deposit of shale that forms a layer in the ground. What can you infer about the area's past environment?

_____

_____

_____

_____

got**it**? ....

○ **I get it!** Now I know that the three major types of sedimentary rocks are _____

_____

○ **I need extra help with** _____

    Go to MY SCIENCE Ⓢ **COACH** *online for help with this subject.*

How Are Sedimentary Rocks Used?

People have used sedimentary rocks throughout history for many different purposes, including for tools and building materials. Chert was used to make spearheads by people who lived in Pennsylvania more than 10,000 years ago. Other people also made arrowheads out of flint for thousands of years. Flint is a hard rock, yet it can be shaped to a point. It forms when small particles of silica settle out of water.

Sedimentary rocks such as sandstone and limestone have been used as building materials for thousands of years. Both types of stone are soft enough to be cut easily into blocks or slabs. The White House in Washington, D.C., is built of sandstone. Today, builders use sandstone and limestone on the outside walls of buildings, such as the building shown in **Figure 4.** Limestone also has industrial uses. For example, it is used in making cement and steel.

FIGURE 4 ....

> **REAL-WORLD INQUIRY**

Building With Limestone

Limestone is a popular building material. However, acid rain reacts with the calcite in limestone, damaging buildings made from it.

✏ **Evaluate the Design** Do the benefits of constructing limestone buildings outweigh the damage acid rain causes to these buildings? Explain.

_____

_____

Carnegie Library (Jeffersonville, Indiana) ▼

Lab zone ® Do the Lab Investigation *Testing Rock Flooring.*

Assess Your Understanding

got it? ....

○ **I get it!** Now I know that throughout history, people have used sedimentary rocks for _____

_____

○ **I need extra help with** _____

Go to MY SCIENCE COACH online for help with this subject.

Metamorphic Rocks

UNLOCK
THE BIG
?

🔑 What Are Metamorphic Rocks?

MY PLANET DIARY

MISCONCEPTION

Rock Dough

Misconception:
Rocks do not change form.

Did you know that heat can change a rock's form without melting it? To understand how, think of what happens when you bake cookies. You might mix flour, eggs, sugar, and baking powder in a bowl. When you bake the raw dough in a hot oven, the dough changes into cookies.

Heat can change rock, too. If hot magma or lava come near rock, the heat can "bake" the rock. The ingredients in the rock—the minerals—might not melt. But the heat can still change the rock into a new form!

Read the text and then answer the question below.

Does rock have to melt in order to change form? Explain.

_____

_____

_____

_____

_____

▷ PLANET DIARY Go to Planet Diary to learn more about how rocks can change form.

Lab®
zone Do the Inquiry Warm-Up
A Sequined Rock.

What Are Metamorphic Rocks?

You may be surprised to learn that heat can change rock like a hot oven changes raw cookie dough. But deep inside Earth, both heat and pressure are much greater than at Earth's surface. When great heat and pressure are applied to rock, the rock can change both its shape and its composition. 🔑 **Any rock that forms from another rock as a result of changes in heat or pressure (or both heat and pressure) is a metamorphic rock.**

Vocabulary
- foliated

Skills
- ↻ Reading: Relate Cause and Effect
- △ Inquiry: Observe

How Metamorphic Rocks Form

Metamorphic rock can form out of igneous, sedimentary, or other metamorphic rock. Many metamorphic rocks are found in mountains or near large masses of igneous rock. Why are metamorphic rocks commonly found in these locations? The answer lies inside Earth.

The heat that can change a rock into metamorphic rock can come from pockets of magma. For instance, pockets of magma can rise through the crust. The high temperatures of these pockets can change rock into metamorphic rock. Collisions between Earth's plates can also push rock down toward the heat of the mantle.

Very high pressure can also change rock into metamorphic rock. For instance, plate collisions cause great pressure to be applied to rocks while mountains are being formed. The pressure can deform, or change the physical shape of, the rock, as shown in **Figure 1**. Also, the deeper that a rock is buried in the crust, the greater the pressure on that rock. Under very high temperature or pressure (or both), the minerals in a rock can be changed into other minerals. At the same time, the appearance, texture, and crystal structure of the minerals in the rock change. The rock eventually becomes a metamorphic rock.

FIGURE 1 ·····························
Metamorphic Rock
The rock in the photograph was once sedimentary rock. Now, it is metamorphic rock.

✎ **Develop Hypotheses** What changed the rock? Make sure your answer explains the rock's current appearance.

_____

_____

_____

_____

_____

Deformed metamorphic rock in eastern Connecticut ▲

........................✎........................
⟲ Relate Cause and Effect
Read the text on this page. Underline each sentence that describes how one type of rock changes into another type of rock.

How Metamorphic Rocks Are Classified

While metamorphic rocks are forming, intense heat changes the size and shape of the grains, or mineral crystals, in the rock. Extreme pressure squeezes rock so that the mineral grains may line up in flat, parallel layers. **⌐ Geologists classify metamorphic rocks according to the arrangement of the grains making up the rocks.**

Foliated Rocks Metamorphic rocks that have their grains arranged in either parallel layers or bands are said to be foliated. **Foliated** describes the thin, flat layering found in most metamorphic rocks. For instance, the crystals in granite can be flattened to create the foliated texture of gneiss. Slate is also a common foliated rock. Heat and pressure change the sedimentary rock shale into slate. Slate is basically a denser, more compact version of shale. But as shale changes into slate, the mineral composition of the shale can change.

Nonfoliated Rocks Some metamorphic rocks are nonfoliated. The mineral grains in these rocks are arranged randomly. Marble and quartzite are metamorphic rocks that have a nonfoliated texture. Quartzite forms out of quartz sandstone. The weakly cemented quartz particles in the sandstone recrystallize to form quartzite, which is extremely hard. Quartzite looks smoother than sandstone, as shown in **Figure 2.** Finally, marble usually forms when limestone is subjected to heat and pressure deep beneath the surface.

FIGURE 2 ···························
Presto!
Great heat and pressure can change one type of rock into another.

✎ **Classify** Label each rock *sedimentary,* *igneous,* or *metamorphic.* Indicate whether the metamorphic rocks are foliated. Then shade the correct arrowhead to show which rock can form from the other rock.

Granite

Gneiss

Heat and pressure

Quartzite

Sandstone

Heat and pressure

How Metamorphic Rocks Are Used Marble and slate are two of the most useful metamorphic rocks. Marble has an even grain, so it can be cut into thin slabs or carved into many shapes. And marble is easy to polish. So architects and sculptors use marble for many statues and buildings, such as the Tower of Pisa. Like marble, slate comes in many colors, including gray, red, and purple. Because it is foliated, slate splits easily into flat pieces. These pieces can be used for roofing, outdoor walkways, and as trim for stone buildings. **The metamorphic rocks marble and slate are important materials for building and sculpture.**

Tower of Pisa ▶

apply it!

Although marble, quartzite, and slate are all metamorphic rocks, they are used in different ways.

❶ Observe Look around your school or neighborhood. What examples of metamorphic rock can you find? How is each metamorphic rock used? Write your answers in the notebook at the right.

❷ CHALLENGE Why are chess pieces sometimes made of marble?

_____
_____
_____

Lab zone Do the Quick Lab *How Do Grain Patterns Compare?*

Assess Your Understanding

1a. Define What is a metamorphic rock?

_____
_____
_____
_____
_____

b. Identify Faulty Reasoning Suppose great heat completely melts a certain deposit of rock, which then hardens into new rock. You might think that the new rock is metamorphic. But it isn't. Why not?

_____
_____
_____

got it?

○ **I get it!** Now I know that certain metamorphic rocks are used for _____

○ **I need extra help with** _____

Go to my science COACH online for help with this subject.

The Rock Cycle

🔑 **What Is the Rock Cycle?**

MY PLANET DIARY

Rolling Along

The Himalaya Mountains are eroding at a rate of about 2.5 millimeters per year. That's about one tenth as fast as your fingernails grow! But the Himalayas were formed millions of years ago. So imagine the total mass of rock that has fallen down the mountain and that has then been swept out to sea. Over millions of years, the piled weight of eroded particles will squeeze the bits together on the sea floor. New rock will form. Then, ancient bits of the Himalayas will be recycled inside new rock.

FUN FACT

Read the text and then answer the question.

How could small pieces of the Himalayas form new rock?

_____

_____

▶ PLANET DIARY Go to **Planet Diary** to learn more about the rock cycle.

Lab zone® Do the Inquiry Warm-Up *Recycling Rocks.*

What Is the Rock Cycle?

Natural forces act on the Himalayas. In fact, rock in Earth's crust is always changing. 🔑 **Forces deep inside Earth and at the surface produce a slow cycle that builds, destroys, and changes the rocks in the crust.** The rock cycle is a series of processes that occur on Earth's surface and in the crust and mantle that slowly change rocks from one kind to another. For example, weathering can break down granite into sediment that later forms sandstone.

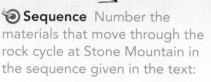

Vocabulary
- rock cycle

Skills
- Reading: Sequence
- Inquiry: Classify

One Pathway Through the Rock Cycle

There are many pathways by which rocks move through the rock cycle. For example, Stone Mountain, near Atlanta, Georgia, is made of granite. The granite in Stone Mountain, shown in **Figure 1,** formed millions of years ago below Earth's surface as magma cooled.

After the granite had formed, the forces of mountain building slowly pushed the granite upward. Then, over millions of years, weathering and erosion began to wear away the granite. Today, particles of granite constantly break off the mountain and become sand. Streams carry the sand to the ocean. What might happen next?

Over millions of years, layers of sand might pile up on the ocean floor. Slowly, the sand would be compacted by its own weight. Or perhaps calcite that is dissolved in the ocean water would cement the particles together. Over time, the quartz that once formed the granite of Stone Mountain could become sandstone, which is a sedimentary rock.

Sediment could keep piling up on the sandstone. Eventually, pressure would compact the rock's particles until no spaces were left between them. Silica, the main ingredient in quartz, would replace the calcite cement. The rock's texture would change from gritty to smooth. After millions of years, the standstone would have changed into the metamorphic rock quartzite.

Sequence Number the materials that move through the rock cycle at Stone Mountain in the sequence given in the text:

_____ Sand

_____ Granite

_____ Quartzite

FIGURE 1 ·······················
Stone Mountain
The granite in Stone Mountain is moving through the rock cycle.

Answer the questions.

1. **Classify** As shown in the photograph, trees can grow on the mountain. Their roots might break up the granite. What step of the rock cycle do the trees play a role in?

_____

2. **CHALLENGE** Does the rock cycle stop after the quartzite has formed? Explain.

_____
_____
_____
_____
_____
_____

The Rock Cycle

How do rocks form?

FIGURE 2 ·······························

✎ **› INTERACTIVE ART** Be a Rock Star!
Through melting, weathering and erosion, and heat and pressure, the rock cycle constantly changes rocks from one type into another type.

Interpret Diagrams Study the diagram. Then fill in each blank arrow with the correct term: *melting, weathering and erosion,* or *heat and pressure.* (*Hint:* To fit your answers, abbreviate "weathering and erosion" as "w & e.")

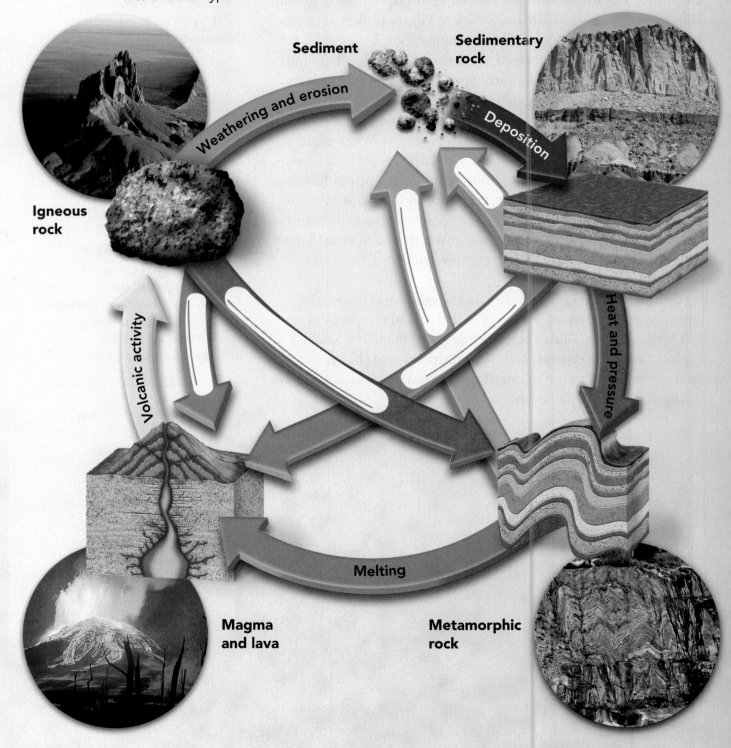

Sediment

Sedimentary rock

Weathering and erosion

Deposition

Igneous rock

Volcanic activity

Heat and pressure

Magma and lava

Melting

Metamorphic rock

The Rock Cycle and Plate Tectonics

The changes of the rock cycle are closely related to plate tectonics. Recall that Earth's lithosphere is made up of huge plates. These plates move slowly over Earth's surface as the result of convection currents in Earth's mantle. As the plates move, they carry the continents and ocean floors with them. Plate movements help drive the rock cycle by helping to form magma, the source of igneous rocks.

Where oceanic plates move apart, magma formed from melted mantle rock moves upward and fills the gap with new igneous rock. Where an oceanic plate is subducted beneath a continental plate, magma forms and rises. The result is a volcano made of igneous rock. A collision of continental plates may push rocks so deep that they melt to form magma, leading to the formation of igneous rock.

Sedimentary rock can also result from plate movement. For example, the collision of continental plates can be strong enough to push up a mountain range. Then, weathering and erosion begin. The mountains are worn away. This process leads to the formation of sedimentary rock.

Finally, a collision between continental plates can push rocks down deep beneath the surface. Here, heat and pressure could change the rocks to metamorphic rock.

Conservation of Material in the Rock Cycle

Constructive and destructive forces build up and destroy Earth's landmasses. But as the rock in Earth's crust moves through the rock cycle, material is not lost or gained. For example, a mountain can erode to form sediment, all of which can eventually form new rock.

New rock forms on the ocean floor at the mid-Atlantic ridge. Here, two plates move apart.

❶ (Igneous/Sedimentary) rock forms at point A.

❷ How can rock that is formed at the mid-Atlantic ridge be changed into sedimentary rock?

_____

_____

_____

_____

_____

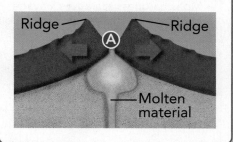

Ridge ——   —— Ridge

Ⓐ

—— Molten material

 Do the Quick Lab
Which Rock Came First?

🔑 Assess Your Understanding

1a. Name The rock cycle builds, destroys, and changes the rock in Earth's (crust/core).

b. **Describe** How do rocks form?

_____

_____

_____

_____

_____

_____

got it? ....

○ **I get it!** Now I know that the rock cycle is _____

_____

_____

○ **I need extra help with** _____

Go to **MY SCIENCE COACH** *online for help with this subject.*

65

2 Study Guide

In the rock cycle, rocks form through three main processes: _____,
_____, and _____.

LESSON 1 Properties of Minerals

🔑 A mineral is a natural solid that can form by inorganic processes and that has a crystal structure and a definite chemical composition.

🔑 Each mineral has characteristic properties.

🔑 Minerals form from cooling of magma and lava, from solutions, or from organic processes.

Vocabulary
- mineral • inorganic • crystal • streak • luster
- Mohs hardness scale • cleavage • fracture
- geode • crystallization • solution • vein

LESSON 2 Classifying Rocks

🔑 To study a rock sample, geologists observe the rock's mineral composition, color, and texture.

🔑 Geologists have classified rocks into three major groups: igneous rock, sedimentary rock, and metamorphic rock.

Vocabulary
- rock-forming mineral • granite • basalt
- grain • texture • igneous rock
- sedimentary rock • metamorphic rock

LESSON 3 Igneous Rocks

🔑 Igneous rocks are classified by their origin, texture, and mineral composition.

🔑 People throughout history have used igneous rock for tools and building materials.

Vocabulary
- extrusive rock
- intrusive rock

LESSON 4 Sedimentary Rocks

🔑 Most sedimentary rocks form by weathering, erosion, deposition, compaction, cementation.

🔑 Three major types of sedimentary rocks are clastic rocks, organic rocks, and chemical rocks.

🔑 People use sedimentary rocks for tools and building materials.

Vocabulary
- sediment • weathering • erosion
- deposition • compaction • cementation
- clastic rock • organic rock • chemical rock

LESSON 5 Metamorphic Rocks

🔑 Any rock that forms from another rock as a result of changes in heat or pressure (or both) is a metamorphic rock.

🔑 Geologists classify metamorphic rocks according to the arrangement of the grains making up the rocks.

🔑 The metamorphic rocks marble and slate are important materials for building and sculpture.

Vocabulary
- foliated

LESSON 6 The Rock Cycle

🔑 Forces deep inside Earth and at the surface produce a slow cycle that builds, destroys, and changes the rocks in the crust.

Vocabulary
- rock cycle

Review and Assessment

LESSON 1 Properties of Minerals

1. Streak is the color of a mineral's
  a. luster.   **b.** cleavage.
  c. powder.   **d.** fracture.

2. During crystallization, _____ are arranged to form a material with a crystal structure.

3. Compare and Contrast Fill in the table to compare the characteristics of a mineral and a material that is not a mineral.

	Hematite	Brick
Natural	✔	✘
Can form by inorganic processes		
Solid		
Crystal structure		
Definite chemical composition		

LESSON 2 Classifying Rocks

4. A rock that forms from many small fragments of other rocks is a(n)
  a. igneous rock.   **b.** sedimentary rock.
  c. metamorphic rock. **d.** extrusive rock.

5. The 20 or so minerals that make up most of the rocks of Earth's crust are known as

_____

Use the photograph to answer Question 6.

6. Interpret Photographs Describe the texture of this rock.

_____

_____

LESSON 3 Igneous Rocks

7. What kind of igneous rock usually contains large crystals?
  a. organic   **b.** clastic
  c. intrusive   **d.** extrusive

8. An igneous rock's color is primarily determined by its _____

9. Relate Cause and Effect What conditions lead to the formation of large crystals in an igneous rock?

_____

_____

10. **Write About It** Describe the texture of granite. Also describe granite's mineral composition and explain granite's origin.

LESSON 4 Sedimentary Rocks

11. You find a deposit of organic limestone. In what type of setting did it probably form?
  a. the ocean   **b.** a volcano
  c. a swamp   **d.** sand dunes

12. Shale is a clastic rock, meaning that it forms when _____ are squeezed or cemented together (or both).

13. Name A certain rock contains large, jagged pieces of other rocks, cemented by fine particles. What type of rock is this? Explain.

_____

_____

_____

14. **Write About It** You find a rock with fossils in it. Is this rock more likely to be a sedimentary rock than an igneous rock? Explain.

67

2 Review and Assessment

LESSON 5 **Metamorphic Rocks**

15. A metamorphic rock in which the grains line up in layers is called a

   a. chemical rock.   **b.** clastic rock.

   c. nonorganic rock.   **d.** foliated rock.

16. Two types of foliated rock are

_____

17. **Infer** Why do you think slate might be denser than shale?

_____

_____

18. **Develop Hypotheses** Why do the crystals in gneiss line up in bands?

_____

_____

_____

LESSON 6 **The Rock Cycle**

19. The process by which metamorphic rock changes to igneous rock begins with

   a. melting.   **b.** erosion.

   c. deposition.   **d.** crystallization.

20. _____ can turn igneous rock into sediment.

21. Write About It Use the diagram to describe two ways metamorphic rock can change into sedimentary rock.

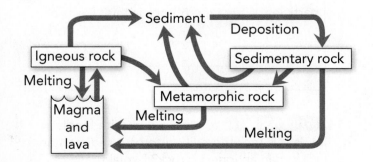

How do rocks form?

22. While hiking through a mountain range, you use a chisel and hammer to remove the three rock samples shown below. Classify the rocks you found as either igneous, sedimentary, or metamorphic. Then, describe the textures of each rock. Also describe the processes that formed each rock.

_____

_____

_____

_____

_____

_____

_____

_____

_____

_____

_____

_____

_____

_____

_____

_____

_____

_____

_____

Standardized Test Prep

Multiple Choice

Circle the letter of the best answer.

1. The diagrams below show four different mineral samples.

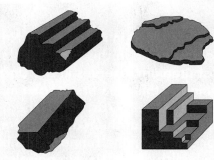

Which mineral property is best shown by the samples?

A crystal structure

B cleavage

C hardness

D color

2. You find a rock in which the grains are arranged in wavy, parallel bands of white and black crystals. What kind of rock have you probably found?

A igneous   **B** sedimentary

C metamorphic   **D** extrusive

3. Which statement best describes how an extrusive igneous rock forms?

A Magma cools quickly on Earth's surface.

B Magma cools slowly to form granite.

C Magma cools quickly below Earth's surface.

D Magma cools slowly beneath Earth's surface.

4. Which process causes many sedimentary rocks to have visible layers?

A eruption   **B** intrusion

C crystallization   **D** deposition

5. If heat and pressure inside Earth cause the texture and crystal structure of a rock to change, what new material is formed?

A metamorphic rock

B sedimentary rock

C igneous rock

D chemical rock

Constructed Response

Use the diagram below and your knowledge of science to help you answer Question 6. Write your answer on a separate piece of paper.

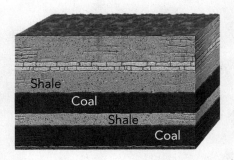

6. Describe the environment that probably existed millions of years ago where these rocks formed. Explain your reasoning.

STRUGGLING TO SURVIVE

An old problem has resurfaced in Arizona and New Mexico. The Navajo homeland in this region rests on one of the richest uranium reserves in the United States. Uranium mining in this area first began in the 1950s and stopped in the 1970s. When the mining companies left, many of them did not remove radioactive waste or seal the mine tunnels. This has greatly affected the health of the Navajo people who live and work near the old mines.

Years later, mining companies have come back to the Navajo homeland and the area around it. This time, they want to use solution mining, which uses water to flush out the uranium ore. This method is less dangerous than underground mining, but it can still contaminate the groundwater. And because the area is mostly desert, mining could use up scarce water.

Uranium is used for fuel in nuclear reactors that generate electricity. These reactors do not add carbon to the atmosphere, so some people think we should use them, instead of coal-fired power plants, to meet our electricity needs. The Navajo who live in an area with both coal and uranium must try to make decisions that will be good for their community both in the present and in the future.

Research It Working in a group, research (a) the uses of uranium, (b) the environmental impact of uranium mining, (c) the effect mining has had on the Navajo people's health, and (d) the effect mining has had on Navajo communities, environment, and people. As a group, write a paper weighing the costs and benefits of using solution mining to extract uranium ore.

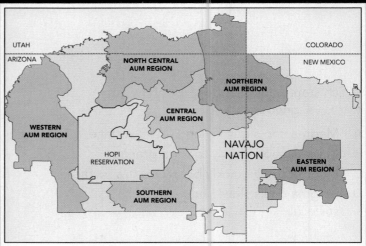

Abandoned Uranium Mines (AUM) on the Navajo Nation

Waiter there's a MINERAL in my soup!

While minerals form part of Earth's crust, they do not simply stay there until somebody picks them up. The minerals that make up Earth's crust are made up of elements that living things need, such as calcium. Over time, the minerals containing elements dissolve in water. Elements become part of our food because vegetables absorb them from the soil. When we eat the vegetables, we also take in the elements.

Calcium is one of the most important elements for your body because it helps build strong bones and teeth. It can be found in dairy products like milk, yogurt, and cheese, as well as broccoli and canned salmon.

Iron helps transport oxygen from your lungs to the rest of your body, and helps form red blood cells. Beef, tuna, eggs, and whole wheat bread are great sources of iron.

Potassium helps your muscles and nervous system work properly. Bananas, tomatoes, oranges, potatoes with skins, and peanuts are rich in potassium.

Zinc helps your immune system stay strong. A healthy immune system helps you fight off illnesses and infections. Zinc can be found in pork, lamb, beans, and lentils.

Design It Plan one day's worth of meals (breakfast, lunch, dinner). Include as many foods rich in essential elements as possible in your plan.

IS THIS CRACK IN EARTH GROWING?

THE BIG ?

How do moving plates change Earth's crust?

You may think that Earth's crust is one huge, solid piece. In fact, Earth's surface is broken into several pieces—like a cracked eggshell. One of the cracks runs through the middle of this lake in Iceland.

▲ **Infer** **Why do you think this crack in Earth's crust might get wider?**

_____

_____

_____

_____

_____

_____

_____

_____

> **UNTAMED SCIENCE** Watch the **Untamed Science** video to learn more about Earth's crust.

Plate Tectonics

3 Getting Started

Check Your Understanding

1. **Background** Read the paragraph below and then answer the question.

> Maria took a train from Oregon to Georgia. The train rode across the entire **continent** of North America. It rode up and down the Rocky Mountains, which form a **boundary** between America's east and west. The conductor said, "These mountains are part of Earth's **crust**."

A **continent** is a large landmass.

A **boundary** is the point or line where one region ends and another begins.

The **crust** is the outer layer of Earth.

• What is the crust?

_____

_____

▶ **MY READING WEB** If you had trouble answering the question above, visit **My Reading Web** and type in *Plate Tectonics.*

Vocabulary Skill

Use Prefixes A prefix is a word part that is added at the beginning of a root or base word to change its meaning. Knowing the meaning of prefixes will help you figure out new words.

Prefix	Meaning	Example
mid-	at or near the middle	mid-ocean ridge, *n.* a chain of mountains that runs along the middle of the ocean floor
sub-	below, beneath, under	subduction, *n.* a process by which part of Earth's crust sinks downward

2. **Quick Check** Choose the word from the table that best completes the sentence below.

• Oceanic crust is pushed beneath continental crust during

_____ .

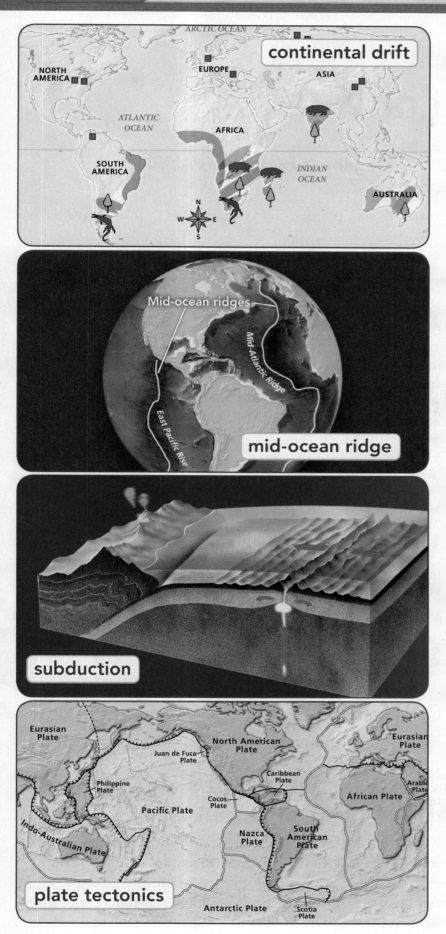

continental drift

mid-ocean ridge

subduction

plate tectonics

Chapter Preview

LESSON 1
- continental drift
- Pangaea
- fossil

⟳ Ask Questions

△ Infer

LESSON 2
- mid-ocean ridge
- sea-floor spreading
- deep-ocean trench
- subduction

⟳ **Relate Text and Visuals**

△ **Develop Hypotheses**

LESSON 3
- plate
- divergent boundary
- convergent boundary
- transform boundary
- plate tectonics
- fault
- rift valley

⟳ **Relate Cause and Effect**

△ **Calculate**

▷ VOCAB FLASH CARDS   For extra help with vocabulary, visit **Vocab Flash Cards** and type in *Plate Tectonics.*

Drifting Continents

UNLOCK THE BIG Q?

🔑 **What Was Wegener's Hypothesis About the Continents?**

my planet Diary

A Puzzled Look

Scientists have long noticed that Earth's continents look as though they could fit together like pieces of a jigsaw puzzle. This was an idea that Alfred Wegener suggested in 1910. "Doesn't the east coast of South America fit exactly against the west coast of Africa, as if they had once been joined?" he asked. "This is an idea I'll have to pursue."

VOICES FROM HISTORY

Communicate **Discuss Wegener's idea with a partner. Then answer the questions.**

1. Why did Wegener think that the continents might once have been joined?

_____

_____

_____

2. If you were Wegener, what other evidence would you look for to show that the continents had once been joined?

_____

_____

▷ **PLANET DIARY** Go to **Planet Diary** to learn more about the continents.

Lab zone® Do the Inquiry Warm-Up *How Are Earth's Continents Linked Together?*

What Was Wegener's Hypothesis About the Continents?

Have you ever looked at a world map and noticed how the coastlines of Africa and South America seem to match up? For many years, scientists made this same observation! In 1910, a German scientist named Alfred Wegener (VAY guh nur) became curious about why some continents look as though they could fit together.

Vocabulary
- continental drift
- Pangaea
- fossil

Skills
- ↻ Reading: Ask Questions
- △ Inquiry: Infer

According to Wegener, the continents of Earth had moved. 🔑 **Wegener's hypothesis was that all the continents were once joined together in a single landmass and have since drifted apart.** Wegener's idea that the continents slowly moved over Earth's surface became known as **continental drift.**

According to Wegener, the continents were joined together in a supercontinent, or single landmass, about 300 million years ago. Wegener called the supercontinent **Pangaea** (pan JEE uh).

Over tens of millions of years, Pangaea began to break apart. The pieces of Pangaea slowly moved to their present locations, shown in **Figure 1.** These pieces became the continents as formed today. In 1915, Wegener published his evidence for continental drift in a book called *The Origin of Continents and Oceans.*

Evidence From Land Features
Land features on the continents provided Wegener with evidence for his hypothesis. On the next page, **Figure 2** shows some of this evidence. For example, Wegener pieced together maps of Africa and South America. He noticed that mountain ranges on the continents line up. He noticed that coal fields in Europe and North America also match up.

Pangaea means "all lands" in Greek. Why is this a suitable name for a supercontinent?

_____
_____
_____
_____

FIGURE 1 ·······
Piecing It All Together
The coastlines of some continents seem to fit together like a jigsaw puzzle.

🖊 **Use the map to answer the questions.**

1. **Interpret Maps** Draw an arrow to match the numbered coast with the lettered coast that seems to fit with it.

   ① ② ③ ④   ⓐ ⓑ ⓒ ⓓ

2. △ **Infer** How would a continent's climate change if it drifted closer to the equator?

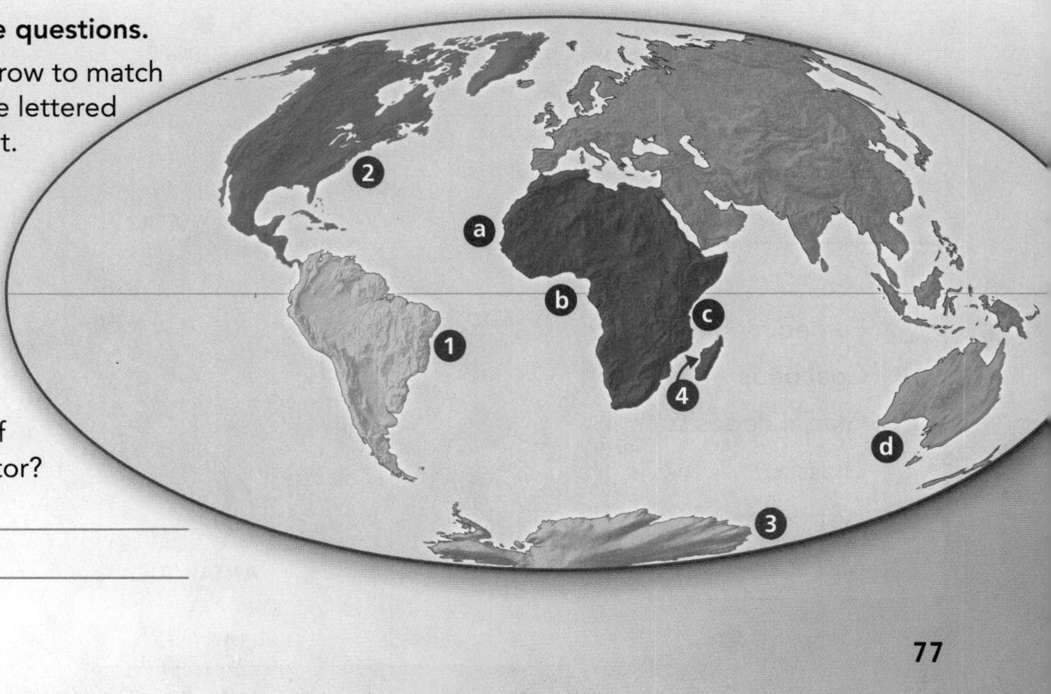

_____
_____

77

FIGURE 2 ··

> INTERACTIVE ART **Pangaea and Continental Drift**

Many types of evidence suggest that Earth's landmasses were once joined together.

Infer On the top map of Pangaea, draw where each piece of evidence on the bottom map would have been found. Use a different symbol or color for each piece of evidence, and provide a key. Then label the continents.

Evidence From Fossils Wegener also used fossils to support his hypothesis for continental drift. A **fossil** is any trace of an ancient organism that has been preserved in rock. For example, *Glossopteris* (glaw SAHP tuh ris) was a fernlike plant that lived 250 million years ago. *Glossopteris* fossils have been found in Africa, South America, Australia, India, and Antarctica, as shown in **Figure 2.** The occurrence of *Glossopteris* on landmasses that are now separated by oceans indicates that Pangaea once existed.

Other examples include fossils of the freshwater reptiles *Mesosaurus* and *Lystrosaurus*. These fossils have also been found in places now separated by oceans. Neither reptile could have swum great distances across salt water. Wegener inferred that these reptiles lived on a single landmass that had since split apart.

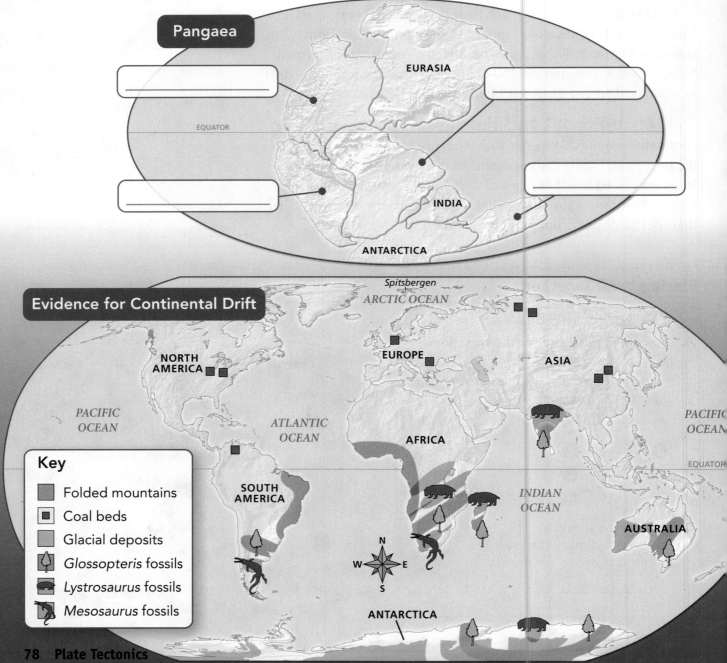

Evidence From Climate Wegener used evidence of climate change to support his hypothesis. As a continent moves toward the equator, its climate gets warmer. As a continent moves toward the poles, its climate gets colder. In either case, the continent carries along with it the fossils and rocks that formed at all of its previous locations.

For example, fossils of tropical plants are found on Spitsbergen, an island in the Arctic Ocean. When these plants lived about 300 million years ago, the island must have had a warm, mild climate. Wegener said the climate changed because the island moved.

Wegener's Hypothesis Rejected Wegener attempted to explain how continental drift took place. He suggested that the continents plowed across the ocean floors. But Wegener could not provide a satisfactory explanation for the force that pushes or pulls the continents. Because Wegener could not identify the cause of continental drift, most geologists of his time rejected his idea.

apply it!

Deep scratches have been found in rocks in South Africa. Such scratches are caused only by glaciers that move across continents. But the climate of South Africa is too mild today for glaciers to form.

1 **Infer** South Africa was once (colder/warmer) than it is today.

2 **CHALLENGE** What can you infer about South Africa's former location?

_____

_____

Lab zone Do the Quick Lab
Moving the Continents.

🔑 Assess Your Understanding

1a. Review Based on evidence from land features, fossils, and climate, Wegener concluded that continents (sink/rise/move).

b. Predict Wegener said that because continents move, they can collide with each other. How could colliding continents explain the formation of mountains?

_____

_____

_____

_____

got it?

○ **I get it!** Now I know Wegener's hypothesis about the continents stated that _____

_____

_____

_____

○ **I need extra help with** _____

Go to **MY SCIENCE ⓢ COACH** *online for help with this subject.*

Sea-Floor Spreading

UNLOCK
THE BIG
?

🔑 **What Are Mid-Ocean Ridges?**

🔑 **What Is Sea-Floor Spreading?**

🔑 **What Happens at Deep-Ocean Trenches?**

MY PLANET DiARY   DISCOVERY

Marie Tharp

Have you ever tried to draw something you can't see? By 1952, geologists Marie Tharp and Bruce Heezen had set to work mapping the ocean floor. Tharp drew details of the ocean floor based on data taken from ships. The data showed how the height of the ocean floor varied. Tharp's maps, which were first published in 1957, helped to confirm the hypothesis of continental drift.

Think about what structures might lie beneath Earth's oceans. Then answer the question.

Do you think the ocean has valleys and mountains? Explain.

_____

_____

_____

_____

> PLANET DIARY Go to **Planet Diary** to learn more about the ocean floor.

Lab ® Do the Inquiry Warm-Up
zone *What Is the Effect of a Change in Density?*

What Are Mid-Ocean Ridges?

When scientists such as Marie Tharp drew maps showing features of the ocean floor, they made a surprising discovery. In certain places, the floor of the ocean appeared to be stitched together like the seams of a baseball! The seams curved along the ocean floors for great distances, as shown in **Figure 1.**

Scientists found that the seams formed mountain ranges that ran along the middle of some ocean floors. Scientists called these mountain ranges **mid-ocean ridges.** 🔑 **Mid-ocean ridges form long chains of mountains that rise up from the ocean floor.**

Vocabulary
- mid-ocean ridge
- deep-ocean trench
- sea-floor spreading
- subduction

Skills
- ↻ **Reading:** Relate Text and Visuals
- △ **Inquiry:** Develop Hypotheses

In the mid-1900s, scientists mapped mid-ocean ridges using *sonar*. Sonar is a device that uses sound waves to measure the distance to an object. Scientists found that mid-ocean ridges extend into all of Earth's oceans. Most mid-ocean ridges lie under thousands of meters of water. Scientists also discovered that a steep-sided valley splits the tops of some mid-ocean ridges. The ridges form the longest mountain ranges on Earth. They are longer than the Rockies in North America and longer than the Andes in South America.

Mid-ocean ridges

Mid-Atlantic Ridge

East Pacific Rise

FIGURE 1 ·····························

Ocean Floors
Mid-ocean ridges rise from the sea floor like stitches on the seams of a baseball.

✎ **Interpret Diagrams** Look at the diagram below. Then use the scale to answer each question. Be sure to measure from the *front* of the diagram.

1. How far below sea level is the peak of the ridge?

_____

2. How high does the ridge rise from the sea floor?

_____

3. [CHALLENGE] How deep below the peak is the valley marking the center of the ridge?

_____

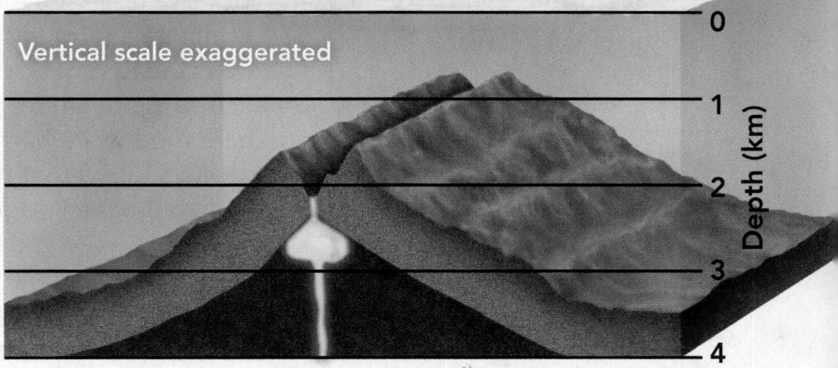

Vertical scale exaggerated

Depth (km)

0

1

2

3

4

Lab zone® Do the Quick Lab *Mid-Ocean Ridges.*

🔑 Assess Your Understanding

got it? ··

○ **I get it!** Now I know that mid-ocean ridges form _____

_____

○ **I need extra help with** _____

Go to **MY SCIENCE** ⑤ **COACH** *online for help with this subject.*

What Is Sea-Floor Spreading?

By the 1960s, geologists had learned more about mid-ocean ridges. They found that mid-ocean ridges continually add new material to the ocean floor. They called this process **sea-floor spreading.**

Sea-floor spreading begins at a mid-ocean ridge, which forms along a crack in the oceanic crust. Along the ridge, new molten material from inside Earth rises, erupts, cools, and hardens to form a solid strip of rock. 🔑 **Sea-floor spreading adds more crust to the ocean floor. At the same time, older strips of rock move outward from either side of the ridge.**

Figure 2 shows evidence that geologists have found for sea-floor spreading.

Pillow lava on the ocean floor

Evidence From Ocean Material

In the central valley of mid-ocean ridges, scientists have found rocks shaped like pillows. Such rocks form only when molten material hardens quickly after erupting under water.

Ridge

Magnetic striping on both sides of the Juan de Fuca ridge

Evidence From Magnetic Stripes

Rock on the ocean floor forms from molten material. As the material erupts, cools, and hardens, magnetic minerals inside the rock line up in the direction of Earth's magnetic poles. These minerals form unseen magnetic "stripes" on the ocean floor. But the magnetic poles occasionally reverse themselves. So each stripe defines a period when molten material erupted and hardened while Earth's magnetic poles did not change.

Scientists found that the pattern of magnetic stripes on one side of a mid-ocean ridge is usually a mirror image of the pattern on the other side of the ridge. The matching patterns show that the crust on the two sides of the ridge spread from the ridge at the same time and at the same rate.

Ocean floor samples taken in 2006

Evidence From Drilling Samples

Scientists drilled into the ocean floor to obtain rock samples. They found that the farther away from a ridge a rock sample was taken, the older the rock was. The youngest rocks were always found at the center of the ridges. Recall that at the ridge center, molten material erupts and cools to form new crust. The rocks' age showed that sea-floor spreading had taken place.

FIGURE 2 ....

> INTERACTIVE ART **Sea-Floor Spreading**

Some mid-ocean ridges have a valley that runs along their center. Evidence shows that molten material erupts through this valley. The material then hardens to form the rock of the ocean floor.

✎ **Color the right half of the diagram to show magnetic striping. How does your drawing show evidence of sea-floor spreading?**

_____

_____

_____

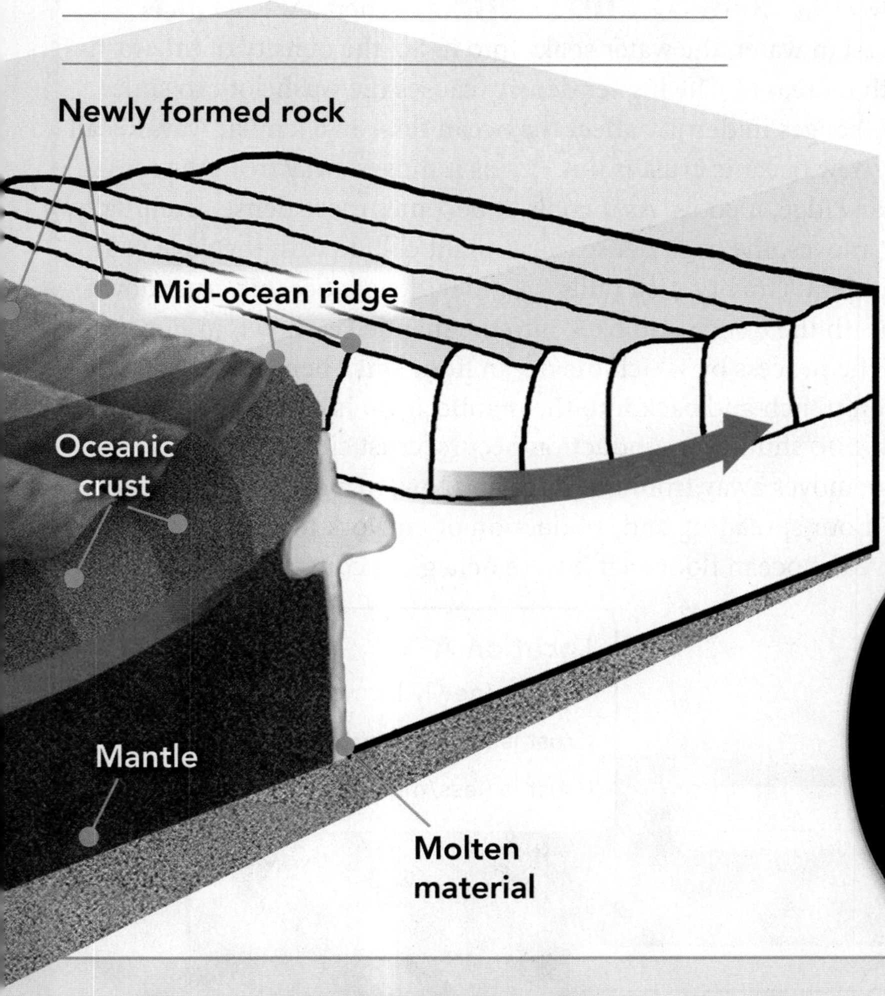

Newly formed rock

Mid-ocean ridge

Oceanic crust

Mantle

Molten material

↻ **Relate Text and Visuals**
How does the diagram show that new crust forms from molten material?

_____

_____

_____

_____

_____

_____

did you know? ....

Scientists used the small submarine *Alvin* to explore the ocean floor. Did you know that *Alvin* was built to withstand the great pressure 4 kilometers down in the ocean?

Alvin, around 1982

Lab zone Do the Quick Lab *Reversing Poles*.

🔑 **Assess Your Understanding**

1a. Review In sea-floor spreading, new crust is added at a (mid-ocean ridge/magnetic stripe).

b. Apply Concepts Suppose Earth's magnetic polarity changed many times over a short period. What pattern of striping at a mid-ocean ridge would you expect to find?

_____

_____

got it?

○ **I get it!** Now I know that sea-floor spreading is the process in which _____

_____

○ **I need extra help with** _____

Go to **my science ⓢ coach** *online for help with this subject.*

83

What Happens at Deep-Ocean Trenches?

Does the ocean floor keep getting wider without stopping? No, eventually the ocean floor plunges into deep underwater canyons. These canyons are called **deep-ocean trenches.** At a deep-ocean trench, the oceanic crust bends downward. 🔑 **In a process taking tens of millions of years, part of the ocean floor sinks back into the mantle at deep-ocean trenches.**

The Process of Subduction

When a washcloth is placed in water, the water soaks into it. So, the density of the washcloth increases. The higher density causes the washcloth to sink.

Changes in density affect the ocean floor in a similar way. Recall that new oceanic crust is hot. But as it moves away from the mid-ocean ridge, it cools. As it cools, it becomes more dense. Eventually, as it moves, the cool, dense crust might collide with the edge of a continent. Gravity then pulls the older, denser oceanic crust down beneath the trench and back into the mantle, as shown in **Figure 3.**

The process by which the ocean floor sinks beneath a deep-ocean trench and back into the mantle again is called **subduction** (sub DUC shun). As subduction occurs, crust closer to a mid-ocean ridge moves away from the ridge and toward a deep-ocean trench. Sea-floor spreading and subduction often work together. They move the ocean floor as if it were on a giant conveyor belt.

FIGURE 3 ·····························

Subduction

Oceanic crust created along a mid-ocean ridge is destroyed at a deep-ocean trench. During the process of subduction, oceanic crust sinks down beneath the trench into the mantle.

✎ **Summarize** Label the mantle, the mid-ocean ridge, and the deep-ocean trench. For locations A and B, circle the correct choice for each statement.

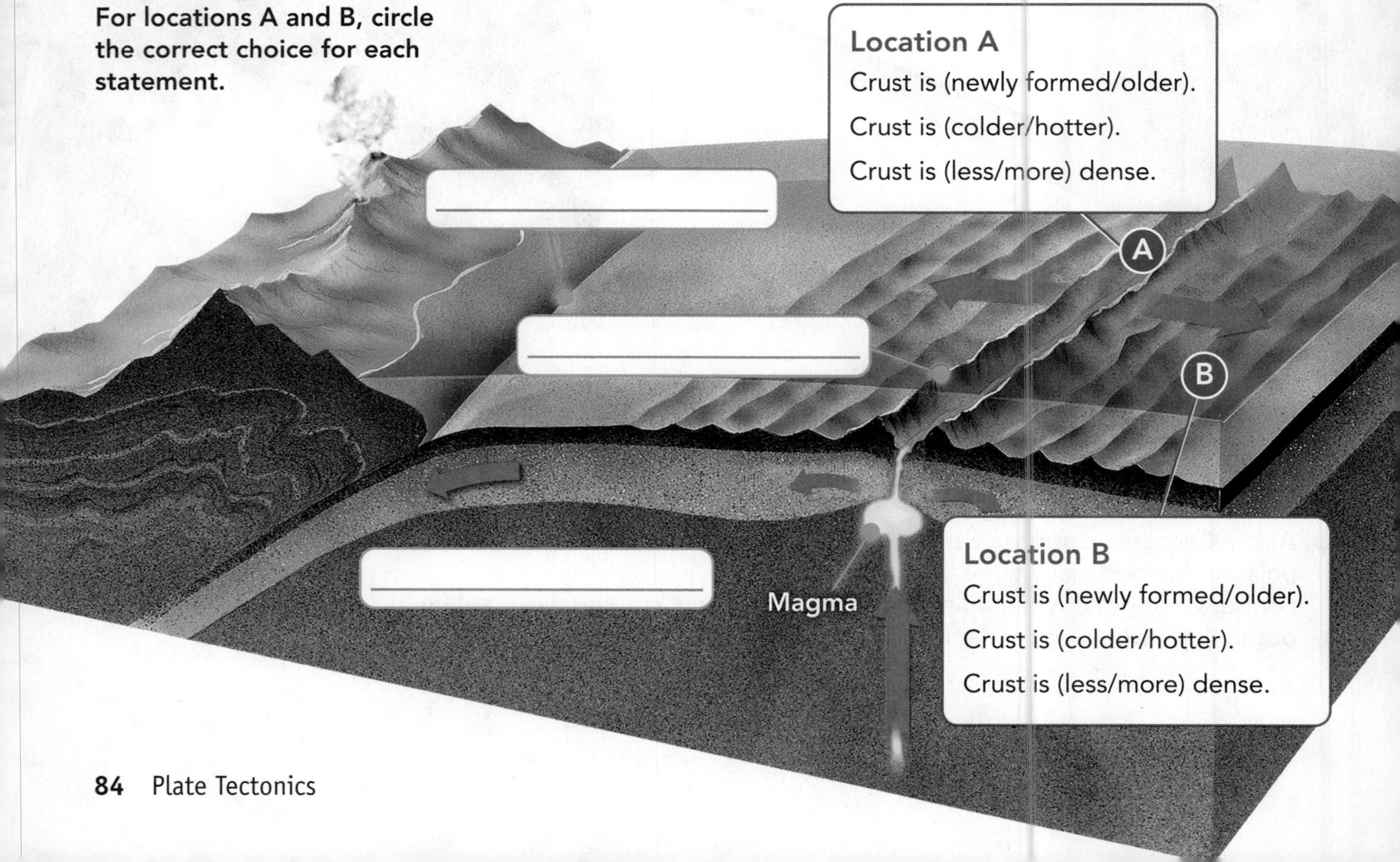

Location A
Crust is (newly formed/older).
Crust is (colder/hotter).
Crust is (less/more) dense.

Location B
Crust is (newly formed/older).
Crust is (colder/hotter).
Crust is (less/more) dense.

Magma

apply it!

The deepest part of the ocean is along the Mariana Trench. This trench is one of several trenches (shown in yellow) in the Pacific Ocean. After reading the main text in this lesson, answer the questions below.

1 Infer At the Pacific Ocean's deep-ocean trenches, oceanic crust is (spread/subducted).

2 Develop Hypotheses The Pacific Ocean is shrinking. Explain this fact in terms of subduction at deep-ocean trenches and spreading at mid-ocean ridges.

_____

_____

_____

_____

_____

_____

Key

— Deep-ocean trench

— Mid-ocean ridge

Subduction and Earth's Oceans

The processes of subduction and sea-floor spreading can change the size and shape of the oceans. Because of these processes, the ocean floor is renewed about every 200 million years. That is the time it takes for new rock to form at the mid-ocean ridge, move across the ocean, and sink into a trench.

The sizes of Earth's oceans are determined by how fast new crust is being created at mid-ocean ridges and how fast old crust is being swallowed up at deep-ocean trenches. An ocean surrounded by many trenches may shrink. An ocean with few trenches will probably grow larger.

For example, the Atlantic Ocean is expanding. This ocean has only a few short trenches. As a result, the spreading ocean floor has almost nowhere to go. Along the continental margins, the oceanic crust of the Atlantic Ocean floor is attached to the continental crust of the continents around the ocean. So as the Atlantic's ocean floor spreads, the continents along its edges also move. Over time, the whole ocean gets wider.

Lab zone Do the Lab Investigation
Modeling Sea-Floor Spreading.

🔑 Assess Your Understanding

2a. Review Subduction takes place at (mid-ocean ridges/deep-ocean trenches).

b. Relate Cause and Effect Why does subduction occur?

_____

_____

_____

_____

got it? ....

○ **I get it!** Now I know that at deep-ocean

trenches _____

_____

○ **I need extra help with** _____

Go to **my science** COACH *online for help with this subject.*

The Theory of Plate Tectonics

UNLOCK THE BIG ?

🗝 **What Is the Theory of Plate Tectonics?**

my planet Diary

Slip-Sliding Away

In 30 million years, this airplane might take one hour longer to fly from New York to London than it takes today. That's because these two cities are moving slowly apart as they ride on pieces of Earth's crust.

THIS TRIP SEEMS TO GET A LITTLE LONGER EACH TIME!

New York

London

Atlantic Ocean

Sea-floor spreading

FUN FACT

Recall the name of your state capital. Then, answer the question below.

Will your state capital be farther from London in 30 million years? Explain.

_____

_____

_____

> PLANET DIARY   Go to **Planet Diary** to learn more about Earth's crust.

Lab® zone   Do the Inquiry Warm-Up
Plate Interactions.

What Is the Theory of Plate Tectonics?

Have you ever dropped a hard-boiled egg? The eggshell cracks into uneven pieces. Earth's lithosphere, its solid outer shell, is like that eggshell. It is broken into pieces separated by cracks. These pieces are called **plates.** Earth's major tectonic plates are shown in **Figure 1.**

Vocabulary

- plate • divergent boundary • convergent boundary
- transform boundary • plate tectonics • fault
- rift valley

Skills

> Reading: Relate Cause and Effect

△ Inquiry: Calculate

Earth's plates meet at boundaries. Along each boundary, plates move in one of three ways. Plates move apart, or diverge, from each other at a **divergent boundary** (dy VUR junt). Plates come together, or converge, at a **convergent boundary** (kun VUR junt). Plates slip past each other along a **transform boundary.**

In the mid-1960s, geologists combined what they knew about sea-floor spreading, Earth's plates, and plate motions into a single theory called **plate tectonics.** ⌾━ **The theory of plate tectonics states that Earth's plates are in slow, constant motion, driven by convection currents in the mantle.** Plate tectonics explains the formation, movement, and subduction of Earth's plates.

Mantle Convection and Plate Motions
What force is great enough to move the continents? Earth's plates move because they are the top part of the large convection currents in Earth's mantle. During subduction, gravity pulls denser plate edges downward, into the mantle. The rest of the plate also moves. The motion of the plates is like the motion of liquid in a pot of soup heating on a stove.

FIGURE 1 ·······································

> REAL-WORLD INQUIRY

Earth's Plates
Plate boundaries divide the lithosphere into large plates.

✎ **Interpret Maps** Draw arrows at all the boundaries of the Pacific plate, showing the directions in which plates move. (*Hint:* First, study the map key.)

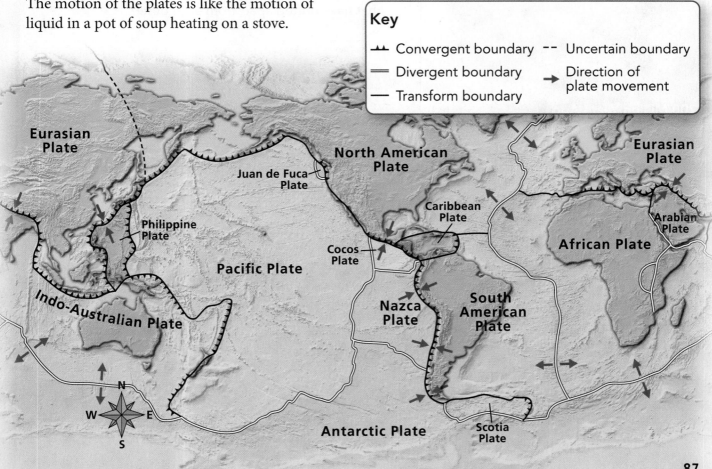

Key

⊥⊥ Convergent boundary

═ Divergent boundary

— Transform boundary

-- Uncertain boundary

→ Direction of plate movement

Eurasian Plate

North American Plate

Juan de Fuca Plate

Caribbean Plate

Eurasian Plate

Arabian Plate

Philippine Plate

Cocos Plate

African Plate

Pacific Plate

Indo-Australian Plate

Nazca Plate

South American Plate

N W E S

Antarctic Plate

Scotia Plate

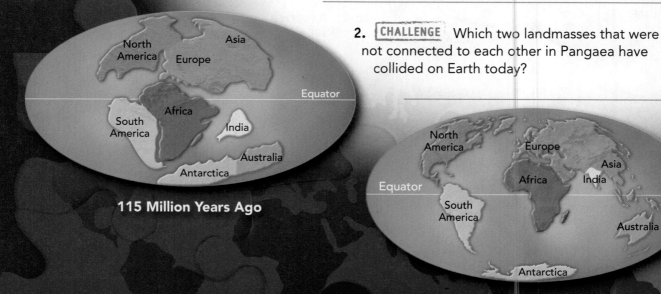

Relate Cause and Effect
What has caused the location of Earth's continents to change over time?

Plate Motions Over Time Scientists use satellites to measure plate motion precisely. The plates move very slowly—from about 1 to 12 centimeters per year. The North American and Eurasian plates move apart at a rate of 2.5 centimeters per year. That's about as fast as your fingernails grow. Because the plates have been moving for tens to hundreds of millions of years, they have moved great distances.

Over time, the movement of Earth's plates has greatly changed the location of the continents and the size and shape of the oceans. As plates move, they change Earth's surface, producing earthquakes, volcanoes, mountain ranges, and deep-ocean trenches. Geologists have evidence that, before Pangaea existed, other supercontinents formed and split apart over the last billion years. Pangaea itself formed when Earth's landmasses moved together about 350 to 250 million years ago. Then, about 200 million years ago, Pangaea began to break apart, as shown in **Figure 2**.

FIGURE 2 ···

> **INTERACTIVE ART** **Plate Motion**

Since the breakup of Pangaea, the continents have taken about 200 million years to move to their present location.

✎ **Use the maps to answer the questions.**

1. **Interpret Maps** List three examples of continents that have drifted apart from each other.

   _____

   _____

   _____

   _____

2. **CHALLENGE** Which two landmasses that were not connected to each other in Pangaea have collided on Earth today?

   _____

200 Million Years Ago

Pangaea   Equator

North America Europe Asia

South America Africa India

Australia

Antarctica

Equator

115 Million Years Ago

North America Europe Asia

Africa India

South America

Equator

Australia

Antarctica

Earth Today

Plate Boundaries

Plate Boundaries Recall that the edges of Earth's plates meet at plate boundaries. **Faults**—breaks in Earth's crust where rocks have slipped past each other—form along these boundaries. Convection currents in Earth's mantle cause the plates to move. As the plates move, they collide, pull apart, or grind past each other. These movements produce great changes in Earth's surface and on the ocean floor. These changes include the formation of volcanoes, mountain ranges, and deep-ocean trenches.

Divergent Boundaries Can a crack in Earth's crust be so wide that people can walk through it? In Iceland it can! There, two plates move slowly away from each other. **Figure 3** shows part of the crack that has formed as these two plates have moved apart over time.

Recall that plates move away from each other at a divergent boundary. Most divergent boundaries occur along the mid-ocean ridges, where new crust is added during sea-floor spreading. But in a few places, the mid-ocean ridge rises above sea level. Volcanic activity of the mid-Atlantic ridge is also seen in Iceland.

Where pieces of Earth's crust diverge on land, a deep valley called a **rift valley** forms. Several rift valleys make up the East African rift system. There, the crust is slowly pulling apart over a wide area.

FIGURE 3 ·······················

Breaking Up Is Hard to Do

Two plates separate to form a great crack in Iceland, marking a divergent boundary.

✎ **Interpret Diagrams** Draw arrows on the diagram to show how plates move at a divergent boundary. Then describe how the plates move.

_____

_____

_____

Vocabulary Prefixes Read the text about the three types of plate boundaries. Circle the correct meaning of each prefix given here.

_Di-_ = (away/together/along)

Con- = (away/together/along)

Trans- = (away/together/along)

do the
math! ·····················

Plates move at very slow rates. These rates are from about 1 to 12 cm per year. To calculate rates of motion, geologists use the following formula.

$$\text{Rate} = \frac{\text{Distance}}{\text{Time}}$$

◢ **Calculate** The Pacific plate is sliding past the North American plate. In 10 million years, the plate will move 500 km. What is the Pacific plate's rate of motion? Express your answer in centimeters per year.

FIGURE 4 ···

The Andes

The Andes Mountains formed at a convergent boundary.

✎ **Interpret Diagrams** Draw arrows on the diagram to show how plates move when they converge. Then describe how the plates move.

_____

_____

_____

Convergent Boundaries The Andes Mountains run for 8,900 kilometers along the west coast of South America. Here, two plates collide. Recall that a boundary where two plates come together, or collide, is called a convergent boundary.

What happens when two plates collide? The density of the plates determines which one comes out on top. Oceanic crust becomes cooler and denser as it spreads away from the mid-ocean ridge. Where two plates carrying oceanic crust meet at a trench, the plate that is more dense sinks under the less dense plate.

A plate carrying oceanic crust can also collide with a plate carrying continental crust. Oceanic crust is more dense than continental crust. The more dense oceanic crust can push up the less dense continental crust. This process has formed the Andes, as shown in **Figure 4.** Meanwhile, the more dense oceanic crust also sinks as subduction occurs. Water eventually leaves the sinking crust and rises into the wedge of the mantle above it. This water lowers the melting point of the mantle in the wedge. As a result, the mantle partially melts and rises up as magma to form volcanoes.

Two plates carrying continental crust can also collide. Then, neither piece of crust is dense enough to sink far into the mantle. Instead, the collision squeezes the crust into high mountain ranges.

EXPLORE THE BIG ❓ Earth's Changing Crust

How do moving plates change Earth's crust?

FIGURE 6 ···

▶ **ART IN MOTION** As plates move, they produce mountains, volcanoes, and valleys as well as mid-ocean ridges and deep-ocean trenches.

✎ **Identify** Fill in the blanks with the correct terms from the list on the next page. (*Hint:* Some points use more than one term.)

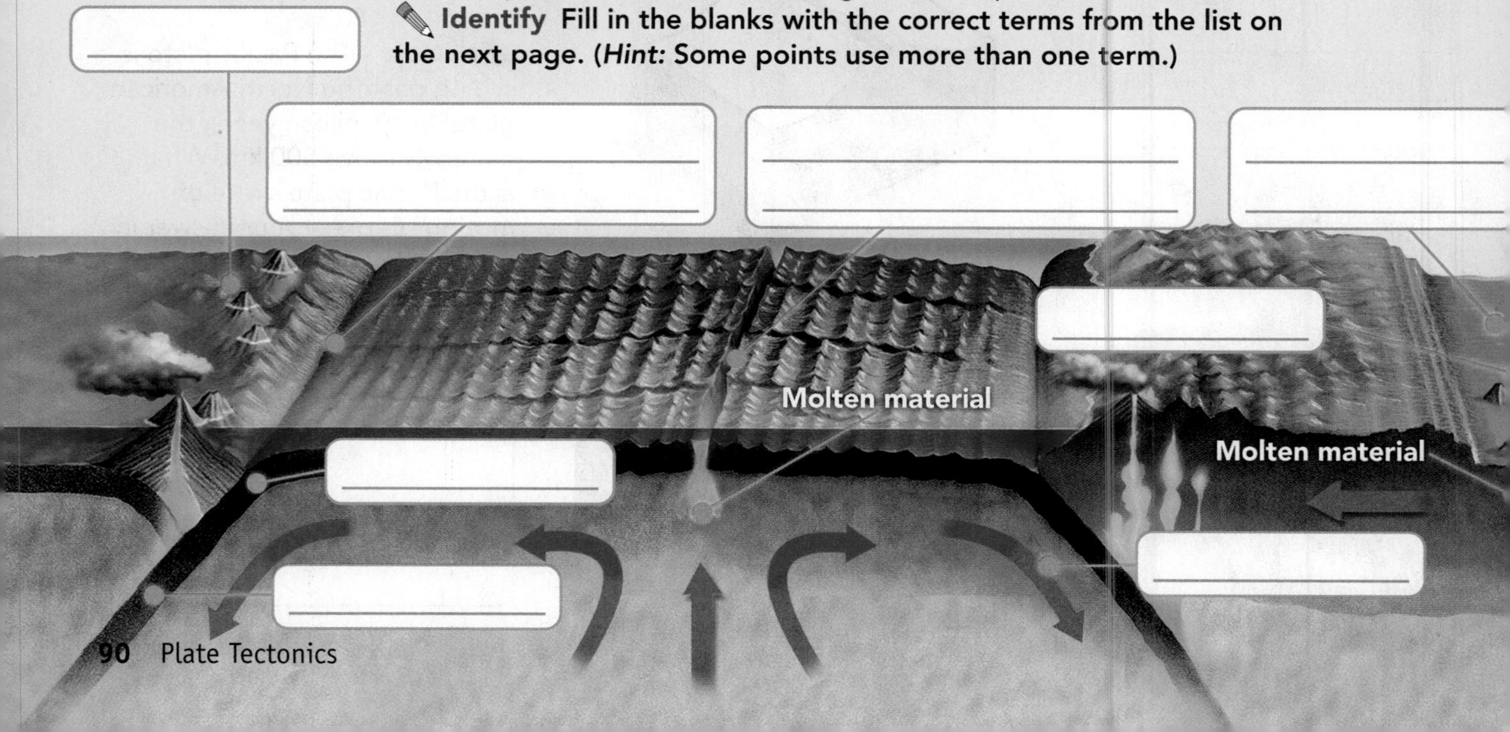

Molten material

Molten material

Transform Boundaries Recall that a transform boundary is a place where two plates slip past each other, moving in opposite directions. Beneath the surface of a transform boundary, the sides of the plates are rocky and jagged. So, the two plates can grab hold of each other and "lock" in place. Forces inside the crust can later cause the two plates to unlock. Earthquakes often occur when the plates suddenly slip along the boundary that they form. However, crust is neither created nor destroyed at transform boundaries. The San Andreas fault, shown in **Figure 5,** is one example of a transform boundary.

Rift valley	Mountains	Convection
Volcanoes	Subduction	Oceanic crust
Sea-floor spreading	Mid-ocean ridge	Convergent boundary
Transform boundary	Continental crust	Deep-ocean trench
Divergent boundary		

FIGURE 5 ·······························

Fault Line

The San Andreas fault in California marks a transform boundary.

✎ **Interpret Diagrams** Draw arrows on the diagram to show how plates move at a transform boundary. Then describe how the plates move.

_____

_____

_____

Lab zone ® Do the Quick Lab *Mantle Convection Currents.*

🔑 Assess Your Understanding

1a. Review Moving plates form convergent, divergent, or _____ boundaries.

b. ANSWER THE BIG **? Summarize** How do moving plates change Earth's crust?

_____

_____

_____

_____

_____

_____

_____

_____

_____

got it? ··································

○ **I get it!** Now I know that the three types of plate boundaries are _____

_____

○ **I need extra help with** _____

Go to **MY SCIENCE** Ⓢ **COACH** *online for help with this subject.*

91

New crust forms at _____. Crust is subducted and destroyed at _____. Mountains form where plates _____.

LESSON 1 Drifting Continents

🔑 Wegener's hypothesis was that all the continents were once joined together in a single landmass and have since drifted apart.

Vocabulary
- continental drift
- Pangaea
- fossil

LESSON 2 Sea-Floor Spreading

🔑 Mid-ocean ridges form long chains of mountains that rise up from the ocean floor.

🔑 Sea-floor spreading adds more crust to the ocean floor. At the same time, older strips of rock move outward from either side of the ridge.

🔑 In a process taking tens of millions of years, part of the ocean floor sinks back into the mantle at deep-ocean trenches.

Vocabulary
- mid-ocean ridge
- sea-floor spreading
- deep-ocean trench
- subduction

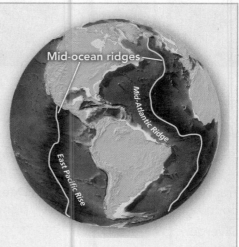

LESSON 3 The Theory of Plate Tectonics

🔑 The theory of plate tectonics states that Earth's plates are in slow, constant motion, driven by convection currents in the mantle.

Vocabulary
- plate
- divergent boundary
- convergent boundary
- transform boundary
- plate tectonics
- fault
- rift valley

Review and Assessment

LESSON 1 Drifting Continents

1. What did Wegener think happens during continental drift?

   a. Continents move.   **b.** Continents freeze.

   c. The mantle warms.   **d.** Convection stops.

2. Wegener thought that all the continents were once joined together in a supercontinent that he called _____.

3. **Draw** The drawing shows North America and Africa. Circle the parts of the coastlines of the two continents that were joined in Pangaea.

North America

Africa

4. **Make Judgments** Wegener proposed that mountains form when continents collide, crumpling up their edges. Was Wegener's idea about how mountains form consistent with his hypothesis of continental drift? Explain.

_____

_____

_____

_____

5. **Write About It** Michelle is a scientist working in Antarctica. She learns that fossils of *Glossopteris* have been found on Antarctica. Her colleague Joe, working in India, has also found *Glossopteris* fossils. Write a letter from Michelle to her colleague explaining how these fossils could be found in both places. Define *continental drift* in your answer and discuss how it explains the fossil findings.

LESSON 2 Sea-Floor Spreading

6. In which areas does subduction of the ocean floor take place?

   a. rift valleys   **b.** the lower mantle

   c. mid-ocean ridges   **d.** deep-ocean trenches

7. A mid-ocean ridge is a _____

_____

that rises up from the ocean floor.

8. **Compare and Contrast** Look at the diagram. Label the area where new crust forms.

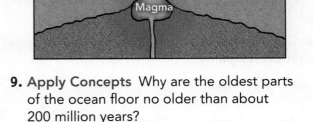

Oceanic plate   Oceanic plate

Magma

9. **Apply Concepts** Why are the oldest parts of the ocean floor no older than about 200 million years?

_____

_____

_____

10. **Sequence** Place the following steps of sea-floor spreading in their correct sequence.

   A. The molten material cools and hardens, forming a strip of rock along the ocean floor.

   B. The strip of rock moves away from the ridge.

   C. Molten material from inside Earth rises to the ocean floor at a mid-ocean ridge.

_____

11. **Write About It** How is pillow lava evidence of sea-floor spreading?

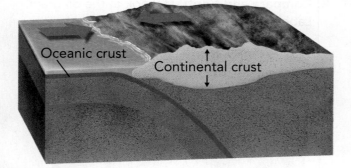

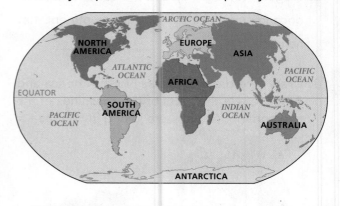

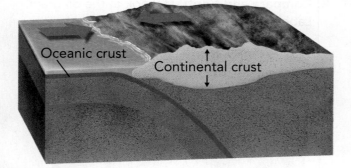

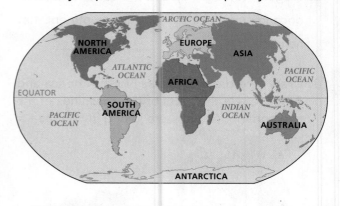

LESSON 3 **The Theory of Plate Tectonics**

12. At which boundary do two plates pull apart?

    a. convergent   **b.** transform

    c. divergent   **d.** mantle-crust

13. When a divergent boundary occurs on land, it forms a _____.

Use the diagram to answer Questions 14–15.

Oceanic crust

Continental crust

14. Classify What type of plate boundary is shown in the diagram?

_____

15. Predict What type of landforms will result from the plate movement shown in the diagram?

_____

16. Compare and Contrast How does the density of oceanic crust differ from that of continental crust? Why is this difference important?

_____

_____

_____

17. math! It takes 100,000 years for a plate to move about 2 kilometers. What is the rate of motion in centimeters per year?

_____

APPLY
THE BIG
How do moving plates change Earth's crust?

18. Summarize Suppose Earth's landmasses someday all move together again. Describe the changes that would occur in Earth's oceans and Earth's landmasses. Use the map and the theory of plate tectonics to explain your ideas.

ARCTIC OCEAN

NORTH AMERICA   EUROPE   ASIA

ATLANTIC OCEAN   AFRICA   PACIFIC OCEAN

EQUATOR

PACIFIC OCEAN   SOUTH AMERICA   INDIAN OCEAN   AUSTRALIA

ANTARCTICA

_____

_____

_____

_____

_____

_____

_____

_____

_____

_____

_____

_____

_____

_____

_____

_____

_____

_____

_____

_____

_____

_____

Standardized Test Prep

Multiple Choice

Circle the letter of the best answer.

1. The diagram shows a process in Earth's crust.

Which statement best describes the process in the diagram?

A Converging plates form mountains.

B Converging plates form volcanoes.

C Diverging plates form mountains.

D Diverging plates form a rift valley.

2. What is one piece of evidence that caused Wegener to think that continents moved?

A He found an old map of the world that showed movement.

B He found similar fossils on different continents that are separated by oceans.

C He proved his hypothesis with an experiment that measured movement.

D He observed the continents moving with his own eyes.

3. Which of the following is evidence for sea-floor spreading?

A matching patterns of magnetic stripes found in the crust of the ocean floor

B new rock found farther from mid-ocean ridges than older rock

C pieces of different crust found on different continents

D changes in climate on the continent of Africa

4. What happens to new oceanic crust at a mid-ocean ridge?

A It forms new mountains under the water.

B It climbs up the mantle to form a trench.

C It gets hotter and sinks into a trench.

D It is so dense that gravity pulls it into a deep-ocean trench.

5. What force causes the movement of Earth's plates?

A convection currents

B pressure

C sound waves

D cooling

Constructed Response

Use the map below and your knowledge of science to help you answer Question 6. Write your answer on a separate piece of paper.

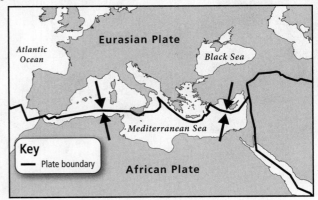

6. The African plate is moving toward the Eurasian plate at a rate of a few centimeters per year. How will this area change in 100 million years? In your answer, consider how the continents will change and how the Mediterranean Sea will change.

ALVIN:2.0

AN EXTREME MAKEOVER

For years, *Alvin*, the world's oldest research submarine, has worked hard. *Alvin* carries scientists deep into the ocean. The research submarine has made over 4,400 dives—some as deep as 4,500 meters beneath the water's surface. With the help of *Alvin*, scientists have discovered everything from tube worms to the wreck of the *Titanic*. But *Alvin* allows scientists to see only the top 63 percent of the ocean. The rest of the ocean lies even deeper than 4,500 meters, where *Alvin* can't go.

Enter *Alvin* 2.0—*Alvin's* replacement. It is bigger and faster, with more windows and improved sensors. It can go down to 6,500 meters and carry heavier samples. Even better, *Alvin* 2.0 allows scientists to see most of the ocean—only 1 percent of the ocean lies deeper than 6,500 meters!

With better and deeper access to the ocean, scientists are excited about all of the new and weird discoveries they'll make with *Alvin* 2.0.

▼ Presenting . . . the new *Alvin!*

Design It Research more about *Alvin* 2.0's features. Think about a new feature that you would like to add to *Alvin* 2.0. What needs would your feature meet? Draw or describe a design for the part, and explain how it will work on the new model.

Museum of Science

An Ocean Is Born

In one of the hottest, driest places in the world, Earth's crust is cracking.

In the Afar region of Ethiopia, Earth's tectonic plates are moving apart. Here, Earth's crust is so thin that magma has been able to break through the surface. As the plates drifted farther apart, the crust sank to form a valley that is 59 kilometers long!

Today volcanoes, earthquakes, and hydrothermal fields tell us how thin the crust is, and how the plates are pulling apart. Eventually, this valley could sink deep enough to allow salt water from the nearby Red Sea to move in and form an ocean. This ocean could split Africa apart. Although it could take millions of years for an actual ocean to form, scientists are excited to witness the steps that will lead to its birth.

Research It Research a major change in Earth's surface caused by plate movement. Try to find at least two different accounts of the event. Create a timeline or a storyboard showing when and how the change occurred.

▲ Tectonic plates are pulling apart in this dry, hot area in the Afar region of Ethiopia.

▲ Lava seeps out of a crack in the lava lake on top of Erfa Ale, the highest mountain in the Afar region. Scientists must wear protective clothing in this extremely hot, dangerous environment.

97

WHAT COULD CAUSE THIS BUILDING TO TOPPLE?

Why do earthquakes occur more often in some places than in others?

Earthquakes can strike without a moment's notice. The ground can buckle and buildings can topple, as happened to this building in Taiwan in 1999. These disasters may seem like random events. But the structure of Earth suggests a different conclusion. **Predict** Do you think geologists can predict where and when an earthquake will occur? Explain.

_____

_____

_____

_____

_____

_____

> **UNTAMED SCIENCE** Watch the **Untamed Science** video to learn more about earthquakes.

CHAPTER

Earthquakes 4

4 Getting Started

Check Your Understanding

1. **Background** Read the paragraph below and then answer the question.

> Ann's parents couldn't move the huge boulder from their yard. The **force** of their pushing didn't budge the rock. "Let's crush it," said Ann's mom. She went on, "Smaller pieces will each have smaller **mass** and **volume.** Then we can move the rock one piece at a time."

A **force** is a push or pull exerted on an object.

Mass is a measure of the amount of matter an object contains and its resistance to movement.

Volume is the amount of space that matter occupies.

• What features of the boulder make it hard to move?

_____

> **MY READING WEB** If you had trouble completing the question above, visit **My Reading Web** and type in *Earthquakes*.

Vocabulary Skill

Identify Multiple Meanings Some familiar words have more than one meaning. Words you use every day may have different meanings in science. Look at the different meanings of the words below.

Word	Everyday Meaning	Scientific Meaning
fault	*n.* blame or responsibility Example: The team's loss was not the fault of any one person.	*n.* a crack or break in rock along which rock surfaces can slip Example: A fault ran through the cliff.
focus	*v.* to concentrate Example: Focus your attention on reading, writing, and arithmetic.	*n.* the area where rock that is under stress begins to break, causing an earthquake Example: The focus of the earthquake was 70 kilometers below Earth's surface.

2. **Quick Check** Circle the sentence below that uses the scientific meaning of the word *fault.*
   • Errors in the test were the test writer's **fault.**
   • The San Andreas **fault** runs along the coast of California.

plateau

strike-slip fault

earthquake

seismogram

Chapter Preview

LESSON 1
- stress
- tension
- compression
- shearing
- normal fault
- reverse fault
- strike-slip fault
- plateau

↻ Relate Cause and Effect
▲ Make Models

LESSON 2
- earthquake
- focus
- epicenter
- P wave
- S wave
- surface wave
- seismograph
- Modified Mercalli scale
- magnitude
- Richter scale
- moment magnitude scale

↻ Sequence
▲ Infer

LESSON 3
- seismogram

↻ Identify the Main Idea
▲ Predict

> **VOCAB FLASH CARDS** For extra help with vocabulary, visit **Vocab Flash Cards** and type in *Earthquakes.*

Forces in Earth's Crust

UNLOCK THE BIG ?

🔑 **How Does Stress Change Earth's Crust?**

🔑 **How Do Faults Form?**

🔑 **How Does Plate Movement Create New Landforms?**

my PLANET DiARY

Still Growing!

Mount Everest in the Himalayas is the highest mountain on Earth. Climbers who reach the peak stand 8,850 meters above sea level. You might think that mountains never change. But forces inside Earth push Mount Everest at least several millimeters higher each year. Over time, Earth's forces slowly but constantly lift, stretch, bend, and break Earth's crust in dramatic ways!

MISCONCEPTION

✏️ **Communicate** Discuss the following question with a classmate. Write your answer below.

How long do you think it took Mount Everest to form? Hundreds of years? Thousands? Millions? Explain.

_____

_____

_____

_____

▶ **PLANET DIARY** Go to **Planet Diary** to learn more about forces in Earth's crust.

Lab zone® Do the Inquiry Warm-Up *How Does Stress Affect Earth's Crust?*

How Does Stress Change Earth's Crust?

Rocks are hard and stiff. But the movement of Earth's plates can create strong forces that slowly bend or fold many rocks like a caramel candy bar. Like the candy bar, some rocks may only bend and stretch when a strong force is first applied to them. But beyond a certain limit, all rocks in Earth's brittle upper crust will break.

Forces created by plate movement are examples of stress. **Stress** is a force that acts on rock to change its shape or volume. Geologists often express stress as force per unit area. Because stress increases as force increases, stress adds energy to the rock. The energy is stored in the rock until the rock changes shape or breaks.

Vocabulary
- stress • tension • compression • shearing
- normal fault • reverse fault • strike-slip fault • plateau

Skills
↻ Reading: Relate Cause and Effect
△ Inquiry: Make Models

Three kinds of stress can occur in the crust—tension, compression, and shearing. 🔑 **Tension, compression, and shearing work over millions of years to change the shape and volume of rock.** Most changes in the crust occur only very slowly, so that you cannot directly observe the crust bending, stretching, or breaking. **Figure 1** shows the three types of stress.

Tension Rock in the crust can be stretched so that it becomes thinner in the middle. This process can make rock seem to act like a piece of warm bubble gum. The stress force that pulls on the crust and thins rock in the middle is called **tension.** Tension occurs where two plates pull apart.

Compression One plate pushing against another plate can squeeze rock like a giant trash compactor. The stress force that squeezes rock until it folds or breaks is called **compression.** Compression occurs where two plates come together.

Shearing Stress that pushes a mass of rock in two opposite directions is called **shearing.** Shearing can cause rock to break and slip apart or to change its shape. Shearing occurs where two plates slip past each other.

FIGURE 1 ·····················
▶ ART IN MOTION **Stress in Earth's Crust**
Stress can push, pull, or squeeze rock in Earth's crust.
✏ **Apply Concepts Look at the pair of arrows in the second diagram. These arrows show how tension affects rock. Draw a pair of arrows on the third diagram to show how compression affects rock. Then, draw a pair of arrows on the bottom diagram to show how shearing acts on rock.**

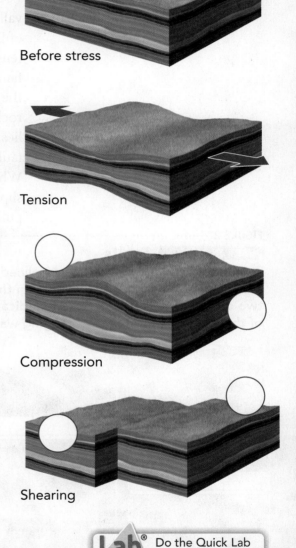

Before stress

Tension

Compression

Shearing

Lab zone ® Do the Quick Lab Effects of Stress.

🔑 **Assess Your Understanding**

got it? ···

○ **I get it!** Now I know that stress changes Earth's crust by changing the _____

_____

○ **I need extra help with** _____

Go to MY SCIENCE ⑤ COACH online for help with this subject.

How Do Faults Form?

Recall that a fault is a break in the rock of the crust where rock surfaces slip past each other. Most faults occur along plate boundaries, where the forces of plate motion push or pull the crust so much that the crust breaks. 🔑 **When enough stress builds up in rock, the rock breaks, creating a fault.** There are three main types of faults: normal faults, reverse faults, and strike-slip faults.

Normal Faults The Rio Grande River flows through a wide valley in New Mexico. Here, tension has pulled apart two pieces of Earth's crust, forming the valley. Where rock is pulled apart by tension in Earth's crust, normal faults form. In a **normal fault,** the fault cuts through rock at an angle, so one block of rock sits over the fault, while the other block lies under the fault. The block of rock that sits over the fault is called the *hanging wall.* The rock that lies under the fault is called the *footwall.* The diagram of the normal fault in **Figure 2** shows how the hanging wall sits over the footwall. When movement occurs along a normal fault, the hanging wall slips downward. Normal faults occur where two plates diverge, or pull apart.

FIGURE 2 ···

▶ ART IN MOTION Faults

The three main types of faults are defined by the direction in which rock moves along the fault. ✏️ **Observe In the descriptions below the first two diagrams, fill in the blanks to indicate how rock moves. In both of these diagrams, label the hanging wall and footwall.**

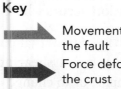

Key

→ Movement along the fault

→ Force deforming the crust

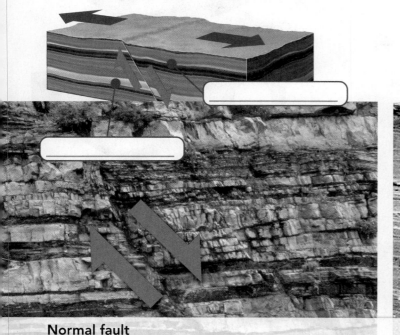

Normal fault

In a normal fault, the hanging wall _____ _____ relative to the footwall.

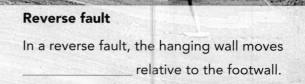

Reverse fault

In a reverse fault, the hanging wall moves _____ relative to the footwall.

Reverse Faults

The northern Rocky Mountains rise high above the western United States and Canada. These mountains were gradually lifted up over time by movement along reverse faults. A **reverse fault** has the same structure as a normal fault, but the blocks move in the reverse direction. That is, the hanging wall moves up and the footwall moves down. **Figure 2** shows a reverse fault. Reverse faults form where compression pushes the rock of the crust together.

Strike-Slip Faults

The hilly plains in southern California are split by the San Andreas fault, shown in **Figure 2.** Here, shearing has produced a strike-slip fault. In a **strike-slip fault,** the rocks on either side of the fault slip past each other sideways, with little up or down motion. A strike-slip fault that forms the boundary between two plates is called a transform boundary. The San Andreas fault is an example of a transform boundary.

Lab zone® Do the Quick Lab *Modeling Faults.*

apply it!

The low angle of a thrust fault allows rock in the hanging wall to be pushed great distances. For example, over millions of years, rock along the Lewis thrust fault in Glacier National Park has moved 80 kilometers.

1 Identify Based on the arrows showing fault movements in the diagram, a thrust fault is a type of (normal fault/reverse fault).

2 CHALLENGE Why might the type of rock in the hanging wall of the Lewis thrust fault be different from the type of rock in the footwall?

_____
_____
_____
_____

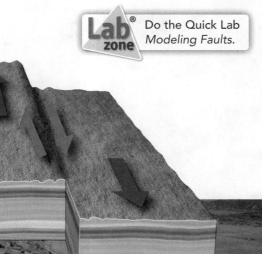

Strike-slip fault

Rocks on either side of a strike-slip fault move past each other.

🔑 Assess Your Understanding

1a. Review When enough stress builds up in brittle rock, the rock breaks, causing a

_____ to form.

b. Infer A geologist sees a fault along which blocks of rock in the footwall have moved higher relative to blocks of rock in the hanging wall. What type of fault is this?

_____

got it? ....

○ **I get it!** Now I know that faults form when _____

_____

○ I need extra help with _____

_____

Go to **MY SCIENCE ⑤ COACH** *online for help with this subject.*

How Does Plate Movement Create New Landforms?

Most changes in the crust occur so slowly that they cannot be observed directly. But what if you could speed up time so that a billion years passed by in minutes? Then, you could watch the movement of Earth's plates fold, stretch, and uplift the crust over wide areas. 🗝️ **Over millions of years, the forces of plate movement can change a flat plain into features such as anticlines and synclines, folded mountains, fault-block mountains, and plateaus.**

Folding Earth's Crust Have you ever skidded on a rug that wrinkled up as your feet pushed it across the floor? Sometimes plate movements can cause Earth's crust to fold much like the rug. Then, rocks stressed by compression may bend without breaking.

How Folds Form Folds are bends in rock that form when compression shortens and thickens Earth's crust. A fold can be a few centimeters across or hundreds of kilometers wide. **Figure 3** shows folds in rock that were exposed when a road was cut through a hillside in California.

....

Vocabulary Identify Multiple Meanings Underline the sentence that uses the scientific meaning of *fold*.

- The rock looked as crushed as my shirts if I don't fold them.
- Rock that bends without breaking may form a fold.

FIGURE 3 ....

Folded Rock

Folds in rock shorten and thicken the Earth's crust. Over time, this process can form mountains.

Make Models Hold down the right edge of this page. Then, push the left edge toward the center of the book. Is this activity a good model for showing how folded rock forms? Explain.

_____

_____

_____

_____

_____

_____

_____

_____

Place your fingers here and push the left edge of the page.

How Anticlines and Synclines Form Geologists use the terms *anticline* and *syncline* to describe upward and downward folds in rock. A fold in rock that bends upward into an arch is an anticline (AN tih klyn), as shown in **Figure 4.** A fold in rock that bends downward to form a V shape is a syncline (SIN klyn). Anticlines and synclines are found in many places where compression forces have folded the crust. The central Appalachian Mountains in Pennsylvania are folded mountains made up of anticlines and synclines.

How Folded Mountains Form The collision of two plates can cause compression and folding of the crust over a wide area. Folding produced some of the world's largest mountain ranges. The Himalayas in Asia and the Alps in Europe formed when pieces of the crust folded during the collision of two plates. These mountains formed over millions of years.

FIGURE 4 ·······························

Anticlines and Synclines
Compression can cause folds in the crust. Two types of folding are anticlines, which arch up, and synclines, which dip down.
Relate Cause and Effect Draw arrows to show the direction in which forces act to compress the crust. (*Hint:* Review the information on compression in this lesson.) Then label the anticline and the syncline.

✎

Relate Cause and Effect
When two normal faults cause valleys to drop down on either side of a block of rock, what type of landform results?

_____

_____

Stretching Earth's Crust If you traveled by car from Salt Lake City to Los Angeles, you would cross the Great Basin. This region contains many mountains separated by broad valleys, or basins. The mountains form from tension in Earth's crust that causes faulting. Such mountains are called fault-block mountains.

How do fault-block mountains form? Where two plates move away from each other, tension forces create many normal faults. Suppose two normal faults cause valleys to drop down on either side of a block of rock. This process is shown in the diagram that accompanies the photograph in **Figure 5.** As the hanging wall of each normal fault slips downward, the block in between now stands above the surrounding valleys, forming a fault-block mountain.

FIGURE 5 ···

Tension and Normal Faults
As tension forces pull the crust apart, two normal faults can form a fault-block mountain range, as you can see in the diagram below. The mountain range in the photograph is in the Great Basin. Valleys can also form as a result of two normal faults.

✎ **Predict** Label the hanging wall and the two footwalls in diagram A. In diagram B, draw the new position of the hanging wall after movement occurs. Describe what happens.

_____

_____

_____

_____

Fault-block mountains

A Before movement occurs along the faults.

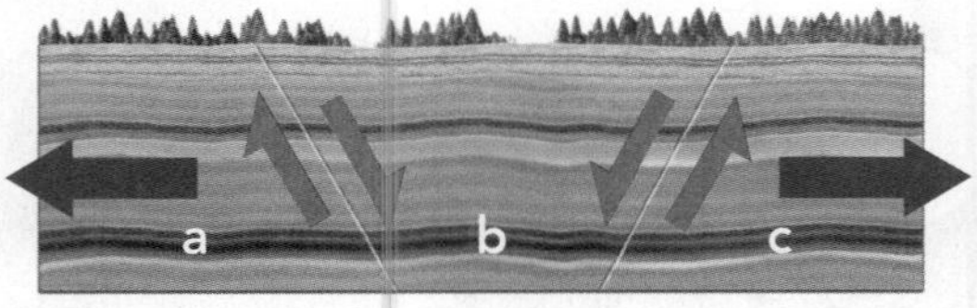

a. _____

b. _____

c. _____

B Draw the outcome after movement occurs along the faults.

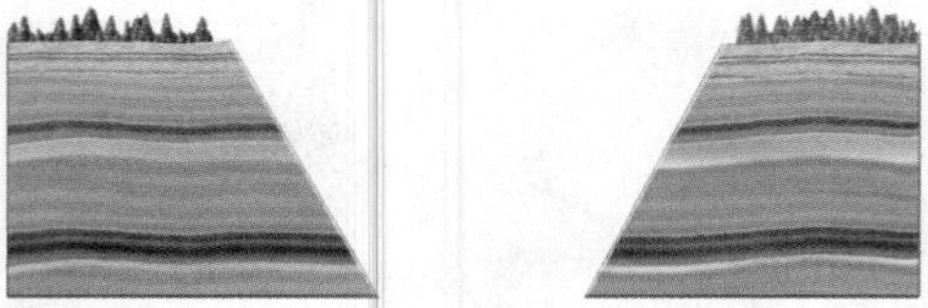

Key

→ Movement along the fault

➡ Force deforming the crust

Uplifting Earth's Crust The forces that raise mountains can also uplift, or raise, plateaus. A **plateau** is a large area of flat land elevated high above sea level. Some plateaus form when forces in Earth's crust push up a large, flat block of rock. Like a fancy sandwich, a plateau consists of many different flat layers, and is wider than it is tall. Forces deforming the crust uplifted the Colorado Plateau in the "Four Corners" region of Arizona, Utah, Colorado, and New Mexico. **Figure 6** shows one part of that plateau in northern Arizona.

FIGURE 6 ·····················
The Kaibab Plateau
The Kaibab Plateau forms the North Rim of the Grand Canyon. The plateau is the flat-topped landform in the right half of the photograph.

Look at the sequence of drawings below. In your own words, describe what happens in the last two diagrams.

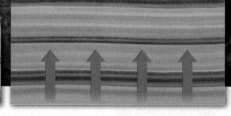

A flat, layered block of rock lies somewhere in Earth's crust.

_____
_____
_____
_____

_____
_____
_____
_____

Lab zone® Do the Quick Lab *Modeling Stress.*

🔑 Assess Your Understanding

2a. Review Normal faults often occur when two plates (come together/pull apart).

b. Interpret Diagrams Look at the diagram that accompanies the photograph in **Figure 5.** Does the block of rock in the middle move up as a result of movement along the normal faults? Explain.

_____
_____
_____
_____
_____

got**it?**

○ **I get it!** Now I know that plate movements create new features by _____

_____
_____
_____
_____

○ **I need extra help with** _____

_____

Go to MY SCIENCE ⓢ COACH online for help with this subject.

Earthquakes and Seismic Waves

🗝 **What Are Seismic Waves?**

🗝 **How Are Earthquakes Measured?**

🗝 **How Is an Epicenter Located?**

my planet diary

Witness to Disaster

On May 12, 2008, a major earthquake struck China. American reporter Melissa Block was conducting a live radio interview in that country at the moment the earthquake struck.

"What's going on?" Block asked. She remained on the air and continued: "The whole building is shaking. The whole building is SHAKING."

Block watched as the ground moved like waves beneath her feet. The top of the church across the street started to fall down. For minutes, the ground continued to vibrate under Block's feet. The earthquake that day killed about 87,000 people.

—NPR.com

DISASTER

✏️ **Communicate Discuss these questions with a group of classmates. Write your answers below.**

1. What does Melissa Block's experience tell you about the way the ground can move during an earthquake?

_____

_____

2. How do you think you would react during an earthquake or other disaster?

_____

_____

_____

▶ **PLANET DIARY** Go to **Planet Diary** to learn more about earthquakes.

Lab zone ® Do the Inquiry Warm-Up *How Do Seismic Waves Travel Through Earth?*

Vocabulary

- earthquake • focus • epicenter • P wave
- S wave • surface wave • seismograph
- Modified Mercalli scale • magnitude • Richter scale
- moment magnitude scale

Skills

↻ Reading: Sequence
△ Inquiry: Infer

What Are Seismic Waves?

Earth is never still. Every day, worldwide, several thousand earthquakes are detected. An **earthquake** is the shaking and trembling that results from movement of rock beneath Earth's surface. Most earthquakes are too small to notice. But a large earthquake can crack open the ground, shift mountains, and cause great damage.

Cause of Earthquakes The forces of plate movement cause earthquakes. Plate movements produce stress in Earth's crust, adding energy to rock and forming faults. Stress increases along a fault until the rock slips or breaks, causing an earthquake. In seconds, the earthquake releases an enormous amount of stored energy. Some of the energy released during an earthquake travels in the form of seismic waves. ⊶ **Seismic waves are vibrations that are similar to sound waves. They travel through Earth carrying energy released by an earthquake.** The speed and path of the waves in part depend on the material through which the waves travel.

Earthquake   Path of seismic waves

• A

• B

C

apply it!

Earthquakes start below the surface of Earth. But an earthquake's seismic waves do not carry energy only upward, toward Earth's surface. They also carry energy downward, through Earth's interior.

❶ Look at the drawing showing Earth's interior. At which point(s) can seismic waves be detected?

○ A only
○ A and B
○ A, B, and C

❷ △ Infer At which point do you think the seismic waves will have the most energy? Why?

_____

_____

_____

_____

Sequence Number the following in the order in which seismic waves would be felt:

___ At an earthquake's epicenter

___ At a distance of 500 km from the earthquake's focus

___ At the earthquake's focus

Types of Seismic Waves

Like a pebble thrown into a pond, the seismic waves of an earthquake race out in every direction from the earthquake's focus. The **focus** (FOH kus) is the area beneath Earth's surface where rock that was under stress begins to break or move. This action triggers the earthquake. The point on the surface directly above the focus is called the **epicenter** (EP uh sen tur).

Most earthquakes start in the lithosphere, within about 100 kilometers beneath Earth's surface. Seismic waves carry energy from the earthquake's focus. This energy travels through Earth's interior and across Earth's surface. That happened in 2002, when a powerful earthquake ruptured the Denali fault in Alaska, shown in **Figure 1.**

There are three main categories of seismic waves. These waves are P waves, S waves, and surface waves. But an earthquake sends out only P and S waves from its focus. Surface waves can develop wherever P and S waves reach the surface.

FIGURE 1

▶ **INTERACTIVE ART** **Seismic Waves**
The diagram shows how seismic waves traveled during an earthquake along the Denali fault.

✎ **Explain** Match the two points in the diagram to the two terms below them. Then, write a short, science-based news article that describes how, why, and where the earthquake took place. Include a headline.

earthBL🜨G

ENTRY 1

Write your headline here.

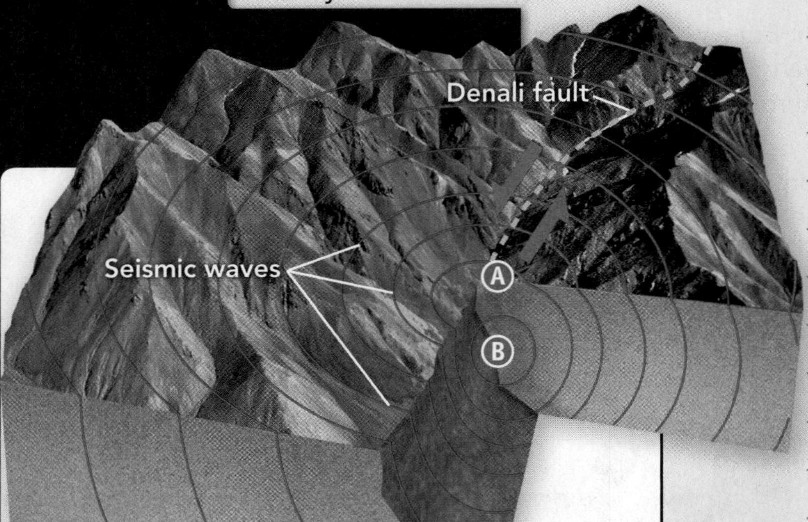

Denali fault

Seismic waves

Ⓐ
Ⓑ

Focus   Point _____

Epicenter   Point _____

P Waves The first waves to arrive are primary waves, or P waves. **P waves** are seismic waves that compress and expand the ground like an accordion. Like the other types of seismic waves, P waves can damage buildings. Look at **Figure 2A** to see how P waves move.

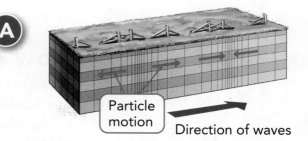

Particle motion

Direction of waves

S Waves After P waves come secondary waves, or S waves. **S waves** are seismic waves that can vibrate from side to side (as shown in **Figure 2B**) or up and down. Their vibrations are at an angle of 90° to the direction that they travel. When S waves reach the surface, they shake structures violently. While P waves travel through both solids and liquids, S waves cannot move through liquids.

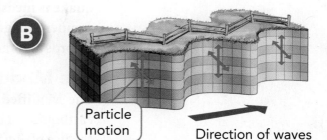

Particle motion

Direction of waves

Surface Waves When P waves and S waves reach the surface, some of them become surface waves. **Surface waves** move more slowly than P and S waves, but they can produce severe ground movements. These waves produce movement that is similar to waves in water, where the water's particles move in a pattern that is almost circular. Surface waves can make the ground roll like ocean waves (**Figure 2C**) or shake buildings from side to side.

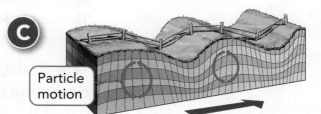

Particle motion

Direction of waves

FIGURE 2 ···

P, S, and Surface Waves
Earthquakes release stored energy as seismic waves.
✎ **Describe Draw a line from each type of seismic wave to the movement it causes.**

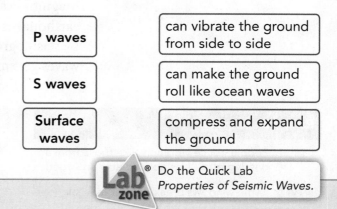

P waves	can vibrate the ground from side to side
S waves	can make the ground roll like ocean waves
Surface waves	compress and expand the ground

Lab zone ® Do the Quick Lab *Properties of Seismic Waves.*

🔑 **Assess Your Understanding**

1a. Review The energy released by an earthquake moves out from the earthquake's

_____ in the form of seismic waves.

b. Predict Small earthquakes occur along a certain fault several times a year. Why might geologists worry if no earthquakes occur for 25 years?

_____

_____

_____

got it? ···

○ **I get it!** Now I know that seismic waves are_____

_____

○ I need extra help with _____

Go to **my science coach** *online for help with this subject.*

How Are Earthquakes Measured?

Geologists monitor earthquakes by measuring the seismic waves they produce. This is done in two ways. 🔑 **The amount of earthquake damage or shaking that is felt is rated using the Modified Mercalli scale. The magnitude, or size, of an earthquake is measured on a seismograph using the Richter scale or moment magnitude scale.** A **seismograph** is an instrument that records and measures an earthquake's seismic waves.

The Modified Mercalli Scale

The **Modified Mercalli scale** rates the amount of shaking from an earthquake. The shaking is rated by people's observations, without the use of any instruments. This scale is useful in regions where there aren't many instruments to measure an earthquake's strength. The table in **Figure 3** describes the 12 steps of the Mercalli scale. To rank examples of damage, look at the photographs in **Figure 3**.

The Richter Scale

An earthquake's **magnitude** is a single number that geologists assign to an earthquake based on the earthquake's size. There are many magnitude scales. These scales are based on the earliest magnitude scale, called the **Richter scale**. Magnitude scales like the Richter scale rate the magnitude of small earthquakes based on the size of the earthquake's waves as recorded by seismographs. The magnitudes take into account that seismic waves get smaller the farther a seismograph is from an earthquake.

Rank	Description
I–III	People notice vibrations like those from a passing truck. Unstable objects disturbed.
IV–VI	Some windows break. Plaster may fall.
VII–IX	Moderate to heavy damage. Buildings jolted off foundations.
X–XII	Great destruction. Cracks appear in ground. Waves seen on surface.

FIGURE 3 ···

> **INTERACTIVE ART** **Modified Mercalli Scale**
The Modified Mercalli scale uses Roman numerals to rate the damage and shaking at any given location, usually close to the earthquake. ✎ **Classify Assign a Modified Mercalli rating to each photograph.**

The Moment Magnitude Scale

Geologists use the **moment magnitude scale** to rate the total energy an earthquake releases. News reports may mention the Richter scale, but the number quoted is almost always an earthquake's moment magnitude. To assign a magnitude to an earthquake, geologists use data from seismographs and other sources. The data allow geologists to estimate how much energy the earthquake releases. **Figure 4** gives the magnitudes of some recent, strong earthquakes.

Comparing Magnitudes An earthquake's moment magnitude tells geologists how much energy was released by an earthquake. Each one-point increase in magnitude represents the release of roughly 32 times more energy. For example, a magnitude 6 earthquake releases 32 times as much energy as a magnitude 5 earthquake.

An earthquake's effects increase with magnitude. Earthquakes with a magnitude below 5 are small and cause little damage. Those with a magnitude above 6 can cause great damage. The most powerful earthquakes, with a magnitude of 8 or above, are rare. In the 1900's, only three earthquakes had a magnitude of 9 or above. More recently, the 2004 Sumatra earthquake had a magnitude of 9.2.

FIGURE 4 ⋯⋯⋯⋯⋯⋯⋯⋯⋯⋯⋯⋯⋯⋯⋯⋯⋯

Earthquake Magnitude

The table gives the moment magnitudes of some recent earthquakes.

Magnitude	Location	Date
9.2	Sumatra (Indian Ocean)	December 2004
7.9	China	May 2008
7.6	Turkey	August 1999
6.6	Japan	October 2004
5.4	California	July 2008

[CHALLENGE] Approximately how many times stronger was the earthquake in Turkey than the earthquake in Japan?

did you know?

About 98 percent of Antarctica is covered by ice. Large shifts in the ice here can cause "ice quakes." Did you know that these "ice quakes" can be the equivalent of magnitude 7 earthquakes?

Lab zone® Do the Quick Lab *Measuring Earthquakes.*

🔑 Assess Your Understanding

2a. Identify The _____ scale rates earthquakes based on the amount of energy that is released.

b. Infer Suppose the moment magnitude of an earthquake is first thought to be 6, but is later found to be 8. Would you expect the earthquake damage to be more or less serious? Why?

_____

_____

_____

got it?⋯⋯⋯⋯⋯⋯⋯⋯⋯⋯⋯⋯⋯⋯⋯⋯

○ **I get it!** Now I know that to measure earthquakes, geologists use seismic waves to determine _____

_____

○ I need extra help with _____

_____

Go to MY SCIENCE ⬛ COACH *online for help with this subject.*

How Is an Epicenter Located?

When an earthquake occurs, geologists try to pinpoint the earthquake's epicenter. Why? Locating the epicenter helps geologists identify areas where earthquakes may occur in the future.

🔑 **Geologists use seismic waves to locate an earthquake's epicenter.** To do this, they use data from thousands of seismograph stations set up all over the world. However, you can use a simpler method to find an earthquake's epicenter.

Recall that seismic waves travel at different speeds. P waves arrive at a seismograph first. Then S waves follow close behind. Look at the graph, P and S Waves, below. Suppose you know when P waves arrived at a seismograph after an earthquake, and when S waves arrived. You can read the graph to find the distance from the seismograph to the epicenter. Notice that the farther away an earthquake is from a given point, the greater the time between the arrival of the P waves and the S waves.

Suppose you know the distance of three seismograph stations from an epicenter. You can then draw three circles to locate the epicenter. Look at **Figure 5.** The center of each circle is a particular seismograph's location. The radius of each circle is the distance from that seismograph to the epicenter. The point where the three circles intersect is the location of the epicenter.

do the math!

Seismic Wave Speeds

Seismographs at five observation stations recorded the arrival times of the P and S waves produced by an earthquake. These data were used to draw the graph.

1 Read Graphs What variable is shown on the x-axis of the graph? What variable is shown on the y-axis?

_____

2 Estimate How long did it take the S waves to travel 2,000 km?

_____

3 Estimate How long did it take the P waves to travel 2,000 km?

_____

4 Calculate What is the difference in the arrival times of the P waves and the S waves at 2,000 km? At 4,000 km?

_____

_____

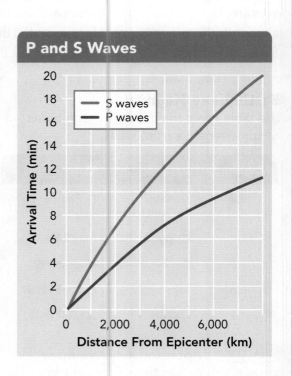

P and S Waves

— S waves
— P waves

Arrival Time (min) vs. Distance From Epicenter (km)

FIGURE 5 ··········

Determining an Earthquake's Epicenter

The map shows how to find the epicenter of an earthquake using data from three seismographic stations. ✎ **Interpret Maps** Suppose a fourth seismographic station is located in San Diego. What was the approximate difference in arrival times of P and S waves here?

_____

Hint: Use the map scale to determine how far San Diego is from the epicenter. Then, use the graph on the previous page to find your answer.

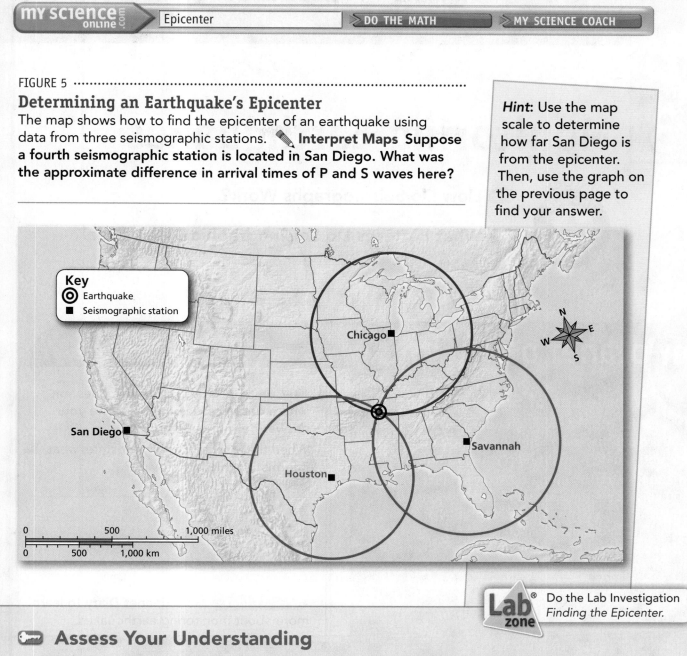

Key
◎ Earthquake
■ Seismographic station

Chicago

San Diego

Houston

Savannah

0   500   1,000 miles
0   500   1,000 km

Lab zone ® Do the Lab Investigation *Finding the Epicenter.*

🗝 Assess Your Understanding

3a. Review Geologists use _____ to locate an earthquake's epicenter.

b. Identify What can geologists measure to tell how far an earthquake's epicenter is from a particular seismograph?

_____

_____

c. Apply Concepts Suppose an earthquake occurs somewhere in California. Could a seismograph on Hawaii be used to help locate the epicenter of the earthquake? Why or why not?

_____

_____

_____

_____

got it? ··

○ **I get it!** Now I know that geologists can locate an earthquake's epicenter by using_____

_____

○ **I need extra help with** _____

Go to MY SCIENCE ⬤ COACH *online for help with this subject.*

Monitoring Earthquakes

UNLOCK THE BIG ?

🔑 **How Do Seismographs Work?**

🔑 **What Patterns Do Seismographic Data Reveal?**

MY PLANET DiARY

Whole Lot of Shaking Going On

Is the ground moving under your school? A project that will monitor shaking underneath the entire nation might help you find out!

In 2004, scientists in the USArray project placed 400 seismographs across the western United States. Every month, 18 seismographs are picked up and moved east, "leapfrogging" the other seismographs. The map below shows one arrangement of the array. The seismic data that are obtained will help scientists learn more about our active Earth!

FUN FACT

✏️ **Communicate** Discuss this question with a group of classmates. Write your answer below.

When the array arrives in your state, what information might it provide?

_____

_____

_____

_____

▶ **PLANET DIARY** Go to **Planet Diary** to learn more about monitoring earthquakes.

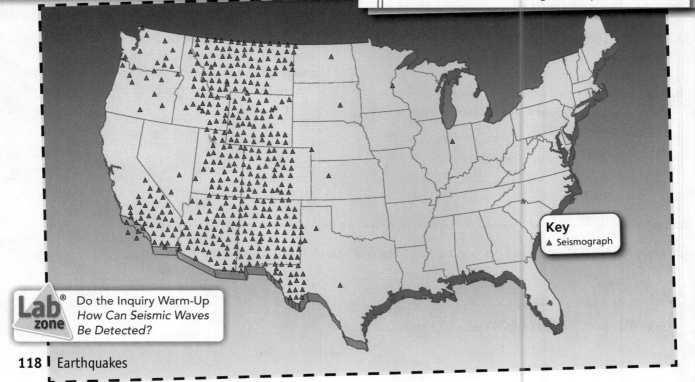

Key
▲ Seismograph

Lab zone® Do the Inquiry Warm-Up *How Can Seismic Waves Be Detected?*

Vocabulary
- seismogram

Skills
- ⟳ Reading: Identify the Main Idea
- △ Inquiry: Predict

How Do Seismographs Work?

Today, seismographs are complex electronic devices. Some laptop computers and car air bags contain similar devices that detect shaking. But a simple seismograph, like the one in **Figure 1,** can consist of a heavy weight attached to a frame by a spring or wire. A pen connected to the weight rests its point on a drum that can rotate. As the drum rotates, the pen in effect draws a straight line on paper wrapped tightly around the drum. ⟳ **Seismic waves cause a simple seismograph's drum to vibrate, which in turn causes the pen to record the drum's vibrations.** The suspended weight with the pen attached moves very little. This allows the pen to stay in place and record the drum's vibrations.

Measuring Seismic Waves When you write a sentence, the paper stays in one place while your hand moves the pen. But in a seismograph, it's the pen that remains stationary while the paper moves. Why is this? All seismographs make use of a basic principle of physics: Whether it is moving or at rest, every object resists any change to its motion. A seismograph's heavy weight resists motion during an earthquake. But the rest of the seismograph is anchored to the ground and vibrates when seismic waves arrive.

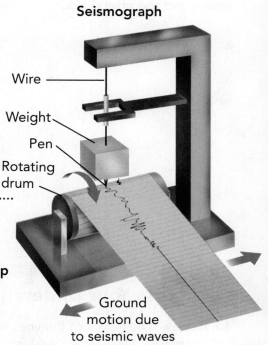

Seismograph

Wire

Weight

Pen

Rotating drum

Ground motion due to seismic waves

FIGURE 1 ·····································

Recording Seismic Waves
In a simple seismograph, a pen attached to a suspended weight records an earthquake's seismic waves.

✏️ **Make Models** To mimic the action of a seismograph, hold the tip of a pencil on the right edge of the seismograph paper below. Have a classmate pull the right edge of the book away from your pencil while the classmate also "vibrates" the book side to side.

FIGURE 2 ·····················

Seismograms

When an earthquake's seismic waves reach a simple seismograph, the seismograph's drum vibrates. The vibrations are recorded by the seismograph's pen, producing a seismogram, as shown on the top diagram.

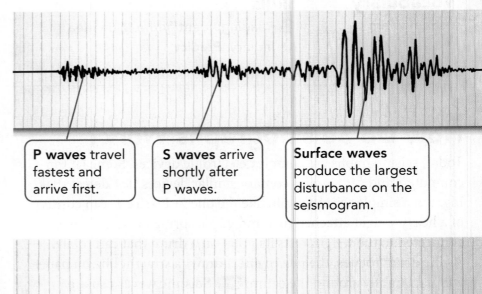

P waves travel fastest and arrive first.

S waves arrive shortly after P waves.

Surface waves produce the largest disturbance on the seismogram.

CHALLENGE An aftershock is a smaller earthquake that occurs after a larger earthquake. Draw the seismogram that might be produced by a seismograph during an earthquake and its aftershock. Label the earthquake and the aftershock.

Reading a Seismogram You have probably seen the zigzagging lines used to represent an earthquake. The pattern of lines, called a **seismogram,** is the record of an earthquake's seismic waves produced by a seismograph. Study the seismogram in **Figure 2.** Notice when the P waves, S waves, and surface waves arrive. The height of the lines drawn by the seismograph is greater for a more severe earthquake or an earthquake closer to the seismograph.

 ® Do the Quick Lab *Design a Seismograph.*

🔑 Assess Your Understanding

1a. Review The height of the lines on a seismogram is (greater/less) for a stronger earthquake.

b. Interpret Diagrams What do the relatively straight, flat portions of the seismogram at the top of **Figure 2** represent?

_____

_____

_____

got it?

○ **I get it!** Now I know that a simple seismograph works when _____

_____

_____

_____

○ **I need extra help with** _____

Go to **MY SCIENCE** ⓢ **COACH** online for help with this subject.

What Patterns Do Seismographic Data Reveal?

Geologists use seismographs to monitor earthquakes. Other devices that geologists use detect slight motions along faults. Yet even with data from many different devices, geologists cannot yet predict when and where an earthquake might strike. 🗝 **But from past seismographic data, geologists have created maps of where earthquakes occur around the world. The maps show that earthquakes often occur along plate boundaries.** Recall that where plates meet, plate movement stores energy in rock that makes up the crust. This energy is eventually released in an earthquake.

Earthquake Risk in North America Earthquake risk largely depends on how close a given location is to a plate boundary. In the United States, two plates meet along the Pacific coast in California, Washington state, and Alaska, causing many faults. Frequent earthquakes occur in California, where the Pacific plate and the North American plate meet along the San Andreas fault. In Washington, earthquakes result from the subduction of the Juan de Fuca plate beneath the North American plate. Recall that during subduction, one plate is forced down under another plate.

✎ **Identify the Main Idea**
Underline the sentence in the second paragraph that describes the main factor in determining earthquake risk for a given location.

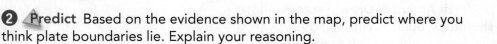

apply it!

The map shows areas where serious earthquakes are likely to occur, based on the location of past earthquakes across the United States.

❶ **Interpret Maps** The map indicates that serious earthquakes are most likely to occur (on the east coast/in the midsection/on the west coast) of the United States.

❷ **Predict** Based on the evidence shown in the map, predict where you think plate boundaries lie. Explain your reasoning.

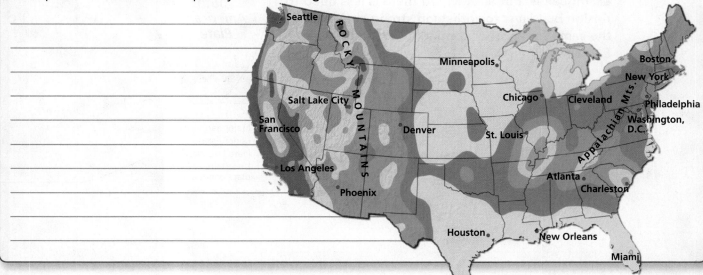

Key

Lowest risk — Highest risk

Earthquake Risk Around the World Many of the world's earthquakes occur in a vast area of geologic activity called the Ring of Fire. In this area, plate boundaries form a ring around the Pacific Ocean. Volcanoes as well as earthquakes are common along these boundaries. The Ring of Fire includes the west coast of Central America and the west coast of South America. Strong earthquakes have occurred in countries along these coasts, where plates converge. Across the Pacific Ocean, the Pacific Plate collides with several other plates. Here, Japan, Indonesia, New Zealand, and New Guinea are seismically very active.

India, China, and Pakistan also have been struck by large earthquakes. In this area of the world, the Indo-Australian Plate collides with the Eurasian Plate. Earthquakes are also common where the Eurasian Plate meets the Arabian and African plates.

EXPLORE THE BIG ? Earthquakes and Plate Tectonics

Why do earthquakes occur more often in some places than in others?

FIGURE 3 ·······················

> **REAL-WORLD INQUIRY** **Earthquakes Around the World**

Earthquakes are closely linked to plate tectonics. The map shows where past earthquakes have occurred in relation to plate boundaries.

✎ **Make Judgments** Draw an outline tracing the plate boundaries that make up the Ring of Fire. Then, look at North America. Draw a star where buildings should be built to withstand earthquakes. Put an X where there is less need to design buildings to withstand strong shaking. Do the same for another continent (not Antarctica). Explain your answers.

_____

_____

_____

_____

_____

_____

_____

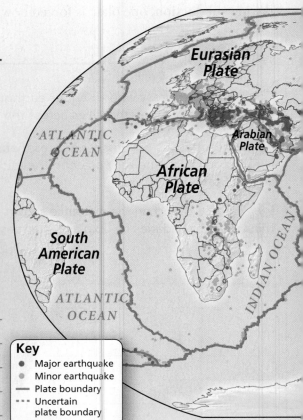

Key
- ● Major earthquake
- ● Minor earthquake
- — Plate boundary
- ··· Uncertain plate boundary

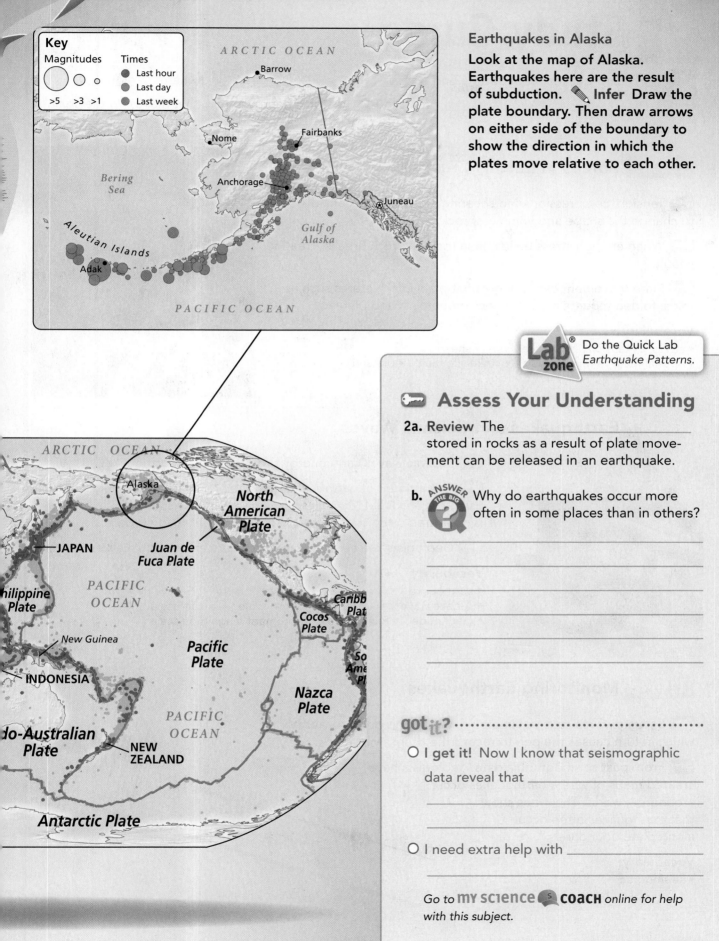

Key

Magnitudes
- >5
- >3
- >1

Times
- Last hour
- Last day
- Last week

ARCTIC OCEAN

Barrow

Nome

Fairbanks

Bering Sea

Anchorage

Juneau

Aleutian Islands

Adak

Gulf of Alaska

PACIFIC OCEAN

ARCTIC OCEAN

Alaska

North American Plate

JAPAN

Juan de Fuca Plate

Philippine Plate

PACIFIC OCEAN

New Guinea

INDONESIA

Pacific Plate

Caribb Plat

Cocos Plate

So Ame Pl

Indo-Australian Plate

NEW ZEALAND

PACIFIC OCEAN

Nazca Plate

Antarctic Plate

Earthquakes in Alaska

Look at the map of Alaska. Earthquakes here are the result of subduction. ✏️ **Infer** Draw the plate boundary. Then draw arrows on either side of the boundary to show the direction in which the plates move relative to each other.

Lab zone® Do the Quick Lab *Earthquake Patterns.*

🔑 **Assess Your Understanding**

2a. Review The _____ stored in rocks as a result of plate movement can be released in an earthquake.

b. ANSWER THE BIG ❓ Why do earthquakes occur more often in some places than in others?

_____
_____
_____
_____
_____
_____
_____

got it? ....

○ **I get it!** Now I know that seismographic data reveal that _____
_____
_____

○ **I need extra help with** _____
_____

Go to **my science** 🅢 **coach** *online for help with this subject.*

123

Study Guide

Earthquakes often occur along _____ , where _____

_____ stores energy in rock that makes up the crust.

LESSON 1 **Forces in Earth's Crust**

🔑 Tension, compression, and shearing work over millions of years to change the shape and volume of rock.

🔑 When enough stress builds up in rock, the rock breaks, creating a fault.

🔑 Plate movement can change a flat plain into features such as folds, folded mountains, fault-block mountains, and plateaus.

Vocabulary
- stress • tension • compression • shearing
- normal fault • reverse fault • strike-slip fault • plateau

LESSON 2 **Earthquakes and Seismic Waves**

🔑 Seismic waves carry energy produced by an earthquake.

🔑 The amount of earthquake damage or shaking that is felt is rated using the Modified Mercalli scale. An earthquake's magnitude, or size, is measured using the Richter scale or moment magnitude scale.

🔑 Geologists use seismic waves to locate an earthquake's epicenter.

Vocabulary
- earthquake • focus • epicenter • P wave • S wave
- surface wave • seismograph • Modified Mercalli scale
- magnitude • Richter scale • moment magnitude scale

LESSON 3 **Monitoring Earthquakes**

🔑 Seismic waves cause a simple seismograph's drum to vibrate, which in turn causes the pen to record the drum's vibrations.

🔑 From past seismographic data, geologists have created maps of where earthquakes occur around the world. The maps show that earthquakes often occur along plate boundaries.

Vocabulary
- seismogram

Surface waves

S waves

P waves

Review and Assessment

LESSON 1 Forces in Earth's Crust

1. Which force squeezes Earth's crust to make the crust shorter and thicker?

  a. tension   **b.** normal

  c. shearing   **d.** compression

2. Rocks on either side of a _____ fault slip past each other with little up and down motion.

3. **List** Give two examples of mountain ranges in the world that have been caused by folding.

_____

_____

_____

4. **Interpret Diagrams** What type of stress is shown in the diagram below?

_____

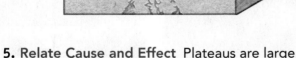

5. **Relate Cause and Effect** Plateaus are large, flat, elevated areas of land. What is one way plateaus can form?

_____

_____

_____

6. **Write About It** Compression causes folds called anticlines and synclines. How do these features resemble each other? How do they differ from one another?

LESSON 2 Earthquakes and Seismic Waves

7. Which of these scales rates earthquake damage at a particular location?

  a. focus   **b.** Modified Mercalli

  c. Richter   **d.** moment magnitude

8. The point on Earth's surface directly above an earthquake's focus is called _____

_____

9. **Interpret Diagrams** Label the diagram to show the directions an S wave travels and vibrates.

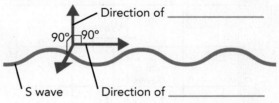

10. **Explain** How is the energy released by an earthquake related to its moment magnitude?

_____

_____

11. **Interpret Data** Can geologists use data from only two seismographic stations to locate an earthquake's epicenter? Explain.

_____

_____

_____

12. **math!** Seismograph A records P waves at 6:05 P.M. and S waves at 6:10 P.M. Seismograph B records P waves at 6:10 P.M. and S waves at 6:25 P.M. What is the difference in the arrival times at each device? Which device is closer to the earthquake's epicenter?

_____

_____

125

Review and Assessment

Monitoring Earthquakes

13. In which type of location is earthquake risk the greatest?

    a. at plate centers   **b.** on big plates

    c. at plate boundaries **d.** on small plates

14. Very high, jagged lines on a seismogram indicate that an earthquake is either _____

_____

Use the graph to answer questions 15–16.

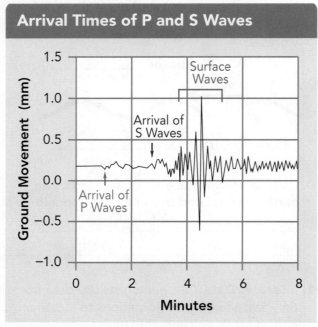

Arrival Times of P and S Waves

15. Read Graphs Which type of seismic waves produced the largest ground movement?

_____

16. Interpret Data What was the difference in arrival times for the P waves and the S waves?

_____

17. **Write About It** There is a high risk of earthquakes along the San Andreas fault in California. What is happening in Earth's crust along the fault to cause this high earthquake risk? Use the theory of plate tectonics in your answer.

 Why do earthquakes occur more often in some places than in others?

18. An architect is hired to design a skyscraper in the Indonesian city of Jakarta, which is near the Ring of Fire. The architect must follow special building codes that the city has written. What might those codes be for and why are they important in Jakarta?

_____

_____

_____

_____

_____

_____

_____

_____

Standardized Test Prep

Multiple Choice

Circle the letter of the best answer.

1. The diagram below shows a mass of rock affected by stress.

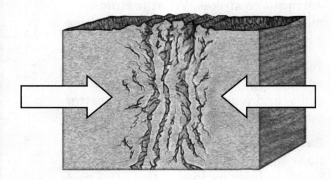

   What type of stress process is shown in this diagram?

   A   pulling apart   B   tension
   C   compression   D   shearing

2. An earthquake occurs along a fault when

   A   energy in the rock along the fault does not change for a long period of time.

   B   stress in the rock along the fault causes the rock to melt.

   C   enough energy builds up in the rock along the fault to cause the rock to break or slip.

   D   energy in the rock along the fault is changed to heat.

3. Which scale would a geologist use to estimate the total energy released by an earthquake?

   A   Modified Mercalli scale

   B   Richter scale

   C   epicenter scale

   D   moment magnitude scale

4. When an earthquake occurs, seismic waves travel

   A   only through the hanging wall.

   B   only through the footwall.

   C   outward from the focus.

   D   inward to the epicenter.

5. Where are the areas that are at greatest risk from earthquakes?

   A   in the center of plates

   B   where plates meet

   C   in the middle of the ocean

   D   where land meets water

Constructed Response

Use the diagram below and your knowledge of science to help you answer Question 6. Write your answer on a separate piece of paper.

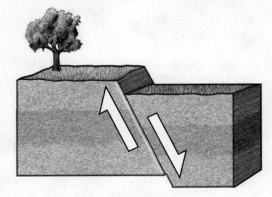

6. Explain the process that forms a normal fault and leads to an earthquake along the fault. Describe the fault, the type of stress that produces it, and events that occur before and during the earthquake.

Seismic-SAFE
BUILDINGS

Suppose you are on the highest floor of a tall building in your town. An earthquake strikes. What features might help the building withstand the powerful effects of an earthquake?

Tension ties firmly "tie" the floors and ceilings of the building to the walls, and work to absorb and scatter earthquake energy.

Base isolators are pads under the first floor that separate, or isolate, the building from its foundation. The pads stop some of an earthquake's energy from entering the building.

Cross braces form a network of steel on the outside of the building to stiffen its frame.

Dampers work like shock absorbers in a car, absorbing some of the energy of seismic waves.

Design It Use cardboard, craft sticks, and modeling clay to build a model of a seismic-safe building. Place your model on a table, and drop a heavy book next to it. Then try bumping the table to shake the model sideways. How well does your building stand up? What changes could you make to improve your structure's stability?

▲ Cross braces on the outside of the building help to support the frame.

What Do the Toads Know?

On May 12, 2008, a strong earthquake struck China. Within days, bloggers claimed that many signs had predicted the earthquake. One blogger wrote that thousands of toads moved through the area just before the earthquake. Another claimed to have seen ponds that emptied and dried up.

Write About It Write an entry that you might post in a blog. Do you believe the bloggers' claims about signs that might predict an earthquake? What evidence would you look for to determine whether the bloggers' claims were scientifically accurate?

FORENSIC SEISMOLOGY

In May 2008, India tested two nuclear devices by exploding them underground. Days later, Pakistan conducted similar tests. The world learned of these tests because these explosions caused seismic waves.

How did geologists know the seismic waves were produced by nuclear explosions and not by earthquakes? Seismic waves from underground nuclear explosions produce a different seismogram pattern than earthquakes do.

Research It Research how the seismograms produced by nuclear explosions differ from those produced by earthquakes, and make a poster illustrating the differences.

▲ An underground nuclear test destroyed these test buildings at Pokaran, India, in 1998.

129

WHAT CAUSED THIS EXPLOSION?

How does a volcano erupt?

Vivid orange and red sparks shower the night sky. A small crowd stands by and watches this beautiful scene light up the night. Could this be a fireworks display gone crazy? You've probably guessed that it is a volcano erupting. This volcano is actually exploding, sending hot gases, ash, and lava into the air. **Infer** **What could cause a volcano to blow up?**

_____

_____

_____

_____

_____

> **UNTAMED SCIENCE** Watch the **Untamed Science** video to learn more about volcanoes.

Volcanoes

5 Getting Started

Check Your Understanding

1. **Background** Read the paragraph below and then answer the question.

> Mr. Carenni said, "For today's activity, let's make a model of Earth's crust. We can think of the **crust** as a thin film of ice resting on top of a much thicker layer of hard, packed snow. Now let's suppose that the ice breaks into pieces. On Earth, these pieces are called **plates.** The edges of the plates are called **boundaries.** "

The **crust** is Earth's rocky, outer layer.

A **plate** is one of the large pieces that Earth's crust is broken into.

Boundaries are lines along which something ends.

- Suppose two pieces of ice are pushed slowly together. What might happen to the edges of the pieces?

_____

_____

> **MY READING WEB** If you had trouble answering the question above, visit **My Reading Web** and type in *Volcanoes.*

Vocabulary Skill

High-Use Academic Words High-use words are words that are used frequently in academic reading, writing, and discussions. These words are different from key terms because they appear in many subject areas.

Word	Definition	Example
surface	*n.* the exterior or outermost layer of an object	The *surface* of Earth is very rocky.
stage	*n.* a point in a process	Middle age is one *stage* of life.
hazard	*n.* a possible danger	Forest fires can be a *hazard* for people living near the woods.

2. **Quick Check** Choose the word from the table that best completes the sentence.

- When a volcano erupts, the lava can be a _____

  for cities and towns nearby.

hot spot

crater

volcanic neck

caldera

Chapter Preview

> **VOCAB FLASH CARDS** For extra help with vocabulary, visit **Vocab Flash Cards** and type in *Volcanoes.*

133

Volcanoes and Plate Tectonics

🔑 **Where Are Volcanoes Found on Earth's Surface?**

my PLaNeT DiaRY

Mountain of Fire, Mountain of Ice

Climbers who struggle up the snow-packed slopes of Mount Erebus on Antarctica may be in for an unpleasant surprise. Balls of scorching molten rock three meters across might come hurtling out of the air and land just steps from climbers' feet! Why? Because Mount Erebus is one of Earth's southernmost volcanoes.

Scientists believe that Mount Erebus lies over an area where material from Earth's mantle rises and then melts. The melted material reaches the surface at Mount Erebus.

Read the text and then answer the question.

How did Mount Erebus form?

_____

_____

_____

_____

_____

_____

▷ PLANET DIARY Go to **Planet Diary** to learn more about volcanoes.

Lab zone® Do the Inquiry Warm-Up *Moving Volcanoes.*

Where Are Volcanoes Found on Earth's Surface?

The eruption of a volcano can be awe-inspiring. Molten material can be spewed high into the atmosphere. Villages can be buried in volcanic ash. A **volcano** is a mountain that forms in Earth's crust when molten material, or magma, reaches the surface. **Magma** is a molten mixture of rock-forming substances, gases, and water from the mantle. When magma reaches the surface, it is called **lava.** After magma and lava cool, they form solid rock.

Vocabulary

- volcano • magma • lava • Ring of Fire
- island arc • hot spot

Skills

↻ **Reading: Relate Text and Visuals**

△ **Inquiry: Develop Hypotheses**

Volcanoes and Plate Boundaries

Are volcanoes found randomly across Earth? No, in general, volcanoes form a regular pattern on Earth. To understand why, look at the map in **Figure 1.** Notice how volcanoes occur in many great, long belts. ☞ **Volcanic belts form along the boundaries of Earth's plates.**

Volcanoes can occur where two plates pull apart, or diverge. Here, plate movements cause the crust to fracture. The fractures in the crust allow magma to reach the surface. Volcanoes can also occur where two plates push together, or converge. As the plates push together, one plate can sink beneath the other plate. Water that is brought down with the sinking plate eventually helps to form magma, which rises to the surface.

The **Ring of Fire,** shown in **Figure 1,** is one major belt of volcanoes. It includes the many volcanoes that rim the Pacific Ocean. The Ring of Fire includes the volcanoes along the coasts of North and South America and those in Japan and the Philippines.

↻ **Relate Text and Visuals**
Volcanoes often form belts along plate boundaries. How does **Figure 1** illustrate that this statement holds true for North America?

_____
_____
_____
_____
_____

FIGURE 1 ··

The Ring of Fire

The Ring of Fire is a belt of volcanoes that circles the Pacific Ocean. As with most of Earth's volcanoes, these volcanoes form along boundaries of tectonic plates.

△ **Develop Hypotheses** Circle a volcano on the map that does not fall along a plate boundary. Why did this volcano form here? Write your answer below. Revise your answer after finishing the lesson.

Original Hypothesis: _____
_____
_____
_____
_____

Revised Hypothesis: _____
_____
_____
_____

Key

▬ Plate boundary

△ Volcano

ASIA

Ring of Fire

NORTH AMERICA

PACIFIC OCEAN

Ring of Fire

SOUTH AMERICA

AUSTRALIA

△ *Mt. Erebus*

ANTARCTICA

135

FIGURE 2 ·····················
> ART IN MOTION

Volcanoes and Converging Boundaries

Volcanoes often form where two plates collide.

✎ **Compare and Contrast**
Shade the arrows to show the direction of plate movement. Then compare and contrast the ways volcanoes form at A and B.

_____

_____

_____

_____

_____

_____

_____

_____

Diverging Boundaries Volcanoes form along the mid-ocean ridges, where two plates move apart. Mid-ocean ridges form long, underwater mountain ranges that sometimes have a rift valley down their center. Along the rift valley, lava pours out of cracks in the ocean floor. This process gradually builds new mountains. Volcanoes also form along diverging plate boundaries on land. For example, large volcanoes are found along the Great Rift Valley in East Africa.

Converging Boundaries Many volcanoes form near converging plate boundaries, where two oceanic plates collide. Through subduction, the older, denser plate sinks into the mantle and creates a deep-ocean trench. Water in the sinking plate eventually leaves the crust and rises into the wedge of the mantle above it. As a result, the melting point of the mantle in the wedge is lowered. So, the mantle partially melts. The magma that forms as a result rises up. This magma can break through the ocean floor, creating volcanoes.

The resulting volcanoes sometime create a string of islands called an **island arc.** Look at **Figure 2.** The curve of an island arc echoes the curve of its deep-ocean trench. Major island arcs include Japan, New Zealand, the Aleutians, and the Caribbean islands.

Volcanoes also occur where an oceanic plate is subducted beneath a continental plate. Collisions of this type produced the volcanoes of the Andes Mountains in South America. In the United States, plate collisions also produced the volcanoes of the Pacific Northwest, including Mount St. Helens and Mount Rainier.

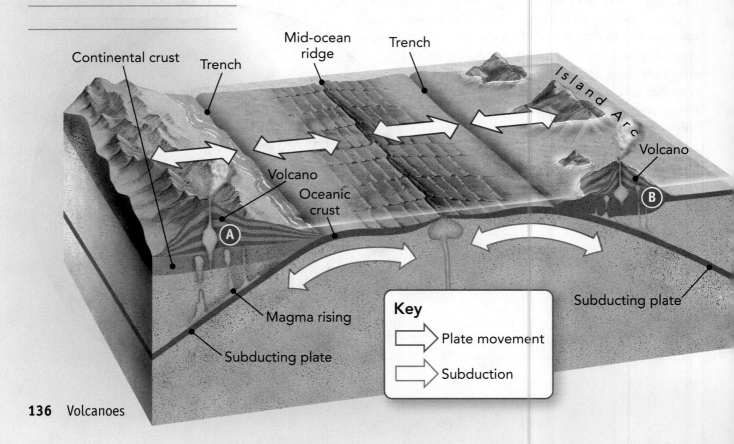

Key
➡ Plate movement
➡ Subduction

Hot Spots

Not all volcanoes form along plate boundaries. Some volcanoes are the result of "hot spots" in Earth's mantle. A **hot spot** is an area where material from deep within Earth's mantle rises through the crust and melts to form magma. 🔑 **A volcano forms above a hot spot when magma erupts through the crust and reaches the surface.** Hot spots stay in one place for many millions of years while the plate moves over them. Some hot spot volcanoes lie close to plate boundaries. Others lie in the middle of plates. Yellowstone National Park in Wyoming marks a huge hot spot under the North American plate.

apply it!

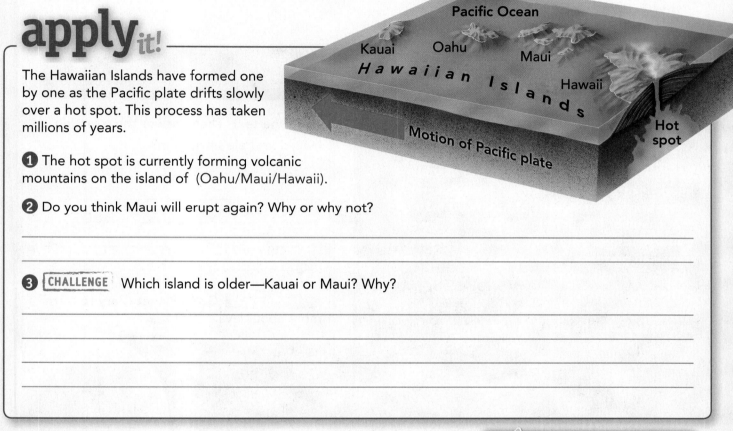

The Hawaiian Islands have formed one by one as the Pacific plate drifts slowly over a hot spot. This process has taken millions of years.

1 The hot spot is currently forming volcanic mountains on the island of (Oahu/Maui/**Hawaii**).

2 Do you think Maui will erupt again? Why or why not?

_____

_____

3 CHALLENGE Which island is older—Kauai or Maui? Why?

_____

_____

_____

_____

🔑 **Assess Your Understanding**

1a. Define A volcano is a mountain that forms in Earth's crust when _____ reaches the surface.

b. Explain Can volcanoes form under water? Why or why not?

_____

_____

Lab zone® Do the Quick Lab *Where Are Volcanoes Found on Earth's Surface?*

got it?

○ **I get it!** Now I know that volcanoes are found in the following two general locations: _____

_____

_____

○ **I need extra help with** _____

Go to MY SCIENCE ⓈCOACH *online for help with this subject.*

Volcanic Eruptions

UNLOCK THE BIG ?

🔑 **What Happens When a Volcano Erupts?**

🔑 **What Are the Stages of Volcanic Activity?**

my PLANET DiaRY

Hotheaded!

Can lava look like hair from the top of your head? It often does in Hawaii! Here, hikers may come across thin strands of hardened material that shimmer like gold in the sunlight. These thin strands are Pele's hair (PAY layz). Pele is the Hawaiian goddess of volcanoes and fire. Her "hair" is actually volcanic glass! It forms when tiny drops of molten lava fly into the air. The wind stretches these drops into threads that are as thin as hair. The glass strands then settle in crevices in the ground, forming clumps.

Read the text. Then answer the question.

How does Pele's hair form?

_____

_____

_____

_____

_____

▷ **PLANET DIARY** Go to **Planet Diary** to learn more about lava.

Lab zone® Do the Inquiry Warm-Up *How Fast Do Liquids Flow?*

What Happens When a Volcano Erupts?

Lava begins as magma. Magma usually forms in the somewhat soft layer of hot, solid rock that lies in the upper mantle, just below a layer of harder rock. The magma is less dense than the material that is around it. So it rises into any cracks in the rock above. If this magma reaches the surface, a volcano can form.

Vocabulary

- magma chamber • pipe • vent • lava flow • crater
- silica • pyroclastic flow • dormant • extinct

Skills

↻ Reading: Outline

△ Inquiry: Communicate

Inside a Volcano A volcano is more than a large, cone-shaped mountain. Inside a volcano is a system of passageways through which magma moves, as shown in **Figure 1.**

- **Magma chamber** All volcanoes have a pocket of magma beneath the surface. Beneath a volcano, magma collects in a **magma chamber.** During an eruption, the magma forces its way through one or more cracks in Earth's crust.
- **Pipe** Magma moves upward through a **pipe,** a long tube that extends from Earth's crust up through the top of the volcano, connecting the magma chamber to Earth's surface.
- **Vent** Molten rock and gas leave the volcano through an opening called a **vent.** Some volcanoes have a single central vent at the top. But volcanoes often have vents on the sides also.
- **Lava flow** A **lava flow** is the spread of lava as it pours out of a vent.
- **Crater** A **crater** is a bowl-shaped area that may form at the top of a volcano around the central vent.

Vocabulary High-Use Academic Words A system is a group of parts that function as a whole. Describe why a volcano might be considered a system.

_____

_____

_____

_____

_____

FIGURE 1 ·······················

> INTERACTIVE ART **Inside a Volcano**
A volcano is made up of many different parts.

✎ **Identify Place each word in its proper place in the diagram.**

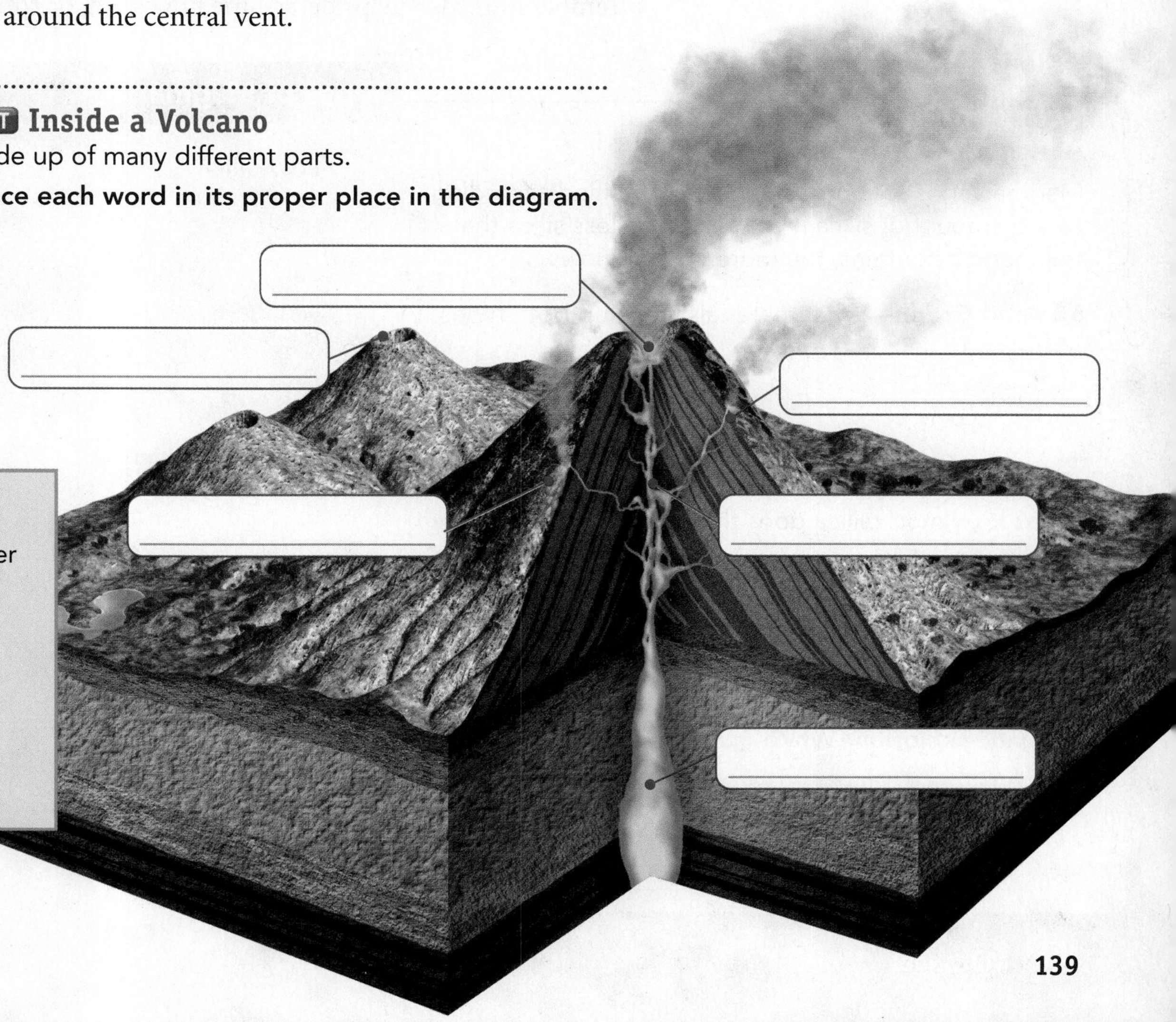

Word Bank

Magma chamber

Pipe

Central vent

Side vent

Lava flow

Crater

A Volcanic Eruption Perhaps you know that dissolved carbon dioxide gas is trapped in every can of soda. But did you know that dissolved gases are trapped in magma? These dissolved gases are under great pressure. During an eruption, as magma rises toward the surface, the pressure of the surrounding rock on the magma decreases. The dissolved gases begin to expand, forming bubbles. These bubbles are much like the bubbles in the soda can. As pressure falls within the magma, the size of the gas bubbles increases greatly. These expanding gases exert great force. **When a volcano erupts, the force of the expanding gases pushes magma from the magma chamber through the pipe until it flows or explodes out of the vent.** Once magma escapes from the volcano and becomes lava, the remaining gases bubble out.

Two Types of Volcanic Eruptions Some volcanic eruptions occur gradually, over days, months, or even years. Others are great explosions. **Geologists classify volcanic eruptions as quiet or explosive.** Whether an eruption is quiet or explosive depends in part on the magma's silica content and whether the magma is thin and runny or thick and sticky. **Silica** is a material found in magma that forms from the elements oxygen and silicon. Temperature also helps determine how fluid, or runny, magma is.

do the
math!

Magma Composition

Magma varies in composition. It is classified according to the amount of silica it contains. The less silica that the magma contains, the more easily it flows.

1 Read Graphs What materials make up both types of magma?

_____

2 Read Graphs Which type of magma has more silica? How much silica does this magma contain?

_____

_____

3 [CHALLENGE] Which of these magmas do you think might erupt in a dramatic explosion? Why?

_____

_____

_____

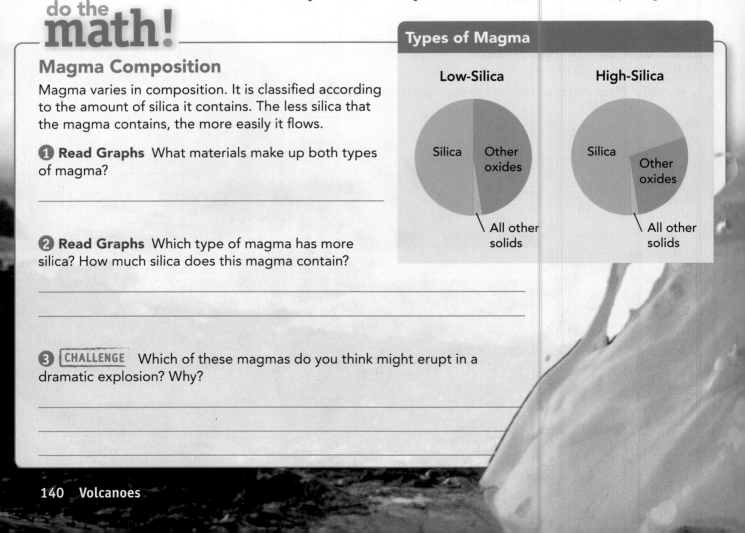

Types of Magma

Low-Silica

Silica | Other oxides

All other solids

High-Silica

Silica | Other oxides

All other solids

Quiet Eruptions A volcano erupts quietly if its magma is hot or low in silica. Hot, low-silica magma is thin and runny and flows easily. The gases in the magma bubble out gently. Low-silica lava oozes quietly from the vent and can flow for many kilometers.

Quiet eruptions can produce different types of lava, as shown in **Figure 2**. The different types of lava harden into different types of rock. Pahoehoe (pah HOH ee hoh ee) forms from fast-moving, hot lava that is thin and runny. The surface of pahoehoe looks like a solid mass of ropelike coils. Aa (AH ah) forms from lava that is cooler and thicker. The lava that aa forms from is also slower-moving. Aa has a rough surface consisting of jagged lava chunks.

Mostly quiet eruptions formed the Hawaiian Islands. On the island of Hawaii, lava pours from the crater near the top of Kilauea. Lava also flows out of long cracks on the volcano's sides. In general, the temperature of magma and lava can range from about 750°C to 1175°C—hot enough to melt copper! Quiet eruptions have built up the island of Hawaii over hundreds of thousands of years.

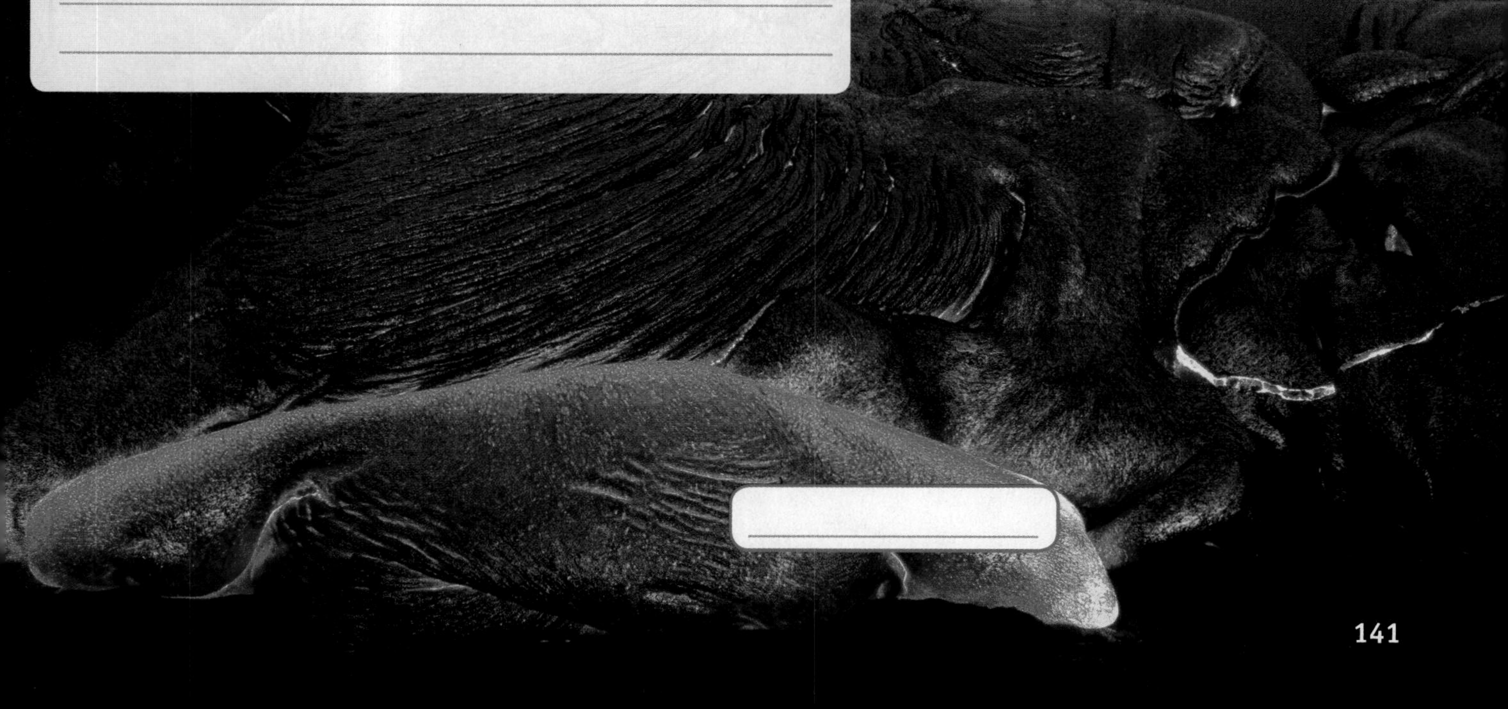

FIGURE 2 ···

Lava From Quiet Eruptions
Quiet eruptions can produce two different types of lava.

✎ **Interpret Photographs** Which lava is hardening to form aa? Which is hardening to form pahoehoe? Write your answers in the spaces provided. Then, in your own words, describe the texture of each type of rock.

_____

_____

_____

_____

_____

_____

········· ✏️ ·················

⊙ Outline Review the text on this page and on the previous page. Then complete the following outline.

Types of Volcanic Eruptions
  1. Quiet eruption
    a. Kilauea
    b. _____
  2. Explosive eruption
    a. _____
    b. High-silica magma

Explosive Eruptions A volcano erupts explosively if its magma is high in silica. High-silica magma is thick and sticky. This type of magma can build up in the volcano's pipe, plugging it like a cork in a bottle. Dissolved gases, including water vapor, cannot escape from the thick magma. The trapped gases build up pressure until they explode. The erupting gases and steam push the magma out of the volcano with incredible force. That's what happened during the eruption of Mount St. Helens in Washington State. This eruption is shown in **Figure 3.**

An explosive eruption throws lava powerfully into the air where it breaks into fragments that quickly cool and harden into pieces of different sizes. The smallest pieces are volcanic ash. Volcanic ash is made up of fine, rocky particles as small as a speck of dust. Pebble-sized particles are called cinders. Larger pieces, called bombs, may range from the size of a golf ball to the size of a car.

FIGURE 3 ···

What a Blast!
The explosive eruption of Mount St. Helens in 1980 blew off the top of the mountain.

✏️ **Explain** Read the text in this section. In your own words, explain how dissolved gases caused Mount St. Helens to erupt explosively.

_____

_____

_____

_____

_____

_____

_____

Before 1980 eruption

During 1980 eruption

After 1980 eruption

Volcano Hazards Both quiet eruptions and explosive eruptions can cause damage far from a crater's rim. For example, during a quiet eruption, lava flows from vents, setting fire to, and often burying, everything in its path. A quiet eruption can cover large areas with a thick layer of lava.

During an explosive eruption, a volcano can belch out a mixture of dangerous materials such as hot rock and ash. This mixture of materials can form a fast-moving cloud that rushes down the sides of the volcano. A **pyroclastic flow** (py roh KLAS tik) is the mixture of hot gases, ash, cinders, and bombs that flow down the sides of a volcano when it erupts explosively. Landslides of mud, melted snow, and rock can also form from an explosive eruption. **Figure 4** shows one result of an explosive eruption.

FIGURE 4 ···

Volcano Hazards

In 1991, Mount Pinatubo in the Philippines erupted explosively.

Communicate **What hazards did Mount Pinatubo present to towns near the volcano? Consider the effects of lava, ash, and gases. Work in a small group. List your answers here.**

_____

_____

_____

_____

_____

_____

_____

Do the Lab Investigation
Gelatin Volcanoes.

Assess Your Understanding

1a. Review Two types of volcanic eruptions are

_____

b. Infer Some volcanoes have great glaciers on their slopes. Why might these glaciers be a hazard if a volcano erupts?

_____

_____

_____

_____

got it?

○ **I get it!** Now I know that when a volcano erupts, the force of the expanding gases

_____

_____

○ I need extra help with _____

Go to MY SCIENCE ⓢ COACH online for help with this subject.

What Are the Stages of Volcanic Activity?

The activity of a volcano may last from less than a decade to more than 10 million years. But most long-lived volcanoes do not erupt continuously. You can see the pattern of activity by looking at the eruptions of volcanoes in the Cascade Range, shown in **Figure 5.** Mount Jefferson has not erupted in at least 15,000 years. Will it ever erupt again? **Geologists often use the terms active, dormant, or extinct to describe a volcano's stage of activity.**

An active, or live, volcano is one that is erupting or has shown signs that it may erupt in the near future. A **dormant,** or sleeping, volcano is a volcano that scientists expect to awaken in the future and become active. An **extinct,** or dead, volcano is a volcano that is unlikely to ever erupt again. For example, hot-spot volcanoes may become extinct after they drift away from the hot spot.

Changes in activity in and around a volcano may give warning shortly before a volcano erupts. Geologists use special instruments to detect these changes. For example, tiltmeters can detect slight surface changes in elevation and tilt caused by magma moving underground. Geologists can also monitor gases escaping from the volcano. They monitor the many small earthquakes that occur around a volcano before an eruption. The upward movement of magma triggers these earthquakes. Also, rising temperatures in underground water may signal that magma is nearing the surface.

Key

→ Direction of plate movement

— Plate boundary

FIGURE 5 ···

Cascade Volcanoes

The Cascade volcanoes have formed as the Juan de Fuca plate sinks beneath the North American plate.

✎ **Develop Hypotheses Answer the questions.**

1. Circle the three volcanoes that appear to be the most active.

2. Why might geologists still consider Mount Jefferson to be an active volcano?

_____

_____

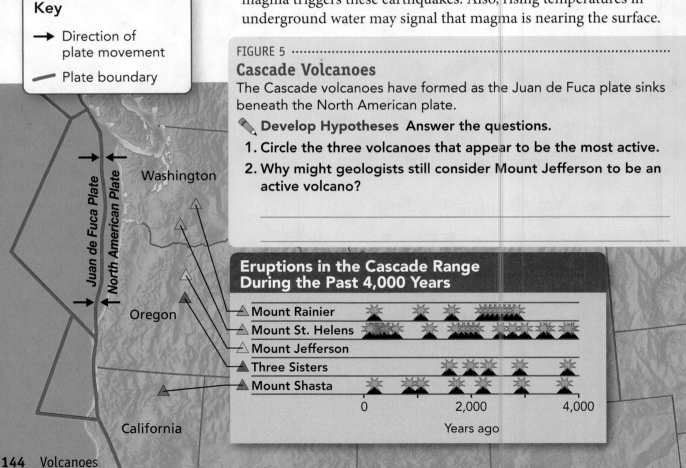

Eruptions in the Cascade Range During the Past 4,000 Years

	0	2,000	4,000
△ Mount Rainier			
△ Mount St. Helens			
△ Mount Jefferson			
▲ Three Sisters			
▲ Mount Shasta			

Years ago

EXPLORE
THE BIG
?

MT. RAINIER

How does a volcano erupt?

FIGURE 6 ···

REAL-WORLD INQUIRY Mount Rainier is part of the Cascade volcanoes. All past eruptions of Mount Rainier have included ash and lava.

Magma at Mount Rainier

60% Silica **40%** Other material

North American plate

Seattle

Mount Rainier

Juan de Fuca plate

✎ **Predict** How might Mount Rainier erupt in the future? Use the information given here. Include the role of plate tectonics in your answer. Also discuss Mount Rainier's history and its current stage of activity. (*Hint:* Look at Figure 5.)

_____

_____

_____

_____

_____

_____

_____

_____

_____

_____

_____

 Do the Quick Lab *Volcanic Stages.*

🔑 Assess Your Understanding

2a. Identify A volcano that is currently erupting is called an (active/dormant/extinct) volcano.

b. ANSWER THE BIG ? How does a volcano erupt?

_____

_____

_____

_____

got it?

○ **I get it!** Now I know that the three stages in the life cycle of a volcano are _____

_____

_____

○ **I need extra help with** _____

_____

Go to **my science** coach online for help with this subject.

Volcanic Landforms

UNLOCK THE BIG ?

🔑 **What Landforms Do Lava and Ash Create?**

🔑 **What Landforms Does Magma Create?**

my planet Diary

Posted by: Jackson

Location: West Hills, California

I was subjected to the sight of an active, dangerous volcano. We were on Hawaii, in a small aircraft over the Big Island.

The volcano was quite large—maybe a few miles in diameter. Out of the top of this volcano, there was an immense pillar of smoke, being blown out to sea by the Hawaiian winds. Judging by the patterns of the hardened lava on the slopes of the volcano, it was a shield volcano. The whole area was literally oozing with volcanic activity. Quite a few large depressions had formed where presumably there had been a magma pocket that collapsed in on itself.

Answer the questions below.

1. What landforms were created by the volcano that Jackson saw?

_____

_____

_____

2. If you had a chance to visit Hawaii, would you prefer to see a volcano from an airplane or from the ground? Explain.

_____

_____

_____

_____

> PLANET DIARY Go to **Planet Diary** to learn more about volcanic landforms.

Lab zone ® Do the Inquiry Warm-Up *How Do Volcanoes Change Land?*

Vocabulary

- caldera • cinder cone • composite volcano
- shield volcano • volcanic neck • dike • sill
- batholith

Skills

↺ Reading: Relate Cause and Effect

△ Inquiry: Predict

What Landforms Do Lava and Ash Create?

Lava has built up much of the islands of Hawaii. In fact, for much of Earth's history, volcanic activity on and beneath Earth's surface has built up Earth's land areas and formed much of the ocean crust. **Volcanic eruptions create landforms made of lava, ash, and other materials. These landforms include shield volcanoes, cinder cone volcanoes, composite volcanoes, and lava plateaus. Other landforms include calderas, which are the huge holes left by the collapse of volcanoes.** A caldera is shown in **Figure 1**.

FIGURE 1 ·············

How a Caldera Forms

Crater Lake in Oregon fills an almost circular caldera.

✎ **Interpret Diagrams** **In your own words, describe what is happening in the sequence of diagrams below.**

Calderas

Large eruptions can empty the main vent and magma chamber beneath a volcano. With nothing to support it, the mountain top may collapse inward. A **caldera** (kal DAIR uh) is the hole left when a volcano collapses. A lake can form, filling the hole. If the volcano erupts again, a steep-walled cone may form in the middle.

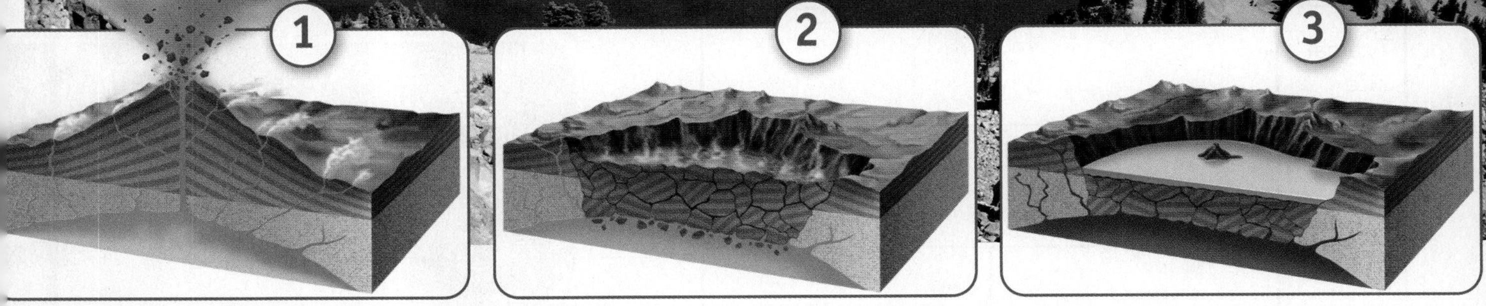

1

2

3

_____
_____
_____
_____
_____

147

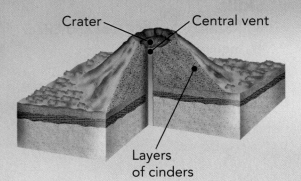

Crater Central vent

Layers
of cinders

Crater Central vent
Lava layer
Ash layer

Cinder Cone Volcanoes

If a volcano's magma has high silica content, it
will be thick and sticky. So the volcano can erupt
explosively, producing ash, cinders, and bombs.
These materials can build up around the vent in
a steep, cone-shaped hill or small mountain that
is called a **cinder cone.** For example, Paricutín
in Mexico erupted in 1943 in a farmer's cornfield.
The volcano built up a cinder cone that was about
400 meters high.

Composite Volcanoes

Sometimes, the silica content of magma can vary.
So eruptions of lava flows alternate with explosive
eruptions of ash, cinder, and bombs. The result is
a composite volcano. **Composite volcanoes** are
tall, cone-shaped mountains in which layers of lava
alternate with layers of ash. Mount Fuji in Japan
and Mount St. Helens in Washington State are
composite volcanoes. Composite volcanoes can
be more than 4,800 meters tall.

FIGURE 2 ···

Volcanic Mountains

Lava from volcanoes cools and hardens to form lava
plateaus and three types of mountains.

✎ **Read the text at the top of these two pages.
Then answer the questions.**

1. **Classify** Identify the type of volcanic landform
   shown in each of the two photographs at the right.
2. **CHALLENGE** Use the graphic organizer to compare
   and contrast two types of volcanoes.

	Volcano Type: _____	Volcano Type: _____
Typical size		
Shape		
How the volcano forms		

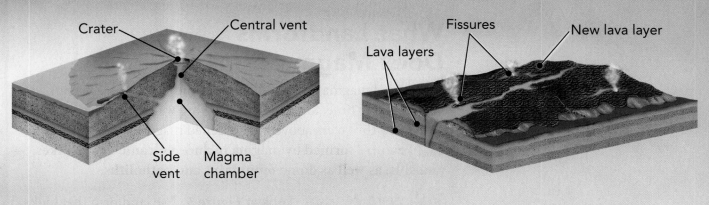

Crater — Central vent

Lava layers — Fissures — New lava layer

Side vent — Magma chamber

Shield Volcanoes

At some spots on Earth's surface, thin layers of lava pour out of a vent and harden on top of previous layers. Such lava flows slowly build a wide, gently sloping mountain called a **shield volcano.** Hot spot volcanoes that form on the ocean floor are usually shield volcanoes. For example, in Hawaii, Mauna Loa rises 9,000 meters from the ocean floor!

Lava Plateaus

Lava can flow out of several long cracks in an area. The thin, runny lava floods the area and travels far before cooling and solidifying. After millions of years, repeated floods of lava can form high, level plateaus. These plateaus are called lava plateaus. The Columbia Plateau is a lava plateau that covers parts of Washington State, Oregon, and Idaho.

 **apply** it!

The Hawaiian Islands are very fertile, or able to support plant growth. In fact, many areas near volcanoes have rich, fertile soil. The rich soil forms after hard lava and ash break down. The ash releases substances that plants need to grow.

1 ◢ **Predict** What type of industry might you expect to find on land near volcanoes?

_____

2 Analyze Costs and Benefits Lava flows could force people to flee their homes on the island of Hawaii. But in 2006, sales from crops on the island totaled over $153 million. Are the risks worth the rewards? Explain.

_____

_____

_____

 Do the Quick Lab *Identifying Volcanic Landforms.*

⚷ Assess Your Understanding

1a. Review Volcanic landforms can be built up by (lava only/ash only/both lava and ash).

b. Explain Suppose lava from a certain volcano has built up a steep, cone-shaped hill around a central vent. What can you conclude about the kind of lava that formed the volcano?

_____

_____

_____

got it?

O **I get it!** Now I know that lava and ash can create the following landforms: _____

_____

_____

O **I need extra help with** _____

Go to MY SCIENCE ⓢ COACH *online for help with this subject.*

What Landforms Does Magma Create?

Sometimes magma cools and hardens into rock before reaching the surface. Over time, forces such as flowing water, ice, or wind may strip away the layers above the hardened magma and expose it. 🔑 **Features formed by magma include volcanic necks, dikes, and sills, as well as dome mountains and batholiths.**

Volcanic Necks Look at **Figure 3**. The landform that looks like a giant tooth stuck in the ground is Shiprock in New Mexico. Shiprock formed when magma hardened in an ancient volcano's pipe. Later, the softer rock around the pipe wore away, exposing the harder rock inside. A **volcanic neck** forms when magma hardens in a volcano's pipe and the surrounding rock later wears away.

Dikes and Sills Magma that forces itself across rock layers hardens into a **dike.** Magma that squeezes between horizontal rock layers hardens to form a **sill.**

⟳ Relate Cause and Effect
What type of landform can be created when magma hardens in a volcano's pipe?
- ◯ Sill
- ◯ Dike
- ◯ Volcanic neck

FIGURE 3 ·······
▶ **INTERACTIVE ART** **Volcanic Necks, Dikes, and Sills**
A dike extends outward from Shiprock, a volcanic neck in New Mexico.

✏️ **Identify** Label the formations. How can you tell which is which?

_____

_____

_____

Volcanic neck

Dike

Sill

CANADA
British
Columbia
batholith

Idaho
batholith

PACIFIC
OCEAN

UNITED STATES

Sierra
Nevada
batholith

Key
▢ Batholith
0   200 mi
0   200 km

Baja
batholith

Dome Mountains

Bodies of hardened magma can create dome mountains. A dome mountain forms when uplift pushes a large body of hardened magma toward the surface. The hardened magma forces the layers of rock to bend upward into a dome shape. Eventually, the rock above the dome mountain wears away, leaving it exposed. This process formed the Black Hills in South Dakota.

Batholiths

How large can landforms created by magma be? Look at the map in **Figure 4**. A **batholith** (BATH uh lith) is a mass of rock formed when a large body of magma cools inside the crust. Batholiths form the core of many mountain ranges. Over millions of years, the overlying rock wears away, allowing the batholith to move upward. Flowing water and grinding ice slowly carve the batholith into mountains.

FIGURE 4 ....
Batholiths
Batholiths are common in the western United States. The mountains shown here are part of the Sierra Nevada batholith.

✎ **Measure** About how long is the Sierra Nevada batholith? (*Hint:* Use the map and map key.)

_____

Do the Quick Lab
How Can Volcanic Activity Change Earth's Surface?

🔑 Assess Your Understanding

2a. Review Dikes and sills are two examples of landforms created when (magma/lava) forces its way through cracks in the upper crust.

b. Identify What feature forms when magma cuts across rock layers?

_____

c. Infer Which is older—a dike or the rock layers the dike cuts across? Explain.

_____

_____

_____

_____

got**it?** ....

○ **I get it!** Now I know that magma creates landforms such as _____

_____

○ **I need extra help with** _____

Go to **my science** ⑤ **coach** *online for help with this subject.*

A volcano erupts when the force of expanding gases pushes _____ from the magma chamber through the _____ until it flows or explodes out of the _____.

LESSON 1 Volcanoes and Plate Tectonics

🔑 Volcanic belts form along the boundaries of Earth's plates.

🔑 A volcano forms above a hot spot when magma erupts through the crust and reaches the surface.

Vocabulary
• volcano • magma • lava
• Ring of Fire • island arc
• hot spot

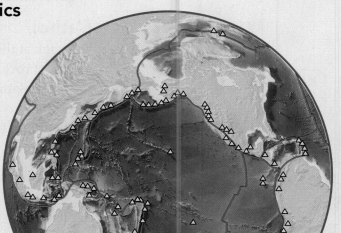

LESSON 2 Volcanic Eruptions

🔑 When a volcano erupts, the force of the expanding gases pushes magma from the magma chamber through the pipe until it flows or explodes out of the vent.

🔑 Geologists classify volcanic eruptions as quiet or explosive.

🔑 Geologists often use the terms active, dormant, or extinct to describe a volcano's stage of activity.

Vocabulary
• magma chamber • pipe • vent • lava flow
• crater • silica • pyroclastic flow • dormant • extinct

LESSON 3 Volcanic Landforms

🔑 Volcanic eruptions create landforms made of lava, ash, and other materials. These landforms include shield volcanoes, cinder cone volcanoes, composite volcanoes, and lava plateaus. Other landforms include calderas, or the huge holes left by the collapse of volcanoes.

🔑 Features formed by magma include volcanic necks, dikes, and sills, as well as dome mountains and batholiths.

Vocabulary
• caldera • cinder cone • composite volcano
• shield volcano • volcanic neck • dike • sill
• batholith

Review and Assessment

LESSON 1 Volcanoes and Plate Tectonics

1. At what point does magma become lava?

   a. below a vent

   b. inside a pipe

   c. at Earth's surface

   d. in Earth's mantle

2. Magma reaches the surface by erupting through a volcano, which is a _____

   _____

   _____

3. **Explain** Does magma consist only of rock-forming materials? Explain.

   _____

   _____

   _____

4. **Relate Cause and Effect** What causes volcanoes to form along a mid-ocean ridge?

   _____

   _____

   _____

   _____

5. **Interpret Diagrams** Look at the diagram below. Draw an arrow to indicate the direction of plate movement.

Oceanic plate

Hot spot

6. **Write About It** What role do converging plates play in the formation of volcanoes?

LESSON 2 Volcanic Eruptions

7. What type of rock forms from thin and runny, fast-moving lava?

   a. pyroclastic

   b. silica

   c. aa

   d. pahoehoe

8. As magma rises to the surface during an eruption, pressure on the magma decreases, allowing gas bubbles to _____

9. **Define** What is an extinct volcano?

   _____

   _____

10. **Predict** How might a volcano be hazardous for plants and animals that live nearby?

    _____

    _____

    _____

    _____

11. A certain volcano has erupted only explosively in the past. Another volcano has erupted only quietly. The magma composition for both volcanoes is shown below. Circle the chart showing the magma composition for the volcano that erupted quietly. Explain.

Silica | Other oxides | All other solids

Silica | Other oxides | All other solids

_____

_____

_____

_____

Volcanic Landforms

12. What type of volcanic mountain is composed of layers of lava that alternate with layers of ash?

    a. cinder cone   **b.** composite volcano

    c. shield volcano   **d.** caldera

13. Sometimes magma creates batholiths, which are _____

_____

_____

14. Name What type of volcano forms when thin layers of lava pour out of a vent and harden on top of previous layers?

_____

Use the illustration to answer the question below.

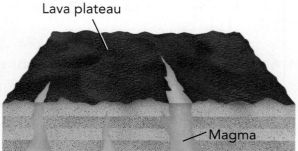

Lava plateau

Magma

15. Infer Why doesn't the type of eruption that produces a lava plateau produce a volcanic mountain instead?

_____

_____

_____

_____

_____

16. Write About It Compare and contrast dikes and sills.

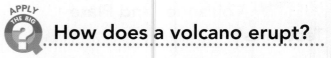

How does a volcano erupt?

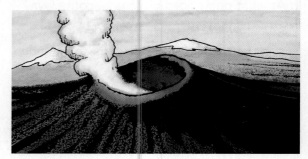

17. You are a blogger who interviews geologists. A certain geologist has just returned from studying a nearby volcano. The geologist tells you that the volcano may soon erupt. Write three questions you would ask the geologist about her evidence, her prediction about the type of eruption that will occur, and about the role of plate tectonics in the eruption. Write an answer for each of your questions.

_____

_____

_____

_____

_____

_____

_____

_____

_____

_____

_____

_____

_____

_____

_____

_____

_____

_____

Standardized Test Prep

Multiple Choice

Circle the letter of the best answer.

1. What volcanic feature is forming in the diagram below?

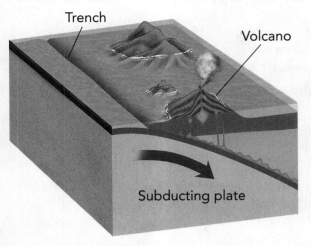

Trench

Volcano

Subducting plate

  A island arc   **B** mid-ocean ridge
  C caldera   **D** diverging boundary

2. Which of the following landforms is formed by magma?

  A caldera

  B dome mountain

  C cinder cone volcano

  D composite volcano

3. What type of feature can form when magma hardens between horizontal layers of rock?

  A volcanic neck   **B** dike
  C cinder cone   **D** sill

4. Which is the first step in the formation of a hot-spot volcano?

  A Material in the mantle rises and melts.

  B Lava erupts and forms an island.

  C Two plates move apart.

  D Magma flows through a pipe.

5. What do we call a volcano that has not erupted in a long time but that scientists believe may erupt sometime in the future?

  A dormant   **B** active

  C extinct   **D** island arc

Constructed Response

Use the diagram below and your knowledge of science to help you answer Question 6. Write your answer on a separate piece of paper.

6. A geologist observes the area around a large volcano. She decides that this volcano must once have had an explosive eruption. What evidence might have led her to this conclusion? Discuss the type of magma that produces an explosive eruption and the rocks that would result from an explosive eruption.

Congratulations, It's an Island!

Island of Surtsey today. People are not allowed to live on the island, but scientists who have permission to research there have built a research station.

On November 15, 1963, a fiery eruption shot out from the icy sea, off the south coast of Iceland, spewing gigantic clouds of ash.

A new island, Surtsey, formed. A volcanic eruption began 130 meters under the sea and forced volcanic ash to the surface. Eventually, the layers of lava and ash formed a volcanic cone that rose above sea level—the birth of Surtsey.

Eruptions continued for nearly four years as steady flows of lava moved outward and cooled in the sea. By the end, Surtsey had an area of 2.7 square kilometers.

It takes a long time for a new island to cool down! At the very base of the island, water flows through layers of loose rocks. When it makes contact with the extremely hot magma chamber deep under the sea, the water evaporates. Steam travels through the layers of porous rock at the base of the island, heating the island up.

To protect Surtsey's environment, the government of Iceland allows only a handful of scientists to visit the delicate new environment. Surtsey is a natural laboratory that gives scientists valuable information on how plant and animal populations begin on a volcanic island.

Research It The arrival of living things on Surtsey is an example of primary succession. Research the organisms that live on Surtsey, or in another area of newly formed lava rock. Make a storyboard showing primary succession on Surtsey or on the area you have researched.

Volcanologists have a seriously hot job. They investigate how, where, and when volcanoes all over the world erupt. You might find a volcanologist studying on the slopes of Mount St. Helens in Washington State, or investigating the crater of Krakatoa in Indonesia. They also try to predict eruptions.

Volcanologists have to take safety very seriously—after all, they work around actively erupting volcanoes! They have to watch out for volcanic gases and landslides. Volcanology is not all about adventures in the field, though. Volcanologists study Earth sciences, math, and physics in order to understand what they observe in the field. They also spend time writing about what they learn, so that other people can learn from their research.

Research It Research the history of a volcano that has been studied by volcanologists. Based on your research, describe how the volcano has erupted and try to predict if and when it might erupt again.

A Dangerous Job

AN EXPLOSIVE SECRET

Scientists once believed that explosive volcanic eruptions could not happen deep under water. Instead, they thought, lava seeped slowly from undersea volcanoes.

But in 2008, scientists found jagged pieces of glassy volcanic rock around undersea volcanoes in the Arctic Ocean. Seeping lava does not cause jagged glassy rocks. Explosive eruptions do.

The Gakkel Ridge is a long crack in the floor of the Arctic Ocean. The two sides of the crack are spreading apart slowly. As a result, gas builds up in pockets of magma beneath the ridge. Eventually the pressure of this gas causes explosive volcanic eruptions. The eruptions release lava, heat, gases, and trace metals into the ocean water. The jagged rocks that scientists found came from these explosions.

Ice cap covering North Pole

▲ The Gakkel Ridge (in red) is located under the Arctic Ocean.

Research It Research volcanic activity along another mid-ocean ridge, such as the Juan de Fuca Ridge. Prepare a graphic organizer comparing the timing, intensity, and volcanic activities along the two mid-ocean ridges.

157

APPENDIX A

Common Minerals

Group 1: Metallic Luster, Mostly Dark-Colored

Mineral/ Formula	Hardness	Density (g/cm³)	Luster	Streak	Color	Other Properties/Remarks
Pyrite FeS_2	6–6.5	5.0	Metallic	Greenish, brownish black	Light yellow	Called "fool's gold," but harder than gold and very brittle
Magnetite Fe_3O_4	6	5.2	Metallic	Black	Iron black	Very magnetic; important iron ore; some varieties known as "lodestone"
Hematite Fe_2O_3	5.5–6.5	4.9–5.3	Metallic or earthy	Red or red brown	Reddish brown to black	Most important ore of iron; used as red pigment in paint
Pyrrhotite FeS	4	4.6	Metallic	Gray black	Brownish bronze	Less hard than pyrite; slightly magnetic
Sphalerite ZnS	3.5–4	3.9–4.1	Resinous	Brown to light yellow	Brown to yellow	Most important zinc ore
Chalcopyrite $CuFeS_2$	3.5–4	4.1–4.3	Metallic	Greenish black	Golden yellow, often tarnished	Most important copper ore; softer than pyrite and more yellow
Copper Cu	2.5–3	8.9	Metallic	Copper red	Copper red to black	Used in making electrical wires, coins, pipes
Gold Au	2.5–3	19.3	Metallic	Yellow	Rich yellow	High density; does not tarnish; used in jewelry, coins, dental fillings
Silver Ag	2.5–3	10.0–11.0	Metallic	Silver to light gray	Silver white (tarnishes)	Used in jewelry, coins, electrical wire, photography
Galena PbS	2.5	7.4–7.6	Metallic	Lead gray	Lead gray	Main ore of lead; used in shields against radiation
Graphite C	1–2	2.3	Metallic to dull	Black	Black	Feels greasy; very soft; used as pencil "lead" and as a lubricant

Group 2: Nonmetallic Luster, Mostly Dark-Colored

Mineral/ Formula	Hardness	Density (g/cm³)	Luster	Streak	Color	Other Properties/Remarks
Corundum Al_2O_3	9	3.9–4.1	Brilliant to glassy	White	Usually brown	Very hard; used as an abrasive; transparent crystals used as "ruby" (red) and "sapphire" (blue) gems
Garnet $(Ca,Mg,Fe)_3$ $(Al,Fe,Cr)_2$ $(SiO_4)_3$	7–7.5	3.5–4.3	Glassy to resinous	White, light brown	Red, brown, black, green	A group of minerals used in jewelry, as a birthstone, and as an abrasive
Olivine $(Mg,Fe)_2SiO_4$	6.5–7	3.3–3.4	Glassy	White or gray	Olive green	Found in igneous rocks; sometimes used as a gem
Augite $Ca(Mg,Fe,Al)$ $(Al,Si)_2O_6$	5–6	3.2–3.4	Glassy	Greenish gray	Dark green to black	Found in igneous rocks
Hornblende $NaCa_2$ $(Mg,Fe,Al)_5$ $(Si,Al)_8O_{22}(OH)_2$	5–6	3.0–3.4	Glassy, silky	White to gray	Dark green, brown, black	Found in igneous and metamorphic rocks

Group 2: Nonmetallic Luster, Mostly Dark-Colored

Mineral/ Formula	Hardness	Density (g/cm³)	Luster	Streak	Color	Other Properties/Remarks
Apatite $Ca_5(PO_4)_3F$	5	3.1–3.2	Glassy	White	Green, brown, red, blue	Sometimes used as a gem; source of the phosphorus needed by plants. Found in bones.
Azurite $Cu_3(CO_3)_2(OH)_2$	3.5–4	3.8	Glassy to dull	Pale blue	Intense blue	Ore of copper; used as a gem
Biotite $K(Mg,Fe)_3$ $AlSiO_{10}(OH)_2$	2.5–3	2.8–3.4	Glassy or pearly	White to gray	Dark green, brown, or black	A type of mica; sometimes used as a lubricant
Serpentine $Mg_6Si_4O_{10}(OH)_8$	2–5	2.2–2.6	Greasy, waxy, silky	White	Usually green	Once used in insulation but found to cause cancer; used in fireproofing; can be in the form of asbestos
Bauxite Aluminum oxides	1–3	2.0–2.5	Dull to earthy	Colorless to gray	Brown, yellow, gray, white	Ore of aluminum, smells like clay when wet; a mixture, not strictly a mineral

Group 3: Nonmetallic Luster, Mostly Light-Colored

Mineral/ Formula	Hardness	Density (g/cm³)	Luster	Streak	Color	Other Properties/Remarks
Diamond C	10	3.5	Brilliant	White	Colorless and varied	Hardest substance; used in jewelry, abrasives, cutting tools
Topaz $Al_2SiO_4(F,OH)_2$	8	3.5–3.6	Glassy	White	Straw yellow, pink, bluish	Valuable gem
Quartz SiO_2	7	2.6	Glassy, greasy	White	Colorless, white; any color when not pure	The second most abundant mineral; many varieties are gems (amethyst, jasper); used in making glass
Feldspar (K,Na,Ca) $AlSi_3O_8$	6	2.6	Glassy	Colorless, white	Colorless, white; various colors	As a family, the most abundant of all minerals; the feldspars make up over 60 percent of Earth's crust
Fluorite CaF_2	4	3.0–3.3	Glassy	Colorless	Purple, light green, yellow, bluish green	Some types are fluorescent (glow in ultraviolet light); used in making steel
Calcite $CaCO_3$	3	2.7	Glassy	White to grayish	Colorless, white	Easily scratched; bubbles in dilute hydrochloric acid; frequently fluorescent
Halite $NaCl$	2.5	2.1–2.6	Glassy	White	Colorless	Perfect cubic crystals; has salty taste
Gypsum $CaSO_4 \cdot 2H_2O$	2	2.3	Glassy, pearly	White	Colorless, white	Very soft; used in plaster of Paris; form known as alabaster used for statues
Sulfur S	2	2.0–2.1	Resinous to greasy	White	Yellow to brown	Used in medicines, in production of sulfuric acid, and in vulcanizing rubber
Talc $Mg_3Si_4O_{10}(OH)_2$	1	2.7–2.8	Pearly to greasy	White	Gray, white, greenish	Very soft; used in talcum powder; also called "soapstone"

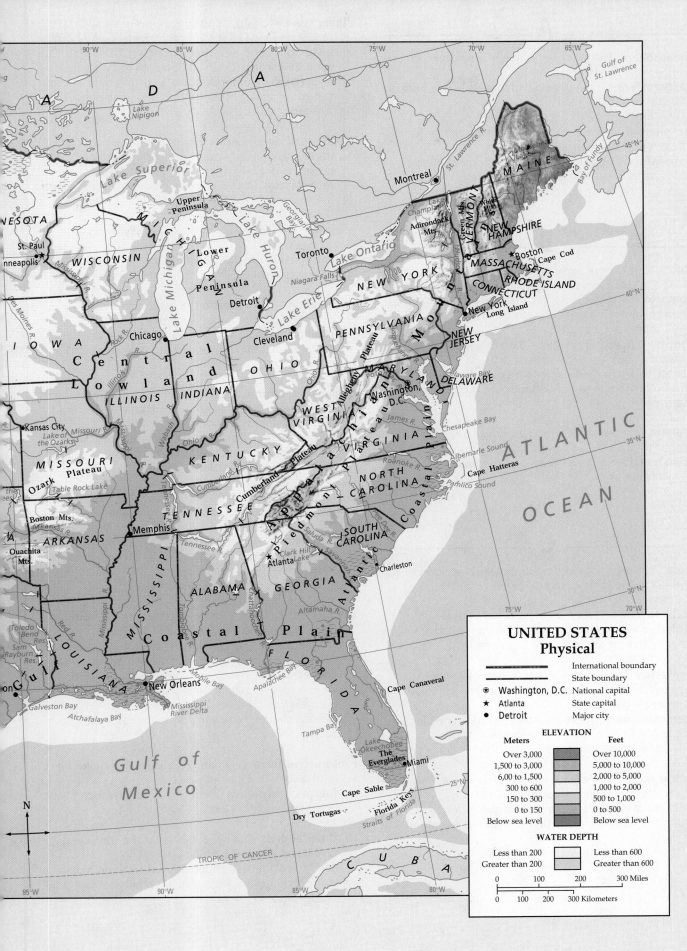

UNITED STATES
Physical

⟐ Washington, D.C.	International boundary	
	State boundary	
★ Atlanta	National capital	
● Detroit	State capital	
	Major city	

ELEVATION

Meters		Feet
Over 3,000		Over 10,000
1,500 to 3,000		5,000 to 10,000
6,00 to 1,500		2,000 to 5,000
300 to 600		1,000 to 2,000
150 to 300		500 to 1,000
0 to 150		0 to 500
Below sea level		Below sea level

WATER DEPTH

Less than 200	Less than 600
Greater than 200	Greater than 600

0   100   200   300 Miles

0   100   200   300 Kilometers

GLOSSARY

A

asthenosphere The soft layer of the mantle on which the lithosphere floats. (14)
astenósfera Capa suave del manto en la que flota la litósfera.

atmosphere The relatively thin layer of gases that form Earth's outermost layer. (6)
atmósfera Capa de gases relativamente delgada que forma la capa exterior de la Tierra.

B

basalt A dark, dense, igneous rock with a fine texture, found in oceanic crust. (13, 45)
basalto Roca ígnea, oscura y densa, de textura lisa, que se encuentra en la corteza oceánica.

batholith A mass of rock formed when a large body of magma cools inside the crust. (151)
batolito Masa de roca formada cuando una gran masa de magma se enfría dentro de la corteza terrestre.

biosphere The parts of Earth that contain living organisms. (7)
biósfera Partes de la Tierra que contienen organismos vivos.

C

caldera The large hole at the top of a volcano formed when the roof of a volcano's magma chamber collapses. (147)
caldera Gran agujero en la parte superior de un volcán que se forma cuando la tapa de la cámara magmática de un volcán se desploma.

cementation The process by which dissolved minerals crystallize and glue particles of sediment together into one mass. (53)
cementación Proceso mediante el cual minerales disueltos se cristalizan y forman una masa de partículas de sedimento.

chemical rock Sedimentary rock that forms when minerals crystallize from a solution. (56)
roca química Roca sedimentaria que se forma cuando los minerales de una solución se cristalizan.

cinder cone A steep, cone-shaped hill or small mountain made of volcanic ash, cinders, and bombs piled up around a volcano's opening. (148)
cono de escoria Colina o pequeña montaña escarpada en forma de cono que se forma cuando ceniza volcánica, escoria y bombas se acumulan alrededor del cráter de un volcán.

clastic rock Sedimentary rock that forms when rock fragments are squeezed together under high pressure. (54)
roca clástica Roca sedimentaria que se forma cuando fragmentos de roca se unen bajo gran presión.

cleavage A mineral's ability to split easily along flat surfaces. (39)
exfoliación Facilidad con la que un mineral se divide en capas planas.

compaction The process by which sediments are pressed together under their own weight. (53)
compactación Proceso mediante el cual los sedimentos se unen por la presión de su propio peso.

composite volcano A tall, cone-shaped mountain in which layers of lava alternate with layers of ash and other volcanic materials. (148)
volcán compuesto Montaña alta en forma de cono en la que las capas de lava se alternan con capas de ceniza y otros materiales volcánicos.

compression **1.** Stress that squeezes rock until it folds or breaks. (103) **2.** The part of a longitudinal wave where the particles of the medium are close together.
compresión **1.** Fuerza que oprime una roca hasta que se pliega o se rompe. **2.** Parte de una onda longitudinal en la que las partículas del medio están muy próximas unas con otras.

conduction **1.** The transfer of thermal energy from one particle of matter to another. (19) **2.** A method of charging an object by allowing electrons to flow from one object to another object through direct contact.
conducción **1.** Transferencia de energía térmica de una partícula de materia a otra. **2.** Método de transferencia de electricidad que consiste en permitir que los electrones fluyan por contacto directo de un cuerpo a otro.

constructive force Any natural process that builds up Earth's surface. (8)
fuerza constructiva Proceso natural que incrementa la superficie de la Tierra.

continental drift The hypothesis that the continents slowly move across Earth's surface. (77)
deriva continental Hipótesis que sostiene que los continentes se desplazan lentamente sobre la superficie de la Tierra.

convection The transfer of thermal energy by the movement of a fluid. (19)
convección Transferencia de energía térmica por el movimiento de un líquido.

convection current The movement of a fluid, caused by differences in temperature, that transfers heat from one part of the fluid to another. (20)
corriente de convección Movimiento de un líquido ocasionado por diferencias de temperatura, que transfiere calor de un punto del líquido a otro.

convergent boundary A plate boundary where two plates move toward each other. (87)
borde convergente Borde de una placa donde dos placas se deslizan una hacia la otra.

crater **1.** A large round pit caused by the impact of a meteoroid. **2.** A bowl-shaped area that forms around a volcano's central opening. (139)
cráter **1.** Gran hoyo redondo que se forma por el impacto de un meteorito. **2.** Área en forma de tazón que se forma en la abertura central de un volcán.

crust The layer of rock that forms Earth's outer surface. (13)
corteza terrestre Capa de rocas que forma la superficie externa de la Tierra.

crystal A solid in which the atoms are arranged in a pattern that repeats again and again. (33)
cristal Cuerpo sólido en el que los átomos siguen un patrón que se repite una y otra vez.

crystallization The process by which atoms are arranged to form a material with a crystal structure. (40)
cristalización Proceso mediante el cual los átomos se distribuyen y forman materiales con estructura de cristal.

D

deep-ocean trench A deep valley along the ocean floor beneath which oceanic crust slowly sinks toward the mantle. (84)
fosa oceánica profunda Valle profundo a lo largo del suelo oceánico debajo del cual la corteza oceánica se hunde lentamente hacia el manto.

density The ratio of the mass of a substance to its volume (mass divided by volume). (20)
densidad Relación entre la masa y el volumen de una sustancia (la masa dividida por el volumen).

deposition Process in which sediment is laid down in new locations. (53)
sedimentación Proceso por el cual los sedimentos se asientan en nuevos sitios.

destructive force Any natural process that tears down or wears away Earth's surface. (9)
fuerza destructiva Proceso natural que destruye o desgasta la superficie de la Tierra.

dike A slab of volcanic rock formed when magma forces itself across rock layers. (150)
dique discordante Placa de roca volcánica formada cuando el magma se abre paso a través de las capas de roca.

divergent boundary A plate boundary where two plates move away from each other. (87)
borde divergente Borde de una placa donde dos placas se separan.

dormant Not currently active but able to become active in the future (as with a volcano). (144)
inactivo Que no está activo en la actualidad pero puede ser activo en el futuro (como un volcán).

E

earthquake The shaking that results from the movement of rock beneath Earth's surface. (111)
terremoto Temblor que resulta del movimiento de la roca debajo de la superficie de la Tierra.

energy The ability to do work or cause change. (5)
energía Capacidad para realizar un trabajo o producir cambios.

epicenter The point on Earth's surface directly above an earthquake's focus. (112)
epicentro Punto de la superficie de la Tierra directamente sobre el foco de un terremoto.

erosion The process by which water, ice, wind, or gravity moves weathered particles of rock and soil. (53)
erosión Proceso por el cual el agua, el hielo, el viento o la gravedad desplazan rocas desgastadas y suelo.

extinct **1.** Term used to refer to a group of related organisms that has died out and has no living members. **2.** Term used to describe a volcano that is no longer active and unlikely to erupt again. (144)
extinto **1.** Término que se refiere a un grupo de organismos que ha muerto y del cual no queda ningún miembro vivo. **2.** Término que describe un volcán que ya no es activo y es poco probable que vuelva a hacer erupción.

GLOSSARY

extrusive rock Igneous rock that forms from lava on Earth's surface. (49)
roca extrusiva Roca ígnea que se forma de la lava en la superficie de la Tierra.

granite A usually light-colored igneous rock that is found in continental crust. (13, 45)
granito Roca generalmente de color claro que se encuentra en la corteza continental.

F

fault A break in Earth's crust along which rocks move. (89)
falla Fisura en la corteza terrestre a lo largo de la cual se desplazan las rocas.

focus The point beneath Earth's surface where rock first breaks under stress and causes an earthquake. (112)
foco Punto debajo de la superficie de la Tierra en el que la roca empieza a romperse debido a una gran fuerza y causa un terremoto.

foliated Term used to describe metamorphic rocks that have grains arranged in parallel layers or bands. (60)
foliación Término que describe las rocas metamórficas con granos dispuestos en capas paralelas o bandas.

fossil The preserved remains or traces of an organism that lived in the past. (78)
fósil Restos o vestigios conservados de un organismo que vivió en el pasado.

fracture 1. The way a mineral looks when it breaks apart in an irregular way. (39) 2. A break in a bone.
fractura 1. Apariencia de un mineral cuando se rompe de manera irregular. 2. Fisura de un hueso.

G

geode A hollow rock inside which mineral crystals have grown. (40)
geoda Roca hueca dentro de la que se forman cristales minerales.

geosphere The densest parts of Earth that include the crust, mantle, and core. (6)
geósfera Partes más densos de la Tierra que incluye la corteza, el manto y el núcleo.

grains The particles of minerals or other rocks that give a rock its texture. (46)
granos Partículas de minerales o de otras rocas que le dan textura a una roca.

H

hot spot An area where magma from deep within the mantle melts through the crust above it. (137)
punto caliente Área en la que el magma de las profundidades del manto atraviesa la corteza.

hydrosphere The portion of Earth that consists of water in any of its forms, including oceans, glaciers, rivers, lakes, groundwater and water vapor. (6)
hidrósfera Parte de la Tierra formada por agua en cualquiera de sus formas, ya sea océanos, glaciares, ríos, lagos, agua subterránea y vapor de agua.

I

igneous rock A type of rock that forms from the cooling of molten rock at or below the surface. (47)
roca ígnea Tipo de roca que se forma cuando se enfrían las rocas fundidas en la superficie o debajo de la superficie.

inner core A dense sphere of solid iron and nickel at the center of Earth. (15)
núcleo interno Esfera densa de hierro y níquel que se encuentra en el centro de la Tierra.

inorganic Not formed from living things or the remains of living things. (33)
inorgánico Que no está formado por seres vivos o por los restos de seres vivos.

intrusive rock Igneous rock that forms when magma hardens beneath Earth's surface. (49)
roca intrusiva (o plutónica) Roca ígnea que se forma cuando el magma se endurece bajo la superficie de la Tierra.

island arc A string of volcanoes that form as the result of subduction of one oceanic plate beneath a second oceanic plate. (136)
arco de islas Cadena de volcanes formados como resultado de la subducción de una placa océanica debajo de una segunda placa océanica.

L

lava Liquid magma that reaches the surface. (134)
lava Magma líquido que sale a la superficie.

lava flow The area covered by lava as it pours out of a volcano's vent. (139)
colada de lava Área cubierta de lava a medida que ésta sale por el ventiladero del volcán.

lithosphere A rigid layer made up of the uppermost part of the mantle and the crust. (14)
litósfera Capa rígida constituida por la parte superior del manto y la corteza.

luster The way a mineral reflects light from its surface. (35)
brillo Manera en la que un mineral refleja la luz en su superficie.

M

magma The molten mixture of rock-forming substances, gases, and water from the mantle. (134)
magma Mezcla fundida de las sustancias que forman las rocas, gases y agua, proveniente del manto.

magma chamber The pocket beneath a volcano where magma collects. (139)
cámara magmática Bolsa debajo de un volcán en la que está acumulado el magma.

magnitude The measurement of an earthquake's strength based on seismic waves and movement along faults. (114)
magnitud Medida de la fuerza de un sismo basada en las ondas sísmicas y en el movimiento que ocurre a lo largo de las fallas.

mantle The layer of hot, solid material between Earth's crust and core. (14)
manto Capa de material caliente y sólido entre la corteza terrestre y el núcleo.

metamorphic rock A type of rock that forms from an existing rock that is changed by heat, pressure, or chemical reactions. (47)
roca metamórfica Tipo de roca que se forma cuando una roca cambia por el calor, la presión o por reacciones químicas.

mid-ocean ridge An undersea mountain chain where new ocean floor is produced; a divergent plate boundary. (80)
cordillera oceánica central Cadena montañosa submarina donde se produce el nuevo suelo oceánico; borde de placa divergente.

mineral A naturally occurring, inorganic solid that has a crystal structure and a definite chemical composition. (32)
mineral Cuerpo sólido inorgánico, de estructura cristalina y composición química definida, que se da en la naturaleza.

Modified Mercalli scale A scale that rates the amount of shaking from an earthquake. (114)
escala modificada de Mercalli Escala que evalúa la intensidad del temblor de un terremoto.

Mohs hardness scale A scale ranking ten minerals from softest to hardest; used in testing the hardness of minerals. (36)
escala de dureza de Mohs Escala en la que se clasifican diez minerales del más blando al más duro; se usa para probar la dureza de los minerales.

moment magnitude scale A scale that rates earthquakes by estimating the total energy released by an earthquake. (114)
escala de magnitud de momento Escala con la que se miden los sismos estimando la cantidad total de energía liberada por un terremoto.

N

normal fault A type of fault where the hanging wall slides downward; caused by tension in the crust. (104)
falla normal Tipo de falla en la cual el labio elevado o subyacente se desliza hacia abajo como resultado de la tensión de la corteza.

O

organic rock Sedimentary rock that forms from remains of organisms deposited in thick layers. (55)
roca orgánica Roca sedimentaria que se forma cuando los restos de organismos se depositan en capas gruesas.

outer core A layer of molten iron and nickel that surrounds the inner core of Earth. (15)
núcleo externo Capa de hierro y níquel fundidos que rodea el núcleo interno de la Tierra.

GLOSSARY

P

P wave A type of seismic wave that compresses and expands the ground. (113)
onda P Tipo de onda sísmica que comprime y expande el suelo.

Pangaea The name of the single landmass that began to break apart 200 million years ago and gave rise to today's continents. (77)
Pangea Nombre de la masa de tierra única que empezó a dividirse hace 200 millones de años y que le dio origen a los continentes actuales.

pipe A long tube through which magma moves from the magma chamber to Earth's surface. (139)
chimenea Largo tubo por el que el magma sube desde la cámara magmática hasta la superficie de la tierra.

plate A section of the lithosphere that slowly moves over the asthenosphere, carrying pieces of continental and oceanic crust. (86)
placa Sección de la litósfera que se desplaza lentamente sobre la astenósfera y que se lleva consigo trozos de la corteza continental y de la oceánica.

plate tectonics The theory that pieces of Earth's lithosphere are in constant motion, driven by convection currents in the mantle. (87)
tectónica de placas Teoría según la cual las partes de la litósfera de la Tierra están en continuo movimiento, impulsadas por las corrientes de convección del manto.

plateau A large landform that has high elevation and a more or less level surface. (109)
meseta Accidente geográfico que tiene una elevación alta y cuya superficie está más o menos nivelada.

pressure The force pushing on a surface divided by the area of that surface. (12)
presión Fuerza que actúa contra una superficie, dividida entre el área de esa superficie.

pyroclastic flow The flow of ash, cinders, bombs, and gases down the side of a volcano during an explosive eruption. (143)
flujo piroclástico Flujo de ceniza, escoria, bombas y gases que corre por las laderas de un volcán durante una erupción explosiva.

R

radiation The transfer of energy by electromagnetic waves. (19)
radiación Transferencia de energía por medio de ondas magnéticas.

reverse fault A type of fault where the hanging wall slides upward; caused by compression in the crust. (105)
falla inversa Tipo de falla en la cual el labio superior se desliza hacia arriba como resultado de compresión de la corteza.

Richter scale A scale that rates an earthquake's magnitude based on the size of its seismic waves. (114)
escala de Richter Escala con la que se mide la magnitud de un terremoto según el tamaño de sus ondas sísmicas.

rift valley A deep valley that forms where two plates move apart. (89)
valle de fisura Valle profundo que se forma cuando dos placas se separan.

Ring of Fire A major belt of volcanoes that rims the Pacific Ocean. (135)
Cinturón de Fuego Gran cadena de volcanes que rodea el océano Pacífico.

rock cycle A series of processes on the surface and inside Earth that slowly changes rocks from one kind to another. (62)
ciclo de la roca Serie de procesos en la superficie y dentro de la Tierra por medio del cual un tipo de roca se convierte lentamente en otro tipo.

rock-forming mineral Any of the common minerals that make up most of the rocks of Earth's crust. (45)
minerales formadores de rocas Uno de los minerales comunes de los que están compuestas la mayoría de las rocas de la corteza de la Tierra.

S

S wave A type of seismic wave in which the shaking is perpendicular to the direction of the wave. (113)
onda S Tipo de onda sísmica que hace que el suelo se mueva en una dirección perpendicular a la onda.

sea-floor spreading The process by which molten material adds new oceanic crust to the ocean floor. (82)
despliegue del suelo oceánico Proceso mediante el cual la materia fundida añade nueva corteza oceánica al suelo oceánico.

sediment Small, solid pieces of material that come from rocks or the remains of organisms; earth materials deposited by erosion. (52)
sedimento Trozos pequeños y sólidos de materiales que provienen de las rocas o de los restos de organismos; materiales terrestres depositados por la erosión.

sedimentary rock A type of rock that forms when particles from other rocks or the remains of plants and animals are pressed and cemented together. (47)
roca sedimentaria Tipo de roca que se forma a partir de la compactación y unión de partículas de otras rocas o restos de plantas y animales.

seismic wave Vibrations that travel through Earth carrying the energy released during an earthquake. (11)
ondas sísmicas Vibraciones que se desplazan por la Tierra, y que llevan la energía liberada durante un terremoto.

seismogram The record of an earthquake's seismic waves produced by a seismograph. (120)
sismograma Registro producido por un sismógrafo de las ondas sísmicas de un terremoto.

seismograph A device that records ground movements caused by seismic waves as they move through Earth. (114)
sismógrafo Aparato con el que se registran los movimientos del suelo ocasionados por las ondas sísmicas a medida que éstas se desplazan por la Tierra.

shearing Stress that pushes masses of rock in opposite directions, in a sideways movement. (103)
cizallamiento Fuerza que presiona masas de roca en sentidos opuestos, de lado a lado.

shield volcano A wide, gently sloping mountain made of layers of lava and formed by quiet eruptions. (149)
volcán en escudo Montaña ancha de pendientes suaves, compuesta por capas de lava y formada durante erupciones que no son violentas.

silica A material found in magma that is formed from the elements oxygen and silicon; it is the primary substance of Earth's crust and mantle. (140)
sílice Material presente en el magma, compuesto por los elementos oxígeno y silicio; es el componente más común de la corteza y el manto de la Tierra.

sill A slab of volcanic rock formed when magma squeezes between layers of rock. (150)
dique concordante Placa de roca volcánica formada cuando el magma a través de capas de roca.

solution A mixture containing a solvent and at least one solute that has the same properties throughout; a mixture in which one substance is dissolved in another. (41)
solución Mezcla que contiene un solvente y al menos un soluto, y que tiene las mismas propiedades en toda la solución; mezcla en la que una sustancia se disuelve en otra.

streak The color of a mineral's powder. (35)
raya Color del polvo de un mineral.

stress A force that acts on rock to change its shape or volume. (102)
presión Fuerza que actúa sobre las rocas y que cambia su forma o volumen.

strike-slip fault A type of fault in which rocks on either side move past each other sideways with little up or down motion. (105)
falla transcurrente Tipo de falla en la cual las rocas a ambos lados se deslizan horizontalmente en sentidos opuestos, con poco desplazamiento hacia arriba o abajo.

subduction The process by which oceanic crust sinks beneath a deep-ocean trench and back into the mantle at a convergent plate boundary. (84)
subducción Proceso mediante el cual la corteza oceánica se hunde debajo de una fosa oceánica profunda y vuelve al manto por el borde de una placa convergente.

surface wave A type of seismic wave that forms when P waves and S waves reach Earth's surface. (113)
onda superficial Tipo de onda sísmica que se forma cuando las ondas P y las ondas S llegan a la superficie de la Tierra.

system A group of parts that work together as a whole. (4)
sistema Partes de un grupo que trabajan en conjunto.

T

tension Stress that stretches rock so that it becomes thinner in the middle. (103)
tensión Fuerza que estira una roca, de modo que es más delgada en el centro.

texture The look and feel of a rock's surface, determined by the size, shape, and pattern of a rock's grains. (46)
textura Apariencia y sensación producida por la superficie de una roca, determinadas por el tamaño, la forma y el patrón de los granos de la roca.

GLOSSARY

transform boundary A plate boundary where two plates move past each other in opposite directions. (87)
borde de transformación Borde de una placa donde dos placas se deslizan, en sentidos opuestos, y se pasan la una a la otra.

V

vent The opening through which molten rock and gas leave a volcano. (139)
ventiladero Abertura a través de la que la roca derretida y los gases salen de un volcán.

vein **1.** A narrow deposit of a mineral that is sharply different from the surrounding rock. (41) **2.** A blood vessel that carries blood back to the heart.
vena Placa delgada de un mineral que es marcadamente distinto a la roca que lo rodea. **2.** Vaso sanguíneo que transporta la sangre al corazón.

volcanic neck A deposit of hardened magma in a volcano's pipe. (150)
cuello volcánico Depósito de magma solidificada en la chimenea de un volcán.

volcano A weak spot in the crust where magma has come to the surface. (134)
volcán Punto débil en la corteza por donde el magma escapa hacia la superficie.

W

weathering The chemical and physical processes that break down rock and other substances. (53)
desgaste Procesos químicos y físicos que erosionan la roca y descomponen otras sustancias.

NDEX

Page numbers for key terms are printed in **boldface** type.

INDEX

Page numbers for key terms are printed in **boldface** type.

INDEX

Page numbers for key terms are printed in **boldface** type.

ACKNOWLEDGMENTS

Staff Credits

The people who made up the *Interactive Science* team—representing composition services, core design digital and multimedia production services, digital product development, editorial, editorial services, manufacturing, and production—are listed below.

Jan Van Aarsen, Samah Abadir, Ernie Albanese, Zareh MacPherson Artinian, Bridget Binstock, Suzanne Biron, MJ Black, Nancy Bolsover, Stacy Boyd, Jim Brady, Katherine Bryant, Michael Burstein, Pradeep Byram, Jessica Chase, Jonathan Cheney, Arthur Ciccone, Allison Cook-Bellistri, Rebecca Cottingham, AnnMarie Coyne, Bob Craton, Chris Deliee, Paul Delsignore, Michael Di Maria, Diane Dougherty, Kristen Ellis, Theresa Eugenio, Amanda Ferguson, Jorgensen Fernandez, Kathryn Fobert, Julia Gecha, Mark Geyer, Steve Gobbell, Paula Gogan-Porter, Jeffrey Gong, Sandra Graff, Adam Groffman, Lynette Haggard, Christian Henry, Karen Holtzman, Susan Hutchinson, Sharon Inglis, Marian Jones, Sumy Joy, Sheila Kanitsch, Courtenay Kelley, Chris Kennedy, Toby Klang, Greg Lam, Russ Lappa, Margaret LaRaia, Ben Leveillee, Thea Limpus, Dotti Marshall, Kathy Martin, Robyn Matzke, John McClure, Mary Beth McDaniel, Krista McDonald, Tim McDonald, Rich McMahon, Cara McNally, Melinda Medina, Angelina Mendez, Maria Milczarek, Claudi Mimo, Mike Napieralski, Deborah Nicholls, Dave Nichols, William Oppenheimer, Jodi O'Rourke, Ameer Padshah, Lorie Park, Celio Pedrosa, Jonathan Penyack, Linda Zust Reddy, Jennifer Reichlin, Stephen Rider, Charlene Rimsa, Stephanie Rogers, Marcy Rose, Rashid Ross, Anne Rowsey, Logan Schmidt, Amanda Seldera, Laurel Smith, Nancy Smith, Ted Smykal, Emily Soltanoff, Cindy Strowman, Dee Sunday, Barry Tomack, Patricia Valencia, Ana Sofia Villaveces, Stephanie Wallace, Christine Whitney, Brad Wiatr, Heidi Wilson, Heather Wright, Rachel Youdelman

Photography

All uncredited photos copyright © 2011 Pearson Education.

Cover, Front and Back
Dorling Kindersley/Getty Images

Front Matter
Page vi, Whit Richardson/Getty Images; **vii,** Matt Theilen/Getty Images; **viii,** Alexander Mustard/Solent News/Rex Feature/AP Images; **ix,** Pata Roque/AP Images; **x,** Digital Vision/Photolibrary; **xi laptop, TV screens, touch-screen phone,** iStockphoto.com; **xiii tr,** iStockphoto.com; **xv br,** JupiterImages/Getty Images; **xviii t,** iStockphoto.com; **xx,** Thomas Kitchin & Victoria Hurst/Getty Images; **xx–xxi,** Marco Simoni/Robert Harding Travel/Photolibrary New York; **xxi,** Reuters/Matangi Tonga Online/Landov.

Chapter 1
Pages xxii–1, Whit Richardson/Getty Images; **3 t,** Janelle Lugge/Shutterstock; **3 m,** Design Pics Inc./Alamy; **3 b,** Rick Price/Nature Picture Library; **4 bkgrnd,** Michael Busselle/Getty Images; **5,** Janelle Lugge/Shutterstock; **6 t,** All Canada Photos/Alamy; **6 m,** InterNetwork Media/Getty Images; **6 b,** Design Pics Inc./Alamy; **7 inset,** Anna Yu/iStockphoto.com; **6–7,** Marvin Dembinsky Photo Associates/Alamy; **8 l,** Dietrich Rose/zefa/Corbis; **8 r,** Philip Dowell/Dorling Kindersley; **9,** David Jordan/AP Images; **10,** Samuel B. Mukasa; **12,** Tracy Frankel/Getty Images; **13 t,** NASA; **13 tm,** Rick Price/Nature Picture Library; **13 bm,** Harry Taylor/Royal Museum of Scotland, Edinburgh/Dorling Kindersley; **13 b,** Harry Taylor/Dorling Kindersley; **14,** NASA; **15,** NASA; **16–17 earth,** NASA; **16–17 stars,** Markus Gann/Shutterstock; **17,** Copyright © 1990 Richard Megna/Fundamental Photographs **18,** Jupiterimages/Brand X/Alamy; **19 l,** Pancaketom/Dreamstime.com; **19 m,** Bloomimage/Corbis; **19 r,** INSADCO Photography/Alamy; **20 t,** Hall/photocuisine/Corbis; **20 b,** tbkmedia.de/Alamy; **21,** NASA; **22 t,** Design Pics Inc./Alamy; **22 m,** NASA; **22 b,** Hall/Photocuisine/Corbis.

Interchapter Feature
Page 26 bkgrnd, Daniel Sambraus/Photo Researchers, Inc.; **26 b,** Courtesy of Michael Wysession; **27 t,** John McConnico/AP Images; **27 b,** Layne Kennedy/Corbis.

Chapter 2
Pages 28–29, Matt Theilen/Getty Images; **31 t,** Javier Trueba/MSF/Photo Researchers, Inc.; **31 m,** Bill Brooks/Alamy; **31 b,** Sandra vom Stein/iStockphoto.com; **32 bkgrnd,** Andrew Romaneschi/iStockphoto.com; **33 l,** Rana Royalty Free/Alamy; **33 r,** Arco Images GmbH/Alamy; **34 l,** Harry Taylor/Dorling Kindersley; **34 r,** Joel Arem/Photo Researchers, Inc.; **35 tl,** Colin Keates/Natural History Museum, London/Dorling Kindersley; **35 tr,** Breck P. Kent; **35 m,** Russ Lappa; **35 bl,** Breck P. Kent; **35 bm,** Breck P. Kent; **35 br,** Charles D. Winters/Photo Researchers, Inc.; **36 t,** Jupiterimages/PIXLAND/Alamy; **36 b all,** Colin Keates/Natural History Museum, London/Dorling Kindersley; **37 No. 6–9,** Colin Keates/Natural History Museum, London/Dorling Kindersley; **37 No. 10,** Dorling Kindersley; **38 tl,** Florea Marius Catalin/iStockphoto.com; **38 tr,** Breck P. Kent; **38 b,** Mark A Schneider/Science Source; **39 t,** John Buitenkant/Science Source; **39 b,** Charles D. Winters/Science Source; **39 m,** Biophoto Associates/Photo Researchers, Inc.; **39 b,** Colin Keates/Natural History Museum, London/Dorling Kindersley; **40,** CLM/Shutterstock; **41 tl,** Jane Burton/Bruce Coleman, Inc.; **41 tr,** John Cancalosi/Getty Images; **41 b,** Javier Trueba/MSF/Photo Researchers, Inc.; **42 l,** Colin Keates/Natural History Museum, London/Dorling Kindersley; **42 r,** Gary Ombler/Oxford University Museum of Natural History/Dorling Kindersley; **44,** Robert Glusic/Corbis; **45 feldspar & granite,** Breck P. Kent; **45 hornblende,** Mark A. Schneider/Photo Researchers, Inc.; **45 mica,** George Whitely/Photo Researchers, Inc.; **45 quartz,** Mark A. Schneider/Photo Researchers, Inc.; **46 slate,** Corbis/Photolibrary New York; **46 diorite, flint, breccia, quartzite, gneiss,** Breck P. Kent; **46 conglomerate,** Dorling Kindersley; **46 b,** Bill Brooks/Alamy; **48 t,** Jon Adamson/iStockphoto.com; **48 b,** All Canada Photos/Alamy; **49 tl,** Dirk Wiersma/Photo Researchers, Inc.; **49 bl & r,** Breck P. Kent; **50,** Breck P. Kent; **51,** Keith Levit/Alamy; **52,** Courtesy of Dr. Beverly Chiarulli; **54 shale,** Joel Arem/Science Source; **54 sandstone,** Jeff Scovil; **54 conglomerate,** Dorling Kindersley; **54 breccia,** Breck P. Kent; **54 No. 1,** Michael P. Gadomski/Photo Researchers, Inc.; **54 No. 2,** Lloyd Cluff/Corbis; **54 No. 3,** John S. Shelton; **54 No. 4,** Sandra vom Stein/iStockphoto.com; **55 l inset,** Andreas Einsiedel/Dorling Kindersley; **55 l bkgrnd,** Corbis Premium RF/Alamy; **55 r inset,** Breck P. Kent; **55 r bkgrnd,** Martin Strmiska/Alamy; **56,** K-PHOTOS/Alamy; **57,** Daniel

Dempster Photography/Alamy; **58 l,** Radius Images/Alamy; **58 r,** Sergey Peterman/Shutterstock; **59,** Phil Dombrowski; **60 tl,** Biophoto Associates/Photo Researchers, Inc.; **60 tr,** Andrew J. Martinez/Photo Researchers, Inc.; **60 bl,** Andrew J. Martinez/Photo Researchers, Inc.; **60 br,** Jeff Scovil; **61,** Phooey/iStockphoto.com; **62 inset,** GlowImages/Alamy; **62 bkgrnd,** Adrian Page/Alamy; **63,** Kevin Fleming/Corbis; **64 tl,** François Gohier/Photo Researchers, Inc.; **64 tr,** Simon Fraser/Photo Researchers, Inc.; **64 bl,** Bern Petit/Breck P. Kent; **64 br,** Gregory G. Dimijian, M.D./Science Source; **66 l,** Breck P. Kent; **66 r,** Kevin Fleming/Corbis; **67,** Don Nichols/iStockphoto.com; **68 tl,** Breck P. Kent; **68 tr,** Andrew J. Martinez/Photo Researchers, Inc.; **68 b,** Breck P. Kent.

Interchapter Feature
Page 70, Loomis Dean/Time Life Pictures/Getty Images; **71,** Jane Stockman/Dorling Kindersley.

Chapter 3
Pages 72–73, Alexander Mustard/Solent News/Rex Feature/AP Images; **76,** Peter Dennis/Dorling Kindersley; **79,** Francois Gohier/Photo Researchers, Inc.; **80,** Joanna Vestey/Corbis; **81,** moodboard/Corbis; **82 t,** OAR/National Undersea Research Program/Photo Researchers, Inc.; **82 m,** Courtesy of USGS; **82 b,** Paul Zoeller/AP Images; **83,** Sandy Felsenthal/Corbis; **86,** Image Source/Getty Images; **88,** Kristy-Anne Glubish/Design Pics/Corbis; **89,** Daniel Sambraus/Science Photo Library; **90,** Blaine Harrington III/Corbis; **91,** James Balog/Getty Images; **92,** Daniel Sambraus/Science Photo Library.

Interchapter Feature
Page 96, Emory Kristof/National Geographic Stock; **97 t,** Radius Images/Alamy; **97 bkgrnd,** Carsten Peter/National Geographic Stock.

Chapter 4
Pages 98–99, Pata Roque/AP Images; **101 t,** Michael Nichols/Getty Images; **101 b,** D. Parker/Photo Researchers Inc.; **102,** vario images GmbH & Co.KG/Alamy; **104 l,** Fletcher & Baylis/Science Source; **104 r,** Marli Miller/University of Oregon; **105,** D. Parker/Photo Researchers Inc.; **106–107,** Martin Bond/Photo Researchers, Inc.; **108,** Bob Krist/Corbis; **109,** Michael Nichols/Getty Images; **110–111,** AFP/Getty Images/Newscom; **114 l,** Photo Japan/Alamy; **114 r,** Koji Sasahara/AP Images; **115,** Ho New/Reuters; **124 t,** D. Parker/Photo Researchers, Inc.; **124 b,** Koji Sasahara/AP Images; **126,** Jewel Samad/AFP/Getty Images.

Interchapter Feature
Page 128, Bruce Leighty/Getty Images; **129 tl,** WENN/Newscom; **129 tr,** Geoff Brightling/Dorling Kindersley; **129 br,** Ajit Kumar/AP Images.

Chapter 5
Pages 130–131, Digital Vision/Photolibrary New York; **133 t,** Danny Lehman/Corbis; **133 b,** Justin Bailie/Aurora Photos/Corbis; **134,** Carsten Peter/Getty Images; **138 inset,** Colin Keates/Natural History Museum, London/Dorling Kindersley; **138 bkgrnd,** Karl Weatherly/Getty Images; **140 tl,** Rainer Albiez/iStockphoto.com; **140–141,** G. Brad Lewis/Omjalla Images; **141 t,** Rolf Schulten/imagebroker/Corbis;

141 b, Stephen & Donna O'Meara/Getty Images; **142 t,** Pat and Tom Leeson/Photo Researchers, Inc.; **142 b,** U.S. Geological Survey/Geologic Inquiries Group; **142 bkgrnd,** Paul Thompson/Photolibrary New York; **143,** Alberto Garcia/Corbis; **145 l,** Courtesy of USGS; **145 r,** G. Brad Lewis/Omjalla Images; **146 b,** Karen Kasmauski/Corbis; **147,** Justin Bailie/Aurora Photos/Corbis; **148 t,** Jeffzenner/Shutterstock, Inc.; **148 b,** Rob Reichenfeld/Dorling Kindersley; **150 inset,** Eric & David Hosking/Photo Researchers, Inc.; **150 bkgrnd,** Danny Lehman/Corbis; **151,** Lee Foster/Alamy; **152 t,** Stephen & Donna O'Meara/Getty Images; **152 b,** Lee Foster/Alamy.

Interchapter Feature
Page 156 t, Arctic Images/Alamy; **156 bkgrnd,** Bettmann/Corbis; **157 t,** Krafft/Explorer/Photo Researchers, Inc.; **157 b,** Tom Van Sant/Corbis.

take note

this space is yours—great for drawing diagrams and making notes

this is your book

you can write in it

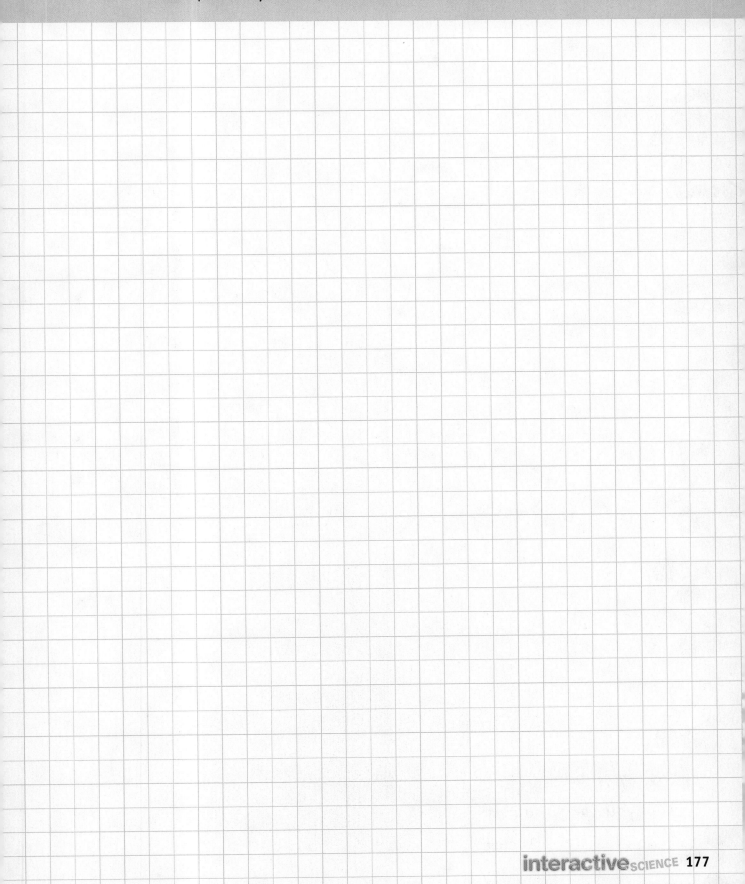

this is your book

you can write in it

178

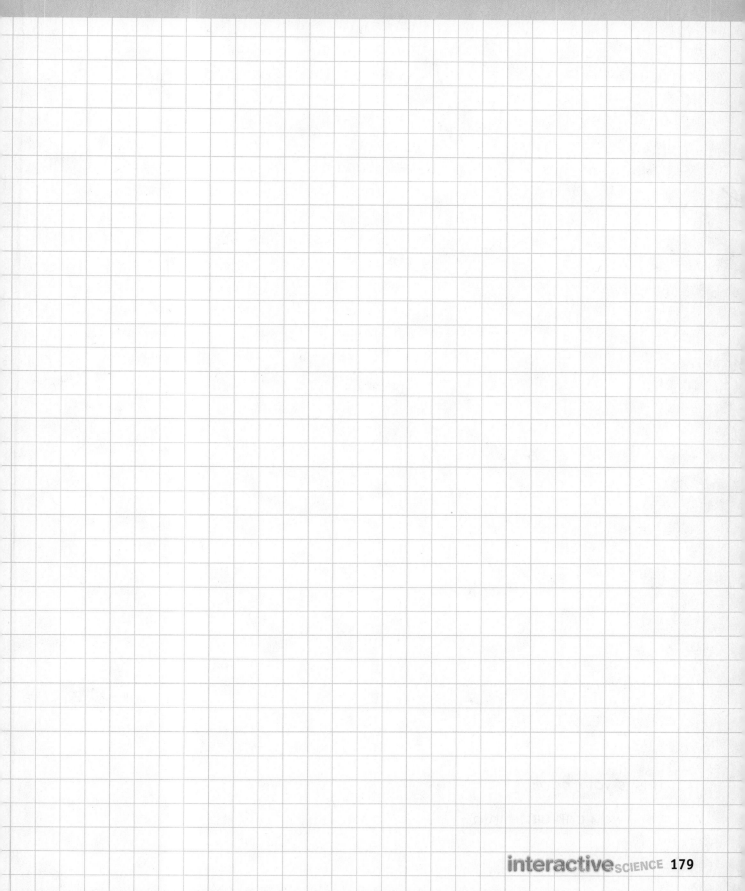

this is your book

you can write in it

this is your book

you can write in it

take note

this space is yours—great for drawing diagrams and making notes

this is your book

you can write in it

184

this is your book

you can write in it